WEST AC
EMERITUS

JESSE H. CHOPER
Professor of Law and Dean Emeritus
University of California, Berkeley

YALE KAMISAR
Professor of Law Emeritus, University of San Diego
Professor of Law Emeritus, University of Michigan

MARY KAY KANE
Professor of Law, Chancellor and Dean Emeritus
University of California, Hastings College of the Law

LARRY D. KRAMER
President, William and Flora Hewlett Foundation

JAMES J. WHITE
Robert A. Sullivan Emeritus Professor of Law
University of Michigan

WEST ACADEMIC PUBLISHING'S LAW SCHOOL ADVISORY BOARD

JOSHUA DRESSLER
Distinguished University Professor Emeritus
Michael E. Moritz College of Law, The Ohio State University

MEREDITH J. DUNCAN
Professor of Law
University of Houston Law Center

RENÉE MCDONALD HUTCHINS
Dean and Joseph L. Rauh, Jr. Chair of Public Interest Law
University of the District of Columbia David A. Clarke School of Law

RENEE KNAKE JEFFERSON
Joanne and Larry Doherty Chair in Legal Ethics &
Professor of Law, University of Houston Law Center

ORIN S. KERR
Professor of Law
University of California, Berkeley

JONATHAN R. MACEY
Professor of Law,
Yale Law School

DEBORAH JONES MERRITT
Distinguished University Professor,
John Deaver Drinko/Baker & Hostetler Chair in Law
Michael E. Moritz College of Law, The Ohio State University

ARTHUR R. MILLER
University Professor, New York University
Formerly Bruce Bromley Professor of Law, Harvard University

GRANT S. NELSON
Professor of Law Emeritus, Pepperdine University
Professor of Law Emeritus, University of California, Los Angeles

A. BENJAMIN SPENCER
Dean & Chancellor Professor of Law
William & Mary Law School

BANKRUPTCY
IN A NUTSHELL®

TENTH EDITION

DAVID G. EPSTEIN
George E. Allen Chair Professor of Law
University of Richmond
Richmond, Virginia

The publisher is not engaged in rendering legal or other professional advice, and this publication is not a substitute for the advice of an attorney. If you require legal or other expert advice, you should seek the services of a competent attorney or other professional.

Nutshell Series, In a Nutshell and the Nutshell Logo are trademarks registered in the U.S. Patent and Trademark Office.

COPYRIGHT © 1973, 1980, 1985, 1991, 1995 WEST PUBLISHING CO.
© West, a Thomson business, 2002, 2005
© 2013 Thomson Reuters
© 2017 LEG, Inc. d/b/a West Academic
© 2021 LEG, Inc. d/b/a West Academic
444 Cedar Street, Suite 700
St. Paul, MN 55101
1-877-888-1330

West, West Academic Publishing, and West Academic are trademarks of West Publishing Corporation, used under license.

Printed in the United States of America

ISBN: 978-1-64708-254-3

To the people teaching bankruptcy law
who make this book necessary

PREFACE

This is a new version of a student text that I first wrote almost 50 years ago in Chapel Hill when I was a "baby" professor of law in the "Southern part of heaven." Since then I have taught bankruptcy or creditors rights at sixteen other law schools and worked as a lawyer on the bankruptcy team of King & Spalding and then Haynes and Boone.

More important, since the last edition there have been significant amendments to the Bankruptcy Code, major court decisions, and meaningful changes in how bankruptcy cases are done and how bankruptcy affects the way deals are done.

Like the prior editions, this book attempts to summarize bankruptcy and state debtor-creditor law. It sets out the rules, the problems, and the answers to those problems that I can answer. It does not attempt to develop the history of the law, to evaluate the law critically or to propose reform of the law. In short, I have attempted to follow West's statement that a nutshell is "a succinct exposition of the law to which a student or lawyer can turn for reliable guidance."

Relatively few cases are mentioned by name. Essentially this book contains citations only to leading, recent or illustrative cases. Virtually no secondary sources are cited. There are, however, numerous references to statutory provisions—particularly Article 9 of the Uniform Commercial

Code and the Bankruptcy Code. Provisions in both the Bankruptcy Code and Article 9 are generally referred to as "section"; however, the different numbering schemes of the two acts should prevent your confusing the two.

This new edition reflects the helpful suggestions of law students, bankruptcy judge clerks, and lawyers who have used prior editions of this book. Just as the first edition benefitted from the work of Pete Chastain, a North Carolina law student, this edition benefitted from the work of Diana Dominguez, a Richmond law student.

I hope this book will help you review or learn bankruptcy law. Bankruptcy law is not always easy, and this is not always an easy book. However, doing bankruptcy law is challenging, interesting and rewarding. Writing this nutshell has been all of these things. I hope that, to at least some extent, reading it is.

DGE

Richmond, Virginia
March 2021

OUTLINE

PART II. WHAT YOU NEED TO KNOW ABOUT BANKRUPTCY

TABLE OF CASES

References are to Pages

BANKRUPTCY
IN A NUTSHELL®

TENTH EDITION

CHAPTER I

INTRODUCTORY MATERIAL

A. WHAT IS THIS BOOK ABOUT—A PREVIEW

This is a book about debtors and creditors. A debtor is a person who owes money to another person (the creditor) because of a loan, credit extended for the purchase of property or service, taxes, a lease, a judgment, a tort claim for damages or any other payment obligation. This book (and your law school course in bankruptcy or debtor-creditor law) is *not* about how or why the obligation was created. This book is about what a debtor or creditor can do under state law, under federal law other than the Bankruptcy Code and under the Bankruptcy Code when a debtor is unable or unwilling to pay that obligation.

This book begins when a debtor-creditor relationship breaks down, not when a debtor-creditor relationship begins. More specifically, this book begins when (1) the debtor-creditor relationship breaks down and (2) the affected debtor and creditors are unable to resolve problems through conversations and negotiations and (3) the dollars at issue are sufficient to warrant creditors' and/or the debtor's hiring attorneys.

Most often, the attorney involved will be a "bankruptcy attorney" (or at least will call themself that). So, most of your law school course and most of this book will be about bankruptcy law.

This book covers both individuals and businesses—both consumer debt and business debt. And, both bankruptcy law and nonbankruptcy law treat individual debtors different from business debtors.

What the previous paragraphs should probably more clearly suggest is that this book is not just about debtors v. creditors but also about creditors v. creditors. A debtor who fails to pay one of its creditors generally fails to pay other creditors. And such a debtor may have the resources to pay some but not all of its debts. The real battle then is among creditors over the debtor's assets, the value of which is less than the total of all of the debts. In such a battle among creditors, the outcome depends on nonbankruptcy concepts such as priorities, liens and priority among liens and the effect that the Bankruptcy Code has on these concepts.

B. SOURCES OF DEBTOR-CREDITOR LAW

This nutshell considers both bankruptcy and nonbankruptcy debtor-creditor law. Bankruptcy law is federal law. The Constitution in article 1, section 8, clause 4 empowers Congress to establish "uniform laws on the subject of Bankruptcies throughout the United States." Congress has acted pursuant to this grant of power and so states are preempted from enacting bankruptcy laws. Bankruptcy laws can be found in Title 11 of the United States Code.

The present bankruptcy statute, generally referred to as the Bankruptcy Code, was enacted in 1978. It replaced the Bankruptcy Act of 1898.

The Bankruptcy Code has been regularly amended since 1978. The most significant amendments were enacted in 1984, 2005, and 2020.

Westlaw of course provides comprehensive coverage of the Bankruptcy Code, cases applying the Bankruptcy Code and books and articles explaining the Bankruptcy Code in FBKR-ALL. And, there are numerous web sites with bankruptcy law information. Consider, for example, American Bankruptcy Institute: *www.abiworld.org*; and U.S. Courts *https://www.uscourts.gov/services-forms/bankruptcy*.

PART I

WHAT YOU NEED TO KNOW ABOUT CREDITORS RIGHTS LAWS OTHER THAN BANKRUPTCY

The nonbankruptcy part of debtor-creditor law is primarily state statutes governing judicial collection law. Much of this state law is codification of early English common law doctrine.

To a large extent, the states' laws share a common design. They agree on the kind of rights available to individual debtors and the kinds of remedies available to creditors, but they disagree widely on the details.

This book focuses on the general design of rights and remedies that are common throughout the country and considers some of the significant state collection law questions that arise throughout the country. That is what you need to know for law school. When, later in practice, you encounter these questions, you will find that each state has one or more "how to" texts for lawyers that fill in the needed details.

CHAPTER II

AN OVERVIEW OF JUDICIAL COLLECTION LAW

A. WHAT CAN CREDITORS DO OUTSIDE OF BANKRUPTCY?

Creditors are generally happy to do nothing. More specifically, creditors are happy to do nothing so long as their debtors are paying them.

When debtors default in paying, creditors will first attempt through "persuasion" to get the debtor to pay "voluntarily." The creditor may even hire a collection agency or attorney to help persuade the debtor. If these nonjudicial collection efforts are unsuccessful, the creditor can resort to the debt collection remedies provided by either (i) creditors' judicial remedies or (ii) the creditor's contract to seize and sell the debtor's assets to satisfy the debt.

1. FORMS OF CREDITORS' JUDICIAL REMEDIES

Let's consider the law of creditors' judicial remedies first. At the broadest level, the law of creditors' judicial remedies involves only three questions: (1) when and how does a creditor gets a lien on property of the debtor, (2) how does a creditor with a lien enforce the lien so as to collect its debt and (3) what is the lien's priority in. relation to third parties' rights to the property, including other creditors' liens and the claims of transferees. These three issues are common to every kind of creditors' remedy.

Why the focus on "liens"? A creditor cannot seize and sell its debtor's property unless it has some property interest in the debtor's property, and the principal way to obtain such an interest is to obtain a "lien" on that property.

Say for example that *C* claims that *D* owes $1,000. *C* can't simply come over to *D*'s apartment and take *D*'s stuff. *C* needs to establish a legal right to be paid $1,000. *C* needs to establish a legal right to *D's* property. *C* needs to obtain a judgment and an execution lien.

This example illustrates the two most important general rules of the law of creditors' remedies: (1) generally a creditor is not able to obtain a lien in the debtor's property until the creditor reduces its claim to judgment[1] and (2) a creditor enforces this judgment through the appropriate postjudgment judicial process.

You should now be asking the questions why is action beyond a judgment necessary. The answer is that a judgment is no more than another form of debt.

A judgment does, however, differ from the original debt in that a judgment is the State's recognition of

---

[1] There is a very narrow exception to the general rule that a creditor cannot obtain a judicial lien until it has obtained a judgment. In a narrow group of situations, a creditor can obtain a prejudgment "attachment lien." Because of due process concerns, attachment liens do not often occur in practice (and will not occur on your exam.)

the legitimacy of the creditor's claim against the debtor. Along with this recognition a willingness by the state to use its coercive power to enforce this lien and otherwise collect the amount of the judgment forcibly from the debtor's property (both real and personal) if the judgment debtor does not pay "voluntarily."

a. Judgment Liens

But first the judgment creditor must obtain a lien. A judgment creditor can obtain a lien on the debtor's real property by "docketing" (i.e., recording) the judgment in the real property record system in the county in which the real property is located. Such a lien is called a "judgment lien."

A "judgment lien" is one form of a "judicial lien." A "judicial lien" is a lien obtained through litigation—through the creditor's use of the judicial process. A "judgment lien" is thus a judicial lien on the debtor's real property.

b. Execution Liens

A judicial lien on a debtor's personal property is called an "execution lien." Obtaining an execution lien on a debtor's personal property is a bit more complicated than obtaining a judgment lien on a debtor's real property.

A creditor with a judgment initiates the execution process by applying to the court that rendered the judgment (or sometimes a different court depending on where the debtor's property is located) for a *writ of execution*, sometimes referred to as a writ of *Fieri Facias* ("FiFa" because lawyers like to use words that most people don't understand). The writ of execution is typically directed to the sheriff of the county where the property is located. The writ orders the sheriff to seize specified property of the debtor located within the county, sell it, and apply the proceeds in satisfaction of the judgment, after payment of the sheriff's costs. The process varies a bit from state to state,[2] but this is the general pattern.

With a judgment lien on real property or execution lien on personal property, an attorney for a judgment creditor can cause state officials to seize and sell a judgment debtor's property that is encumbered by the judicial lien.

c. Garnishment Liens

To reach a debtor's tangible property held by third persons, and to collect from third parties amounts owed the debtor, there is a special proceeding at law in the nature of an adversary suit against the person who holds the debtor's property or who owes the debtor money. This process is called *garnishment*.

Garnishment is in essence a special form of execution designed for reaching property of the debtor held by a third party The court orders the third party (called the garnishee) to turn over the property, or pay the judgment creditor the amount that the garnishee owed to the debtor.

---

[2] For example, in a few states a lien against personal property arises simply by a central filing of the judgment.

The most common example of garnishment is garnishment of bank accounts. When a creditor tries to collect its judgment against the debtor from funds in the debtor's bank account, it seeks to obtain property of the debtor held by a third person, in this case the bank. In this context, the proper terminology regarding what occurs when, for example, the IRS tries to seize a bank account of delinquent taxpayer, is that the IRS is garnishing the bank account and the bank is the "garnishee."

In addition to bank accounts, a judgment creditor might also seek to garnish the debtor's wages by bringing a garnishment action against the debtor's employer or the cash surrender value of an insurance policy by garnishing the insurer.

2. CREDITORS' JUDICIAL REMEDIES SHORTCOMINGS

If you understood what you just read (and more especially if you did not understand what you just read), then you will understand why

- Most lawyers do not like to do debt collection work.
- Most creditors do not like to pay for this kind of legal work.
- Most law professors do not like to teach judicial collection law.

Happily, judicial collection law has become less important in practice and less important in law school. There are three reasons for this change:

(1) The most important reason for the diminished role of judicial collection law in practice and in law school is the increased role of bankruptcy in practice and in the classroom. Businesses and individuals are more willing to file for bankruptcy. And, as we will see, the filing of a bankruptcy petition not only bars a creditor from continuing its efforts to collect its debt using judicial collection remedies but also can require a creditor who has successfully collected its debt using judicial collection remedies to return what it has collected.

(2) Obtaining a judgment and getting a sheriff to seize and sell property of a debtor can be difficult, time consuming and expensive.

(3) Obtaining a judgment and getting a sheriff to seize and sell property of a debtor is often unsuccessful as a way of collecting a debt. There is no guarantee that the judgment debtor will have property that can be seized and sold, or that the property will be in the place that the judgment creditor told the sheriff to go look.

And, even if the judgment debtor has property, that property may be encumbered by other creditors' liens that have priority. These other liens may have been created because of (i) a prior judicial collection effort, or (ii) statute, or (iii) agreement.

3. STATUTORY LIENS AND LIENS CREATED BY AGREEMENT

Tax liens, mechanics' liens and landlords' liens are examples of statutory liens. These are liens that arise by operation of law-arise if the debtor fails to pay a debt protected by the statute.

While statutory liens are important, consensual liens are the most common liens. Most debt deals which are large enough to involve lawyers also involve consensual liens.

A big part of bankruptcy practice and a big part of law school bankruptcy courses deals with consensual liens and so a big part of this book deals with consensual liens, For now, you need to understand that: (1) by contract, a creditor can obtain property rights in addition to the rights available to a creditor under generally available state creditors' remedies law; (2) these rights, i.e., these consensual liens, have the effect of limiting the rights of other creditors under creditors' remedies law; and (3) these consensual liens are property rights and so enjoy the constitutional protection afforded to property rights (you know, due process, no takings, and all that Fifth Amendment stuff on your Con Law test). In essence, a creditor with a consensual lien (or any lien for that matter) really has two claims: (1) an *in personam* (or contract) claim against the debtor based on the promise or obligation to pay, and (2) an *in rem* (or property) claim against the collateral.

State law controls the creation and effect of consensual liens. State law tends to categorize the types of consensual liens by the type of property involved. The two basic types of property in this regard are real property (that is, dirt and things built on and attached to the dirt) and personal property (that is, things that are not dirt or attached to dirt, both tangible (goods) and intangible (like accounts receivable)).

There are various devices for creating consensual liens on real property; i.e., the mortgage, the deed of trust, and the installment land-sale contract. When properly recorded in the local real estate records, these instruments establish the lender's *priority* in the property over other parties, such as other creditors and purchasers, that might claim an interest in the land.

When the creditor and debtor create a consensual lien on personal property or fixtures, the governing law is Uniform Commercial Code, Article 9. All 50 states have adopted Article 9 (yes, *even* Louisiana). Article 9 provides for only one kind of consensual lien on personal property, the "Article 9 security interest."

"Security interest" is Article 9's term for a consensual lien on personal property. Other Article 9 terms that you will encounter in this book are "secured party" and "perfection." A "secured party" under Article 9 is a creditor with a security interest. Perfection refers to action taken by the secured party to establish the priority of its security interest over other parties with an interest in the same property, including creditors with judgment liens. Perfection is usually, but not always, accomplished by filing what's known as a UCC financing statement in the appropriate state government office.

B. WHAT CAN A DEBTOR DO OUTSIDE OF BANKRUPTCY?

There is not much that debtor can do outside of bankruptcy to fix its debt problems. At least not much that a debtor can do without the help and support of its creditors.

1. EXEMPT PROPERTY

If the debtor is an individual (that is, a flesh and blood human), state and some nonbankruptcy federal laws exempt certain property of the debtor from the collection efforts by judgment creditors. At most, these exemption statutes enable a debtor to protect some of their property, or at least part of the value of their property, from execution by their creditors.

State exemption laws vary significantly from state to state. In most states, the amount of property that a debtor can designate as exempt, and retain free from execution, is very limited—enough to assure only a subsistence level of living for the debtor and her dependents. And, in all states, creditors with a mortgage or other lien on property that is designated as exempt are not covered by exemption law; they are themselves "exempt" from it, and therefore can still seize and sell that property free from the exemption law claim. If, for example, Bank has a mortgage on *D*'s house and *D* defaults, First Bank can seize and sell *D*'s house even if *D* has designated the house as *D*'s exempt homestead.

All exemption statutes do is leave an individual debtor with some property. Exemption statutes do not enable a person with debt problems to "fix" the problems.

2. WORKOUT AGREEMENTS

A debtor can try to work out some sort of debt repayment agreement with its creditors. Professors who teach first year contracts courses call these agreements "compositions" and "extensions." Real lawyers call these agreements "workout agreements." Their creditor clients call these agreements "haircuts" (or worse).

Whatever you call these agreements, they are "agreements" and only bind the creditors who agree. If even one creditor refuses to participate in the workout agreement, that dissenting creditor, can in essence, "blow up" any deal by suing on its debt and using the execution process to seize and sell assets of the debtor that are essential to the debtor's performing its workout obligations to the assenting creditors.

C. WHY BANKRUPTCY?

If you understand the material in this Chapter of the book, then you know the answer to the question "Why bankruptcy."

To summarize:

First, judicial collection law focuses on each individual creditor's collection effort against the debtor; it is not concerned with the rights of creditors as a group.[3]

Second, judicial collection law is "grab law," meaning that the creditor that reaches the debtor's property first gets all the value of that property, at least until its judgment is satisfied, before later creditors get anything. (If you come from a big family, think about mealtime and you probably get the idea.)

Third, because the race goes to the swiftest, once creditors get the idea that the debtor may be experiencing financial difficulties, the feeding frenzy begins and any hope the debtor might have had of reversing its fortunes are out the door, literally and figuratively.

Fourth, because the judicial collection process calls for the forced sale of the debtor's property at auction, judicial collection law produces notoriously low

---

[3] There is an infrequently used exception to this statement known as an "assignment for the benefits of creditors" or "ABC." An ABC is a state law, usually statutory, procedure that allows a debtor to voluntarily liquidate its assets in order to pay creditors. Specifically, the debtor will transfer title to all of its nonexempt assets to an assignee that acts as a representative for the debtor's creditors. While creditors will often cooperate with debtor's seeking to use an ABC, there is no way of making them do so. Also, and perhaps most importantly, the debtor cannot obtain a general discharge of debts remaining unpaid after its assets are liquidated and distributed in an ABC, because of the "Impairment of Contracts" clause of the Constitution. In addition to ABC's, there are a variety of both state and federal statutes that call for appointment of a "receiver" under various circumstances, including insolvency of the debtor, to take possession of the debtor's assets with the intent to sell them and disburse the proceeds to creditors according to the priority of their interests. While not unimportant in certain specialized situations, there is not a well-developed body of "receivership law."

values for the debtor's property; *i.e.*, much lower than what would be attained if the property could be sold in an orderly, market transaction.

And so, the rest of the book is about bankruptcy.

PART II

WHAT YOU NEED TO KNOW ABOUT BANKRUPTCY[1]

In general, a law student or practicing lawyer needs to be able to answer four questions about bankruptcy:

(1) How does a bankruptcy case begin?

(2) What happens during a bankruptcy case?

(3) How does a bankruptcy case end?

(4) How can a later bankruptcy affect transactions?

The bankruptcy law answers to these questions turn on the form of bankruptcy involved.

---

1 I understand that the title of this part of the book is somewhat misleading. "MORE THAN WHAT YOU NEED TO KNOW ABOUT BANKRUPTCY" is probably more accurate for law students. Many law school profs will not cover all of this stuff.

CHAPTER III

BANKRUPTCY: AN OVERVIEW

Initially, four basic differences between bankruptcy and state debtor-creditor law should be noted.

First, bankruptcy law is federal law.

Second, state law focuses on individual action by a particular creditor and puts a premium on prompt action by a creditor. The first creditor to take meaningful extrajudicial or judicial collection action is the one most likely to be paid. Bankruptcy, on the other hand, compels collective creditor collection action and emphasizes equality of treatment, rather than a race of diligence. While bankruptcy law does not require equal treatment for all creditors, all creditors within a single class are treated the same. After the commencement of a bankruptcy case, a creditor cannot improve its position vis-a-vis other creditors by seizing the assets of the debtor.

Third, the prospects for debtor relief are much greater in bankruptcy. For individual debtors, this bankruptcy relief may take the form of relief from further personal liability for debts because of a discharge. While no debtor is guaranteed a discharge, most individual debtors do receive a discharge. "One of the primary purposes of the bankruptcy act is to 'relieve the honest debtor from the weight of oppressive indebtedness and permit him to start afresh. . . .' " Local Loan Co. v. Hunt, 292 U.S. 234 (1934). For business debtors, this bankruptcy relief may take the form of a restructuring of debts by reason of a confirmed Chapter 11 plan.

Fourth, the vocabulary of bankruptcy law is different from the vocabulary of state collection law. The Bankruptcy Code uses technical terms such as "automatic stay" and "impairment" that are not a part of state law. And, the Bankruptcy Code uses terms such as "debtor" and "redemption" that are a part of state law differently than state law. Accordingly, it is very important that you consistently and persistently check for the statutory definitions of terms used in the Bankruptcy Code.

A. BANKRUPTCY LAW

Article I of the Constitution empowers Congress to "establish uniform laws on the subject of Bankruptcies throughout the United States." For most of the 20th century, bankruptcy law was the Bankruptcy Act of 1898, commonly referred to as the "Bankruptcy Act." It was replaced in 1978 by a law commonly referred to as the "Bankruptcy Reform Act of 1978" or "Bankruptcy Code." The Bankruptcy Code has been regularly amended; the most comprehensive bankruptcy amendments were enacted in 1984, 2005, and 2019.

This book will introduce you to bankruptcy one concept at a time: stays, then property of the estate, then exempt property, then. . . . That is the easiest way to gain an initial understanding of bankruptcy law. As one of the great bankruptcy teachers, Steve Riesenfeld, observed, "Bankruptcy law is a series of lumps. Do not make mashed potatoes out of it."

The book will also explore some of the connections or relationships of these various concepts. For example, a determination that a doctor's malpractice insurance is property of the estate when she files for bankruptcy can affect the application of the automatic stay to creditors' efforts to collect under that insurance. The various bankruptcy concepts are connected or related.

Judge Grant expressed the same thought much more eloquently in In re Depew, 115 B.R. 965 (1989):

> The Bankruptcy Code is not a fragmented and disconnected collection of miscellaneous rules. It is a complex tapestry of ideas. The colors and patterns that are woven into its fabric combine to compliment and reinforce each other. In order to create a single unifying theme—the equitable treatment of creditors and financial relief for over-burdened debtors. In doing so, the tensions between these seemingly inconsistent objectives have been balanced and harmonized. Consequently, title 11's various provisions should not be viewed in isolation. Instead, the interpretation should reflect the interplay between all of its different parts, so that the Bankruptcy Code can operate as a coherent whole. The meaning given to any one portion must be consistent with the remaining provisions of the Bankruptcy Code.

The Bankruptcy Code divides the substantive law of bankruptcy into the following chapters:

Chapter 1, General Provisions, Definitions and Rules of Construction

Chapter 3, Case Administration

Chapter 5, Creditors, the Debtor, and the Estate

Chapter 7, Liquidation

Chapter 9, Adjustment of the Debts of a Municipality

Chapter 11, Reorganization

Chapter 12, Adjustment of the Debts of a Family Farmer With Regular Annual Income

Chapter 13, Adjustment of the Debts of an Individual With Regular Income

Chapter 15, Ancillary and Other Cross-Border Cases

The provisions in Chapters 1, 3 and 5 apply in every bankruptcy case, unless otherwise specified. Accordingly, if you are working on a problem in a Chapter 11 case, it will be necessary to deal with the provisions of Chapters 1, 3, 5 and 11.

It is also necessary to deal with the Bankruptcy Rules. Pursuant to the authority of 28 USC § 2075, the United States Supreme Court promulgated Bankruptcy Rules. These rules, not the Federal Rules of Civil Procedure, "govern procedure in cases under title II of the Code," Rule 1001. The Bankruptcy Rules are divided into ten parts. Each part governs a different stage of the bankruptcy process. For example, Part 1 of the Rules, Rule 1002 through Rule 1019 deals with issues related to commencement of cases.

Bankruptcy law is also in large part state law. I am not here suggesting that there are state bankruptcy laws. Since Article I of the Constitution empowers Congress to enact uniform laws of bankruptcy and Congress has enacted such laws, principles of federal supremacy preclude state legislatures from enacting bankruptcy laws. Rather, bankruptcy law is in large part state law because courts applying the federal bankruptcy law look to state law to determine questions such as (1) what are the property rights of the debtor and (2) what are the claims of the creditors to that property. As the Supreme Court stated in Butner v. United States, 440 U.S. 48 (1979):

> Congress has generally left the determination of property rights in the assets of a bankrupt's estate to state law.
>
> Property interests are created and defined by state law. Unless some federal interest requires a different result, there is no reason why such interests should be analyzed differently simply because an interested party is involved in a bankruptcy proceeding.

B. FORMS OF BANKRUPTCY RELIEF

There are two general forms of bankruptcy relief: (1) liquidation and (2) rehabilitation or reorganization.

The Bankruptcy Code provides for these two forms of relief in six separate kinds of bankruptcy cases: (1)

Chapter 7 cases, (2) Chapter 9 cases, (3) Chapter 11 cases, (4) Chapter 12 cases, (5) Chapter 13 cases, and (6) Chapter 15 cases.

This book does not deal with Chapters 9, 12 or 15. Chapter 9 cases involve governmental entities as debtors, and it is infrequently used. Chapter 12 is limited to family farmer bankruptcy. Chapter 15 deals with cross-border insolvency proceeding. This nutshell will deal with the three basic forms of bankruptcy relief: Chapter 7, Chapter 11 and Chapter 13.

The vast majority of bankruptcy cases are Chapter 7 cases. Chapter 7 is entitled "Liquidation." The title is descriptive. In a Chapter 7 case, the trustee collects the nonexempt property of the debtor, converts that property to cash, and distributes the cash to the creditors. The debtor gives up all of the nonexempt property they own at the time of the filing of the bankruptcy petition in the hope of obtaining a discharge. A discharge releases the debtor from any further personal liability for their prebankruptcy debts.

Assume, for example, that *B* owes *C* $2,000. *B* files a Chapter 7 petition. *C* only receives $300 from the liquidation of *B*'s assets. If *B* receives a bankruptcy discharge, *C* will be precluded from pursuing *B* for the remaining $1,700.

As the preceding paragraph implies, every Chapter 7 case under the bankruptcy laws does not result in a discharge. Section 727(a) considered infra, lists a number of grounds for withholding a discharge. And, even if the debtor is able to obtain a discharge, she will not necessarily be freed from all creditors' claims. Section 523, considered infra, sets out specific exceptions to discharge.

Chapters 11 and 13 generally deal with debtor rehabilitation or reorganization, not liquidation, of the debtor's assets. In a Chapter 11 or 13 case creditors usually look to future earnings of the debtor, not the property of the debtor at the time of the filing of the bankruptcy proceeding, to satisfy their claims. The debtor retains its assets and makes payments to creditors, usually from postpetition earnings, pursuant to a court approved plan.

Chapter 11, like Chapter 7, is available to all forms of debtors—individuals, partnerships, limited liability companies and corporations. Chapter 13 can be used only by individuals with (i) a "regular income" as defined in section 101(27) (ii) who have unsecured debts and secured debts that do not exceed the dollar amounts in section 109(e)[1].

C. BANKRUPTCY COURTS AND BANKRUPTCY JUDGES

1. UNDER THE BANKRUPTCY ACT OF 1898

The Bankruptcy Act of 1898 provided for "bankruptcy referees." Originally, the judicial role of bankruptcy referees was relatively minor. The referee was primarily an administrator and

---

[1] These dollar amounts are adjusted periodically pursuant to section 104 to reflect changes in the Consumer Price Index.

supervisor of bankruptcy cases, not a judicial officer. Amendments to the Bankruptcy Act of 1898 made the bankruptcy referee more of a judicial officer. In 1973, the Bankruptcy Rules changed the title of the office from "bankruptcy referee" to "bankruptcy judge."

2. UNDER THE PRESENT LAW

Congress deals with the bankruptcy court system separately from the substantive law of bankruptcy. The substantive law of bankruptcy is now in title 11 of the United States Code; the law relating to allocation of judicial power over bankruptcy is in title 28.

Title 28 does not use the term "bankruptcy referee." Section 152 of title 28 provides for "bankruptcy judges" to be appointed by the United States courts of appeals. Section 151 of title 28 states that these bankruptcy judges "shall constitute a unit of the district court to be known as the bankruptcy court." Under title 28, the bankruptcy court is not really a separate court; rather, it is a part of the district court.

Accordingly, the grant of jurisdiction over bankruptcy matters is to the district court, 28 USC § 1334. The federal district judges then refer bankruptcy matters to the bankruptcy judges pursuant to 28 USC § 157.

It is important to understand the differences between 28 USC § 1334 and 28 USC § 157. Section 1334 grants jurisdiction over bankruptcy cases and proceedings; all grants of jurisdiction are to the district court. Neither the phrase "bankruptcy court" nor the phrase "bankruptcy judge" appears in section 1334. Remember, however, that the bankruptcy judge is a unit of the district court under section 151. Thus, a grant of jurisdiction to the "district court" does not preclude the bankruptcy judge from playing a role in bankruptcy litigation.

Section 157 spells out the role that the bankruptcy judge is to play in bankruptcy litigation. Section 157 is entitled "Procedures" and deals with referral of matters from the "district court" to the bankruptcy judge. Section 157 is not a jurisdictional provision; it does not grant jurisdiction to the bankruptcy judges.

In summary, section 1334 speaks to what district courts can do and is jurisdictional. Section 157 deals with what the bankruptcy judges can do and is procedural.

The allocation of judicial power and responsibility over bankruptcy matters is one of the most controversial and complex areas of bankruptcy law and practice. I believe that you will find it easier to deal with the bankruptcy jurisdiction issues after you have gained a greater understanding of the substantive law of bankruptcy. Accordingly, bankruptcy jurisdiction issues will not be dealt with until later in this book.

D. TRUSTEES

In every Chapter 7 case, every Chapter 12 case, every Chapter 13 case and some Chapter 11 cases,[2] there will be not only a bankruptcy judge but also a bankruptcy trustee. Generally, the bankruptcy trustee will be a private citizen, not an employee of the federal government.

A bankruptcy trustee is an active trustee. According to section 323 of the Bankruptcy Code, the bankruptcy trustee is "the representative of the estate." The filing of a bankruptcy petition is said to create an estate consisting generally of the property of the debtor as of the time of the bankruptcy filing. This estate is treated as a separate legal entity, distinct from the debtor. The bankruptcy trustee is the person who sues or may be sued on behalf of the estate.

The powers and duties of a bankruptcy trustee vary from chapter to chapter. Recall that Chapter 7 bankruptcy is essentially liquidation. The duties of a bankruptcy trustee in a Chapter 7 case include

(1) collecting the "property of the estate," i.e., debtor's property as of the time of the filing of the bankruptcy petition;

---

[2] In a "standard" Chapter 11, the bankruptcy court decides whether it is necessary to appoint a trustee, section 1104. Since 2020, a significant number of Chapter 11 cases are Subdivision V Chapter 11 cases. Chapter XVI explains new Subdivision V.

(2) challenging certain prebankruptcy and postbankruptcy transfers of the property of the estate;

(3) selling the property of the estate;

(4) objecting to creditors' claims that are improper;

(5) in appropriate cases, objecting to the debtor's discharge, section 704.

Remember that there will be a bankruptcy trustee in every Chapter 7 case. And, in most Chapter 7 cases, most of the work is done by the Chapter 7 trustee.

There will also be a trustee in every Chapter 13 case, and also in most Chapter 13 cases the trustee does most of the work. But, the person who works as a Chapter 13 trustee is different from the person who works as a Chapter 7 trustee, and the work that they does is different.

A Chapter 7 trustee is generally an attorney in private practice and their trustee work is only a part of their work. For the typical Chapter 13 trustee their Chapter 13 work is a full time job.

The duties of a Chapter 13 trustee also differ significantly from the duties of a Chapter 7 trustee. Section 1302 sets out the duties of a Chapter 13 trustee, and there seems to a considerable overlap between section 1302 and section 702 which sets out the duties of a Chapter 7 trustee.

The major differences between the work of a Chapter 13 trustee and the work of a Chapter 7 trustee mirror the major difference between Chapter 13 and Chapter 7: payments pursuant to a court approved plan as compared with payments pursuant to liquidation. Accordingly, a Chapter 13 trustee does not collect and liquidate the debtor's property. Instead, the Chapter 13 trustee reviews and, where appropriate, contests the debtor's plan of repayment, and, after court approval of the Chapter 13 plan of repayment, serves as disbursing agent for the payments to creditors under the plan.

While there is a bankruptcy trustee in every Chapter 7 case and every Chapter 13 case, until 2020. there was rarely a bankruptcy trustee in a Chapter 11 case. 2019 Bankruptcy Code amendments that became effective in 2020 added a Subchapter V Small Business Debtor Reorganization alternative for small businesses that come within the definition of "debtor" in section 1181.

The typical Chapter 11 case involves a business that continues to operate after the bankruptcy petition is filed. Except for Subchapter V cases, a bankruptcy trustee in a Chapter 11 case takes over the operation of the business. Generally, neither the debtor nor the creditors want that to happen The debtor will usually remain in control of the business after the filing of a Chapter 11 petition; such a debtor is referred to as a "debtor in possession."

The new Subchapter V requires that a trustee be appointed for each case. A Subchapter V trustee, however, does not take over the operation of the business, Instead, a Subchapter V trustee serves as an advisor to facilitate compliance with the requirements of Chapter 11 and the confirmation of a Chapter 11 plan.

E. UNITED STATES TRUSTEES

There was no such thing as a United States trustee until the 1978 bankruptcy legislation. During the debate on the legislation, considerable concern was expressed over the bankruptcy judges' involvement in the administration of bankruptcy cases. While both the House and the Senate seemed to agree that the bankruptcy judge should not perform administrative functions, there was disagreement over who should. The compromise was a United States trustee program.

The United States trustee is a government official, appointed by the Attorney General. More specifically, the Attorney General appoints a United States trustee for each of the various "regions" across the country. Essentially, the United States trustee performs administrative tasks that the bankruptcy judge would otherwise have to perform.

To illustrate, the United States trustee, not the bankruptcy judge, selects and supervises the bankruptcy trustees. Although the United States trustee can act as trustee in a Chapter 7 case or a Chapter 13 case (but not a Chapter 11 case), they are not intended as a substitute for private bankruptcy trustees. The United States trustee is more of a substitute for the bankruptcy judge with respect to supervisory and administrative matters.

CHAPTER IV

COMMENCEMENT, CONVERSION AND DISMISSAL OF A BANKRUPTCY CASE

A bankruptcy case begins with the filing of a petition with the bankruptcy court, section 301. Generally, the debtor files the petition. Such debtor-initiated cases are often referred to as "voluntary." Creditors have a limited right to initiate "involuntary" bankruptcy cases against the debtor under Chapters 7 and 11.

A. VOLUNTARY CASES

Section 301 deals with the commencement of voluntary cases under Chapter 7, 9, 11, 12 or 13. It provides that a bankruptcy petition may be filed by any "entity that may be a debtor under such chapter." Section 109 sets out who is eligible to be a debtor under each chapter.

Section 109(h) makes an individual ineligible to be a debtor under any of the chapters unless within 180 days of her bankruptcy filing she received a briefing from "an approved nonprofit budget and credit counseling agency" approved by the United States trustee under standards set out in section 111. This briefing can be a group briefing; it can be by telephone or the internet.

Section 109(b) contains two limitations on the availability of Chapter 7 (liquidation) relief to a debtor:

(1) The debtor must be a "person." "Person" is defined in section 101 as including partnerships and corporations. A sole proprietorship would not be a "person."

(2) The debtor may not be a railroad, insurance company, or banking institution. Railroads are eligible for bankruptcy relief only under Subchapter IV of Chapter 11; insurance companies and banking institutions are excluded from relief under the Bankruptcy Code because their liquidations are governed by other state and federal regulatory laws.

[For most questions of whether an individual debtor can use Chapter 7 petition, you need to deal not only with section 109(b) eligibility but also with section 707(b) dismissal. Section 707(b) contains detailed provisions for dismissal of Chapter 7 cases filed by an individual debtor with primarily consumer debts upon a finding of "abuse." We will deal with section 707(b) dismissal in the materials on dismissal in this chapter.]

With two exceptions, any person who is eligible to file a petition under Chapter 7 is also eligible to file a petition under Chapter 11, section 109(d). The first exception is railroads. As noted above, railroads are eligible for Chapter 11, but not Chapter 7. The second exception is stockbrokers and commodity brokers; they are eligible for Chapter 7, but not Chapter 11.

Since 2020 individuals or business entities that a (i) are "engaged in business or commercial activities" and (ii) have non-contingent, liquidated debts less than the amount set out in section 1181 may choose to use Subchapter V of Chapter 11.

There are three significant limitations in section 109(e) on the availability of Chapter 13:

(1) The debtor must be an individual. A Chapter 13 petition may not be filed by a corporation or a partnership.

(2) The individual must have "income sufficiently stable and regular to enable such individual to make payments under a [Chapter 13 plan]," sections 101, 109(e). This includes not only wage earners, but also self-employed individuals, and individuals on welfare, pensions, or investment income.

(3) The debtor must have "noncontingent, liquidated" unsecured debts and "noncontingent, liquidated" secured debts less than the limits set out in section 109(e).

Note that not all debts are included in the debt limit. Debts that are contingent or unliquidated are ignored. Note also that all debts are not counted the same. The test is not a single limit but rather two separate limits: first, unsecured debts; and second, secured debts.

Consider the application of these limits to partly secured debt. What if *D* owes *C* $1,500,000 and that debt is secured by property worth $1,100,000?

Most courts would find that *C*'s debt does not disqualify *D* from Chapter 13—that *D*'s obligation to *C* is a secured debt of $1,100,000 and an unsecured debt of $400,000. The statutory basis for such a finding is section 506 of the Bankruptcy Code which provides that a claim is secured only to the extent of the value of the collateral for the debt.

As this example illustrates, a single transaction outside of bankruptcy can create both a secured claim and an unsecured claim in bankruptcy. If *D* borrows $800,000 from *C* in a single transaction with a single set of documents, *C* will have both a secured claim and an unsecured claim if the collateral for the $800,000 loan has a value of less than $800,000.

While too much debt makes a debtor ineligible for Chapter 13, too much assets does not make a debtor ineligible for Chapter 7, 11 or 13. Please note that insolvency is not a condition precedent to any form of voluntary bankruptcy action. A debtor may file a petition under Chapter 7, 9, 11, 12 or 13 even though solvent.

[And, while too much assets does not make any debtor ineligible for any chapter, too much income can make individual debtors whose debts are primarily consumer debts ineligible for Chapter 7. Again, that is because of section 707(b). Again, this will be later in the material in this chapter on dismissal.]

A husband and a wife may file a joint petition for voluntary relief under any chapter that is available to *each* spouse. If a husband and a wife jointly file under Chapter 13, their aggregate debts are subject to the dollar limits in section 109(e).

As the preceding pages examining paragraphs (b), (d), and (e) of section 109 indicate, there are debtors that are eligible for some chapters of bankruptcy relief but not eligible for others. Additionally, there are individual debtors who are not eligible for relief under any chapter: new section 109(f) adds what could be roughly called a "frequent filing" limitation. Under section 109(f), an individual debtor is not eligible to be a debtor under either Chapter 7, 11 or 13, if he or she was a debtor in a bankruptcy case within the last 180 days and that case was:

(1) dismissed by the court for failure of the debtor to abide by court orders or appear before the court; or

(2) dismissed on motion of the debtor following the filing of a request for relief from the automatic stay.

[Note that section 109(f) does not bar an individual who has completed a Chapter 7, 11, or 13 case from immediately filing for bankruptcy again. We will later learn that such "recidivism" can preclude the debtor's receiving a second discharge.]

A voluntary bankruptcy case is commenced when an eligible debtor files a petition. No formal adjudication is necessary; the filing itself operates as an "order for relief," section 301.

B. INVOLUNTARY CASES

Creditors may, under certain circumstances, initiate a bankruptcy case by filing an involuntary petition against the debtor. Section 303 deals with involuntary petitions. It contains a number of significant limitations on involuntary petitions:

(1) Creditors may file involuntary petitions under Chapter 7 or 11 but not Chapter 9, 12 or 13.

(2) Certain debtors are protected from involuntary petitions. Insurance companies, banking institutions, farmers, and charitable corporations cannot be subjected to involuntary petitions.

(3) The petition must be filed by the requisite number of creditors. Generally, three creditors with unsecured claims totaling at least $16,750[1] must join in the petition. If, however, the debtor has less than twelve unsecured creditors, a single creditor with an unsecured claim of $16,750 is sufficient.

While the filing of an involuntary petition effects a commencement of the case, it does not operate as an adjudication, as an order for relief.[2] The debtor has

---

[1] Again the dollar amount is adjusted from time to time pursuant to section 104 to reflect changes in the Consumer Price Index.

[2] To review, all bankruptcy cases—voluntary and involuntary—commence when the petition is filed. Numerous Bankruptcy Code provisions refer to and focus on this event. In voluntary cases, the order for relief also dates from the time when

the right to file an answer. If the debtor does not timely answer the petition, "the court shall order relief," section 303(h). If the debtor does timely answer the petition, the court "shall order relief against the debtor" only if one of the two following grounds for involuntary relief are established.

The first ground for involuntary relief is that the debtor is generally not paying debts as they come due. This is sometimes referred to as "equitable insolvency"; it is different from the definition of insolvency in section 101.

The other possible ground for involuntary relief is that within 120 days before the petition was filed, a general receiver, assignee, or custodian took possession of substantially all of the debtor's property or was appointed to take charge of substantially all of the debtor's property. The appointment of a receiver in a mortgage foreclosure action who takes possession of Greenacre, less than substantially all of the debtor's property, would not be a basis for involuntary relief.

Usually there will be an interval of at least several weeks between the filing of an involuntary petition and the order of relief against the debtor. The bankruptcy court may appoint an interim trustee to take possession of the debtor's property or operate the debtor's business "if necessary to preserve the property of the estate or to prevent loss to the estate,"

---

the petition is filed. In involuntary cases, the order for relief occurs at a later time. See Rules 1011, 1013.

section 303(g). If an interim trustee is appointed, the debtor may regain possession by posting a bond.

Absent appointment of a trustee, the debtor may continue to buy, use, or sell property and to operate its business in the period after the bankruptcy filing and before the order of relief, section 303(f). Sections 502(f) and 507(a)(2) protect third parties who deal with a debtor after an involuntary petition has been filed. Notwithstanding the protection of section 303(f), the filing of an involuntary petition adversely affects the debtor's financial reputation and business operations. Section 303(i) attempts to protect debtors from ill-founded petitions by setting out the following remedies in cases in which an involuntary petition is dismissed after litigation:

(1) The court may grant judgment for the debtor against the petitioning creditors for costs and a reasonable attorney's fee.

(2) If the petition was filed in "bad faith," the court may award "any damages proximately caused by such filing," such as loss of business, and also punitive damages.

C. FOREIGN DEBTORS

A foreign debtor can start its own United States bankruptcy case by filing a voluntary bankruptcy petition if it has a residence or domicile in the United States, a place of business in the United States, or assets in the United States, section 109. Similarly, the creditors of such a foreign debtor may begin a bankruptcy case in the United States by filing an involuntary bankruptcy petition, section 303(b). The Bankruptcy Code treats such foreign debtor filings no differently than filings by or against domestic debtors. Such foreign debtor cases will be independent of any foreign bankruptcy proceedings.

Chapter 15 of the Bankruptcy Code provides an alternative to commencing a full bankruptcy case in the United States. If a bankruptcy case is pending in some foreign country, a "foreign representative" of the debtor in such a case may file a "petition for recognition." Upon the issuance of an order for recognition under section 1517, the automatic stay and selected other provisions of the Bankruptcy Code become effective, section 1519.

D. CONVERSION OF CASES

Remember that there are various forms of bankruptcy relief 13. The party filing a petition elects one of these chapters. For example, an individual might file a petition for relief under Chapter 7 or 11 or 13.

The petitioner's choice of a chapter is sometimes reversible; Chapter 7, Chapter 11, and Chapter 13 have provisions governing conversion of a case filed under that chapter to another chapter. The grounds for conversion vary from chapter to chapter. The Code provides for both voluntary and involuntary conversion.

E. DISMISSAL

The bankruptcy court may dismiss or suspend a voluntary bankruptcy case even though it was filed by an eligible debtor. And, the bankruptcy court may dismiss or suspend an involuntary bankruptcy case even though all of the filing requirements are satisfied.

Each bankruptcy relief chapter has its own dismissal provision. Section 707 governs dismissal of Chapter 7 cases.

A debtor who files a Chapter 7 petition does not have an absolute right to have the bankruptcy case dismissed. Under section 707(a), the standard a bankruptcy court is to apply in ruling on a motion to dismiss is "for cause"; section 707(a) gives two examples of cause. Accordingly, a debtor might find it much easier to "get into" Chapter 7 than it is to "get out."

A debtor might also find it easier to "get into" Chapter 7 than it is to stay in Chapter 7. The court on its own motion or a motion by the United States Trustee or a creditor might dismiss a Chapter 7 petition.

Section 707(b)(1) provides for dismissal of a Chapter 7 petition filed by an individual debtor with primarily consumer debts for "abuse." Again, section 707(b) only applies to individuals whose debts are primarily consumer debts. There are two different ways to establish section 707(b)(1) "abuse":

First way of establishing section 707 "abuse": reading section 707(b)(1) together with section 707(b)(3), "abuse" turns on bad faith filing or "totality of the circumstances of the debtor's financial situation."

Second way of establishing section 707 "abuse": reading section 707(b)(1) together with section 707(b)(2), "abuse" turns on what is generally referred to as a "means test."

The policy reason for the section 707(b) means test is easy to state in class or on an exam. The section 707(b) means test is based on the premise that if debtors can afford to pay their creditors what Congress believes is a meaningful amount they can not use Chapter 7 to avoid paying.

However, the particulars of the section 707(b) means test are hard to explain in class or an exam. You should understand that in real bankruptcy cases, the particulars of the section 707(b)(2) means test will usually not be applicable. Accordingly, for most bankruptcy classes and on most bankruptcy exams, you do not need to know the particulars of section 707.

More specifically, here are the three things I think you need to know about the means test for class and on your exam. First, you need know what "current monthly income" as defined in section 101 is. The word "current in "current monthly income," is misleading, You don't look to what the debtor is earning at the time of the bankruptcy petition, Instead, you look to the debtor's average monthly income for the over the six months before the bankruptcy petition.[3]

Second, you need to know about "median family income" as defined in section 101. I can best explain that term with an example. If D, an Idaho resident who is married but without children files for bankruptcy, the relevant "median family income" would be determined looking to government statistics for median annual income for Idaho families of two.

Third, if the debtor's "current monthly income" times 12 is less than the debtor's "median family income," the debtor "passes" the means test and the Chapter 7 petition is not dismissed. Again, in almost all Chapter 7 bankruptcy cases, the debtor's "current monthly income" multiplied by 12 will be less than "median family income". Accordingly, it will not be necessary to consider the other particulars of the section 707(b)(2) means test.

For those debtors you encounter in the real world or in law school classes with "current monthly income" above "median family income," section 707(b)(2) creates a means test that compares 60 months of "current monthly income" (as defined in section 101) with the total of the following:

---

[3] It is possible to "manipulate" a debtor's "current monthly income." The statutory definition looks to an average of income for the six months prior to the bankruptcy filing. A person who has been earning $2,000 a month can reduce their "current monthly income" from $2,000 to $1,666.66 by not working and not having any income for the month before their bankruptcy filing.

(1) 60 months of expenses measured by Internal Revenue Service expense standards; and

(2) 60 months of other, actual expenses specified in section 707(b)(2); and

(3) payments due on secured and priority debts for the 60 months after the bankruptcy petition date.

In Chapter 11, like Chapter 7, the standard a bankruptcy court is to apply to a motion to dismiss is "for cause." Again, the statute sets out examples of cause, section 1112(b). Again, the "cause" standard applies to both debtor and creditor motions.

In Chapter 13, unlike Chapters 7 and 11, a debtor is given an absolute right to have his or her Chapter 13 case dismissed, section 1307(b). Motions to dismiss filed by creditors in a Chapter 13 case are subject to the "for cause" standard. Section 1307(c) sets out examples of "cause."

In Chapter 7, 11 and 13 cases, a debtor or creditors can also base a motion to dismiss on section 305. Section 305 empowers the bankruptcy court to dismiss or suspend a case if (1) there is a foreign bankruptcy proceeding pending concerning the debtor or (2) "the interests of creditors and the debtor would be better served by such dismissal or suspension."[4]

---

[4] The bankruptcy court may also dismiss a bankruptcy case for failure to pay filing fees.

To illustrate, *D*, Inc., is generally not paying its debts as they come due. *D*, Inc. is trying to negotiate a workout with its creditors. Three of *D*, Inc.'s creditors are dissatisfied with the terms proposed in the workout and file an involuntary Chapter 11 petition against *D*, Inc. The bankruptcy court may decide to dismiss this petition if *D*, Inc. is making progress in negotiating a workout with its creditors.

A section 305 dismissal must be preceded by "notice and a hearing." The decision to dismiss (or not to dismiss) is not appealable. If an involuntary petition is dismissed under section 305, the petitioning creditors are not liable for costs, attorneys' fees or damages under section 303(i).

F. BACK TO THE BEGINNING: CONSEQUENCES OF COMMENCEMENT

The mere filing of a bankruptcy petition (i.e., the "commencement of the case") has important and immediate legal consequences. The most important legal consequence of filing a bankruptcy petition—the automatic stay—is the subject of the next Chapter of this book.

CHAPTER V

STAY OF COLLECTION ACTIONS AND ACTS

After the filing of a bankruptcy petition, a debtor needs immediate protection from the collection efforts of creditors. If the petition is a voluntary Chapter 7, the bankruptcy trustee needs time to collect the "property of the estate" and make pro rata distributions to creditors. If the petition is a voluntary Chapter 11 or Chapter 13, the debtor needs time to prepare a plan. And, if the petition is an involuntary Chapter 7 or Chapter 11, the debtor needs time to controvert the petition. Moreover, since creditors will receive payment through the bankruptcy process or the plan of rehabilitation and some claims will be discharged, continued creditor actions would interfere with orderly bankruptcy administration.

Accordingly, the filing of a voluntary petition under Chapter 7, Chapter 11 or Chapter 13, or the filing of an involuntary petition under Chapter 7 or Chapter 11 automatically "stays," i.e., restrains, creditors from taking further action against the debtor, the property of the debtor, or the property of the estate to collect their claims or enforce their liens, section 362.

There are four stay questions that lawyers (and law students) are asked:

(1) When does the automatic stay become effective? (Time Stay Arises)

(2) What is covered by the automatic stay? (Scope of the Stay)

(3) When does the automatic stay end? (Termination of the Stay)

(4) How can a creditor obtain relief from the stay? (Relief From the Stay)

A. TIME STAY ARISES

The automatic stay is triggered by the filing of a bankruptcy petition. It dates from the time of the filing, not from the time that a creditor receives notice of or learns of the bankruptcy. If *D* files a bankruptcy petition on April 5, the stay becomes effective April 5. The stay dates from April 5 even if creditors do not learn of the bankruptcy until much later. If *C*, not knowing of *D*'s bankruptcy, obtains a default judgment against *D* on April 29, the default judgment violates the automatic stay and is invalid.

B. SCOPE OF THE STAY

1. SECTION 362

Paragraph (a) of section 362 defines the scope of the automatic stay by listing all of the acts and actions that are stayed by the commencement of a bankruptcy case. It is comprehensive and includes virtually all creditor collection activity.

Subparagraphs (1) and (2) of section 362(a) cover most litigation efforts of creditors directed at collecting prebankruptcy debts. Section 362(a)(1) stays creditors from filing collection suits after the bankruptcy petition is filed or from continuing collection suits that were commenced prior to bankruptcy. Section 362(a)(2) bars creditors from enforcing judgments obtained prior to bankruptcy.

Section 362(a)(6) stays "any act to collect . . . ." This phrase has been interpreted as barring informal collection actions such as telephone calls demanding payments and dunning letters.

Subparagraphs (3), (4) and (5) stay virtually all types of secured creditor action against property of the estate or property of the debtor. Creditors are barred from obtaining liens, perfecting liens or enforcing liens after the bankruptcy petition is filed.

Recently, in *City of Chicago, Illinois v. Fulton* (2021), the Supreme Court rejected the argument that a creditor's "mere retention" of property that it had repossessed prior to bankruptcy violated section 362(a)(3). The Court's decision was based on section 542, both of which are explained in Chapter X.

While paragraph (a) of section 362 indicates what is stayed, paragraph (b) of section 362 lists actions that are not stayed. The most important exception is section 362(b)(2) which provides a somewhat limited exception for "domestic support obligations" (as defined in section 101). Such claims can be collected from property that is not "property of the estate." Most of the other section 362(b) exceptions are very narrowly drawn and apply in relatively few bankruptcy cases.

There is an important limitation on the scope of section 362 that is not dealt with in paragraph (b) of section 362. The automatic stay of section 362(a) only covers the debtor, property of the debtor, and property of the estate. It does not protect third parties. Assume, for example, that *D* borrows $3,000 from *C* and *G* guarantees repayment. If *D* files for bankruptcy, section 362(a) will stay *C* from attempting to collect from *D*. Section 362(a) will not, however, protect *G*.

2. SECTION 1301

While section 362(a) will not protect *G*, section 1301 might. By reason of section 1301, the filing of a Chapter 13 petition automatically stays collection action against guarantors and other co-debtors if

(1) the debt is a consumer debt; and

(2) the co-debtor is not in the credit business.

Section 1301's automatic stay of actions against co-debtors applies only in Chapter 13 cases; it is discussed in the chapter of this book dealing with Chapter 13 cases.

3. SECTION 105

Section 105 grants to bankruptcy courts the power to issue orders "necessary or appropriate to carry out the provisions of this title." Courts have used this section 105 power to stay or restrain creditor action against third parties.

There is an important procedural difference between section 105 and sections 362 or 1301. An injunction or stay under section 105 will not be automatic. Rather, it will be granted according to the usual rules for injunctive relief.

There is also an important substantive difference between section 105 and sections 362 or 1301. In acting under section 105, the bankruptcy court is not expressly limited by the restrictions in section 362 or section 1301.

If *D*, Inc. files for bankruptcy, a court cannot use section 362 to prevent creditors of *D*, Inc. from proceeding against *G*, who personally guaranteed *D*, Inc.'s debts. There are, however, numerous reported cases in which courts have invoked section 105 to protect *G* from *D*, Inc.'s creditors during the course of the bankruptcy. Courts that have so ruled have generally emphasized the importance of *G* to the success of *D*, Inc.'s bankruptcy—perhaps *G* is the chief executive officer who needs to devote all of her time and attention to *D*, Inc.'s bankruptcy, perhaps *G* is a possible source of the new funds that *D*, Inc. needs to reorganize.

C. TERMINATION OF THE STAY

Section 362(c)(1) and (2) describe two fairly common situations in which the automatic stay terminates automatically. Section 362(c)(1) provides that the automatic stay ends as to particular property when the property ceases to be property of the estate. Assume for example that *C* has a mortgage on *D* Corp.'s building. *D* Corp. files a bankruptcy petition. *C* is stayed from foreclosing its mortgage. The bankruptcy trustee sells *D* Corp.'s building to *X*. *C* is no longer stayed from foreclosing its lien.[1]

Section 362(c)(2) provides that the automatic stay ends when the bankruptcy case is closed or dismissed or the debtor receives a discharge. The typical Chapter 7 bankruptcy can be completed in a matter of months. In Chapter 11 cases and Chapter 13 cases, however, there can be a gap of several years between the filing of the petition and discharge. Accordingly, unless some action is taken, the stay can last several years.

There are also two grounds for automatic termination of the automatic stay based on the debtor's recent bankruptcy filings. Section 362(c)(3) provides that if the debtor had been the debtor in an earlier bankruptcy case that was dismissed within one year of this bankruptcy case filing, then the automatic stay automatically terminates 30 days after the filing unless the debtor or some other party in interest can show that the second case was filed in good faith. Section 362(c)(4) deals with the even less common situation of a debtor who has had two or more bankruptcy cases dismissed within the past year.

D. RELIEF FROM THE STAY

The bankruptcy court may grant relief from the automatic stay on the "request" of a "party in

---

1 Property also ceases to be property of the estate when it is abandoned to the debtor under section 554. Notwithstanding the language of section 362(c)(1), abandonment does *not* terminate the stay. The stay continues by reason of section 362(a)(5).

interest." The relief will not always take the form of termination of the stay. Section 362(d) provides for "relief" "such as by terminating, annulling, modifying, or conditioning such stay." The Bankruptcy Rules provide that the "request" in section 362 takes the form of a motion, Rules 4001(a), 9014. The facts of the reported cases make clear that the "party in interest" in section 362 is usually a creditor.

What does a creditor have to allege and prove to obtain relief from the stay? The grounds for relief from stay are set out in section 362(d).

1. SECTION 362(d)(1)

Section 362(d)(1) should have been divided into two separate provisions: first, "cause"—a general ground for relief from stay that can be invoked by any creditor and second, "lack of adequate protection of an interest in property"—a more specific ground for relief from stay that can be invoked only by a creditor with a lien.

The general statutory ground for relief from the stay is "for cause," section 362(d)(1). There is very little reported case law on what constitutes "cause" for purposes of section 362(d)(1). Bankruptcy courts routinely find "cause" to lift the stay to allow tort suits against the debtor to go forward in state court to determine liability where the plaintiff agrees that any judgment will be collected only from the liability insurance carrier or some other third party.

Most of the reported section 362(d)(1) cases involve the specific example of cause set out in the statute—"lack of adequate protection of an interest in property of such party in interest." The quoted language raises four questions: (1) who is "the party in interest" (2) what is "the interest in property" (3) from what is it being protected and (4) how much protection is "adequate protection."

The party in interest is the person seeking relief from the stay. Again, the party in interest under this last part of section 362(d)(1) will be a secured creditor.

Only a creditor with a lien, i.e., a secured creditor, has an "interest in property" and not just a right to payment. Note that what is to be protected is the secured creditor's "interest in property," not the secured creditor's right to payment. If, for example, *D* owes *C* $1,000,000 and *C* has a security interest on equipment worth $600,000, section 362(d)(1) contemplates adequate protection of *C*'s $600,000 lien position, rather than *C*'s right to the payment of $1,000,000.

The questions of what interest in property is protected and how much protection is adequate protection are closely related. These questions (and the answers to the questions) are relatively easy in a situation where the collateral is losing value through use, obsolescence or depreciation.

Consider again the above example in which *D* owes *C* $1,000,000, and the debt is secured by equipment with a value of $600,000. Assume that the value of the equipment is declining by $5,000 a month. Section 362(d) contemplates that *C* will be protected in some way from a $5,000 a month loss due to decline in value of the collateral.

A more difficult question was whether section 362(d) also contemplates that a partially secured creditor such as *C* would be protected from a loss due solely to delay in realization of the value of the collateral. The Supreme Court finally resolved that issue in United Savings Association of Texas v. Timbers of Inwood Forest Associates, Ltd., 484 U.S. 365 (1988). There a Chapter 11 debtor, an apartment complex limited partnership, owed more than $4.3 million to *C*, a creditor that had a deed of trust on the apartment complex. The collateral was worth at most $4.25 million and was not depreciating in value. *C* moved for relief from the stay contending that "adequate protection" under section 362(d) included payment to it of "lost opportunity costs." More specifically, *C* argued

(1) part of its "interest in property" is the right to seize and sell its collateral when the debtor defaults;

(2) if the debtor had not filed for bankruptcy, *C* could have sold the apartment complex for $4.25 million;

(3) *C* could have then lent this $4.25 million to another debtor and received interest on this new $4.25 million loan;

(4) accordingly, in order to provide "adequate protection" of *C*'s "interest in the property"

> as contemplated by section 362(d), the automatic stay should be conditioned on the debtor's making monthly payments to *C* equal to the amount that *C* would be receiving in interest payments on a new loan of $4.25 million. In sum, *C*'s argument was that "adequate protection" means that a debtor is compelled to pay a secured creditor for its "lost opportunity costs."

Looking to both legislative history and statutory language such as section 506, the Supreme Court in *Timbers* rejected this argument.

Section 361 does not define "adequate protection"; rather, section 361 specifies three nonexclusive methods of providing adequate protection. The first method of adequate protection specified is periodic cash payments to the lien creditor equal to the decrease in value of the creditors interest in the collateral. If *C* has a security interest in *D*'s car and *D* files a bankruptcy petition, *D* can meet the adequate protection burden of section 362 by making cash payments equal to the depreciation on the car, section 361(1).

Section 361(2) indicates that adequate protection may take the form of an additional lien or substitute lien on other property. Assume, for example, that *D* files a Chapter 11 petition. *C* has a perfected security in *D*'s equipment. *D* needs to use the encumbered equipment to continue operation of its business, to accomplish a successful Chapter 11 reorganization. Such use will, however, decrease the value of the equipment and the value of *C*'s lien in the equipment.

Under section 361(2) adequate protection may take the form of a lien on other property owned by *D*; the new collateral does not necessarily have to be equipment.

Section 361(3) grants the debtor in possession or trustee considerable flexibility in providing adequate protection. Section 361(3) recognizes such other protection, other than providing an administrative expense claim, that will result in the secured party's realizing the "indubitable equivalent" of the value of its interest in the collateral. The term "indubitable equivalent" is not statutorily defined. Even though sections 361 and 362(d) have remained unchanged since 1978, uncertainty remains as to (1) the importance of the "indubitable equivalent" language in section 361, and 361(2) the requirements of the "adequate protection" language in section 362(d).

This uncertainty is attributable in part to the practice of negotiating rather than litigating section 362(d)(1) issues and in part to what is decided in section 362(d)(1) litigation. Section 362(d)(1) does not contemplate that the bankruptcy judge will decide what is adequate protection and mandate that it be provided. Rather, in section 362(d)(1) litigation, the bankruptcy judge merely decides whether what the bankruptcy trustee or debtor in possession has offered is adequate protection.

What if (i) there is section 362(d)(1) litigation, (ii) the bankruptcy judge decides that the debtor is providing adequate protection and (iii) the "adequate protection" ultimately proves to be inadequate? To illustrate, *X* has a perfected security interest in the inventory of *D*. *D* files a Chapter 11 petition. At the time of the petition, *D* owes *X* $100,000, and the encumbered inventory has a value of $60,000. *X* requests relief from the stay. The court concludes that *D*'s offer of a personal guarantee by *G* was "adequate protection," was an "indubitable equivalent." This conclusion turns out to be wrong. When *D*'s Chapter 11 reorganization fails, *G* is insolvent. The value of the inventory now securing *D*'s $100,000 claim is worth only $20,000. Obviously, *X* cannot sue the bankruptcy judge. What can *X* do?

Section 507(b) applies when "adequate protection" proves to be inadequate. It grants an administrative expense priority[2] for the losses. In the above hypo, *X* would have a $40,000 administrative expense priority claim.

Stay litigation under section 362(d) can also involve the term "equity cushion." For example, if *D* owes *S* $500,000 and has *S* has a security interest in *D*'s equipment that is worth $700,000, then there is a $200,000 "equity cushion". While the property is worth $700,000, *S*'s interest in the property is only $500,000. In such a situation, depreciation of $10,000 does a month does not affect *S*'s $500,000 property interest. In such a situation, the "equity cushion" provides the required "adequate protection."

---

[2] The significance of an administrative expense priority is considered infra.

2. SECTION 362(d)(2)

Under section 362(d)(2) a lien creditor can obtain relief from the stay if

(A) the debtor does not have any equity in the encumbered property; AND

(B) the encumbered property is not necessary to an effective reorganization.

The application of section 362(d)(2)(A) would not seem to present any difficult legal issues: generally equity is measured by the difference between the value of the property and the encumbrances against it. If, for example, property has a value of $100,000 and is subject to a $120,000 lien, "the debtor does not have any equity in such property."

A creditor cannot obtain relief from the stay under section 362(d)(2) merely by establishing no equity under (A). Note the conjunction "and" connecting the no equity test of paragraph (A) with paragraph (B). A creditor relying on section 362(d)(2) then must satisfy both (A) and (B).

The language of paragraph (B) of section 362(d)(2) sets out two separate standards, provides two different opportunities for a creditor. The first possible section 362(d)(2)(B) argument for a creditor seeking relief from stay is that the encumbered property is not "necessary." Does the individual debtor need the car in order to get to her job so she can make the payments under her Chapter 13 plan? Does the business debtor need the equipment so that it can manufacture goods to make its Chapter 11 payments? The courts have been much more aggressive in deciding that an individual Chapter 13 debtor does not need a car or house than in deciding that a business debtor does not need equipment or a building.

The second possible section 362(d)(2)(B) argument for a creditor seeking relief from stay is that this debtor cannot reorganize.

Even if the collateral is necessary for the Chapter 11 or 13 debtor's reorganization efforts, the phrase "effective reorganization" in section 362(d)(2)(B) enables a creditor who invokes section 362(d)(2)(B) to question whether the debtor can reorganize.

Dicta in the Supreme Court decision in United Savings Association of Texas v. Timbers of Inwood Forest Associates, Ltd., 484 U.S. 365 (1988), suggests that this should be a meaningful question. "What this requires is not merely a showing that if there is conceivably to be an effective reorganization, the property will be needed for it, but that the property is essential for an effective reorganization *that is in prospect.*"

Let's try a review question to compare section 362(d)(1) and 362(d)(2). *D*, a Chapter 11 debtor owns Redacre which is worth $900,000 and owes $600,000 to *F* who has a first mortgage on Redacre and $700,000 to *S* who has a second mortgage on Redacre.

Under these facts, if *F* seeks stay relief under section 362(d)(1), the court will probably deny relief because *F*'s equity cushion provides adequate protection of *F*s interest in property, On the other hand, if *F* seeks relief under section 362(d)(2), *F* can meet the "no equity" requirement of section 362(d)(2)(A)—$900,000 of collateral and $1,300,000 of debt. Of course, *F* would still need to meet the no "effective reorganization that is in prospect" requirement of section 362(d)(2)(B).

3. SECTION 362(d)(3)

Section 362(d)(3) is available only to a creditor with a lien on "single asset real estate," a phrase defined in section 101. Under section 362(d)(3), a creditor with a lien on "single asset real estate" has a right to relief from stay unless the debtor, within 90 days after the order for relief, has either (A) filed a reorganization plan or (B) started monthly payments.

If the debtor selects alternative A, the plan must be one that has "reasonable possibility of being confirmed within a reasonable time." If the debtor selects alternative B, the amount of the payment must equal interest at "a nondefault contract rate" on the value of the creditor's interest in the real estate.

Alternative B is in essence a partial legislative reversal of the *Timbers* case, discussed earlier. Under section 362(d)(3)(B), an under-secured creditor with a lien on "single asset real estate" has a right to interest—or at least a right to monthly payments equal in amount to interest.

4. SECTION 362(d)(4)

Section 362(d)(4) applies if (1) a creditor has a claim secured by real property and (2) the debtors has made an unauthorized transfer of the encumbered real property or made multiple bankruptcy filings.

362(d)(4) provides for relief from the automatic stay in this case and any other case filed in the next two years but only for creditors secured by real estate.

5. RELATIONSHIP OF SECTION 362(d)(1), SECTION 362(d)(2), SECTION 362(d)(3) AND SECTION 362(d)(4)

Note that section 362(d)(1), section 362(d)(2), section 362(d)(3) and section 362(d)(4) are connected by the conjunction "or." A creditor is entitled to relief from the stay if it is able to establish grounds for relief under either section 362(d)(1), section 362(d)(2), section 362(d)(3) or section 362(d)(4). If, for example, a creditor is able to establish the lack of adequate protection, it is entitled to relief from the stay even though the property is necessary to an effective reorganization.

6. BURDEN OF PROOF IN SECTION 362(d) LITIGATION

Section 362(g) allocates the burden of proof in stay litigation under section 362(d). The creditor or other party requesting the relief has the burden on the issue of whether the debtor has an equity in the property. The debtor or bankruptcy trustee has the burden on all other issues.

CHAPTER VI

PROPERTY OF THE ESTATE

The filing of a bankruptcy petition not only triggers the automatic stay but also creates an estate and in effect transfers the debtor's rights in property to that estate, section 541(a).

A. WHY IS PROPERTY OF THE ESTATE AN IMPORTANT CONCEPT?

"Property of the estate" is one of the most important, basic bankruptcy concepts. The filing of any bankruptcy petition automatically creates an "estate," and that estate includes the assets of the debtor as of the time of the bankruptcy filing, section 541(a).

In a Chapter 7 case, "property of the estate" is collected by the bankruptcy trustee and sold; the proceeds from the sale of the property of the estate are then distributed to creditors, sections 704, 726. In other words, the loss of property of the estate is the primary cost of Chapter 7 bankruptcy to the debtor; the receipt of the proceeds from the sale of property of the estate is the primary benefit creditors derive from a Chapter 7 bankruptcy.

In other kinds of bankruptcy cases, the importance of property of the estate is less obvious. Nonetheless, property of the estate is an important concept in cases filed under Chapter 11 or 13.

In most Chapter 11 cases, the debtor will remain in possession of "property of the estate" as "debtor-in-possession." However, the Chapter 11 debtor-in-possession's use of the property of the estate will be subject to bankruptcy court supervision.

Consider the example of Chapter 11 cases involving business debtors. Successful rehabilitation of a business generally requires continued operation of the business. Continued operation of the business generally requires continued possession and use of the business' property. A debtor will continue to operate its business in Chapter 11 as debtor-in-possession unless a request is made by a "party in interest" for the appointment of a trustee, and the bankruptcy court, after notice and hearing, grants the request.

Recall that since 2020, debtors that meet the requirements of section 1182 can elect to use Subchapter V of Chapter 11. In Subchapter V cases there is a trustee but the debtor will continue to operate the business as a debtor-in-possession.

When a trustee is appointed in a Chapter 11 case that is not a Subchapter V case, the trustee takes possession of property of the estate. Even if a trustee is not appointed in a Chapter 11 case, the debtor-in-possession's use and sale of the property of the estate is subject to the supervision of the bankruptcy judge as provided in section 363. Section 363 is considered later.

While Chapter 13 contemplates that there will be a trustee in every case, a Chapter 13 trustee does not take possession of property of the estate. A debtor who files for Chapter 13 relief retains possession of his property. Again, however, the use and sale of "property of the estate" is subject to the supervision of the bankruptcy court as provided in section 363.

In Chapter 13 cases, the value of the property of the estate determines the minimum amount that must be offered to holders of unsecured claims in the debtor's plan of repayment, section 1325(a)(4). Chapter 11 imposes a similar requirement as to holders of unsecured claims, section 1129(a)(7)(A)(ii).

Finally, a number of general provisions in Chapters 3 and 5 that are applicable in all bankruptcy cases use the phrase "property of the estate." For example, the automatic stay bars a creditor from collecting a claim from property of the estate, section 362(a)(3), (4).

In short, in all bankruptcy cases and in all bankruptcy classes, it is necessary to be able to answer the question "what does property of the estate include?"

B. WHAT DOES PROPERTY OF THE ESTATE INCLUDE?

Section 541 is the primary section to turn to in answering the question "what does property of the estate include?" With only minor exceptions, property of the estate includes all property of the debtor as of the time of the filing of the bankruptcy petition.

1. WHAT IS INCLUDED IN THE PHRASE "INTERESTS OF THE DEBTOR IN PROPERTY AS OF THE COMMENCEMENT OF THE CASE"?

The seven numbered paragraphs of section 541(a) specify what property becomes property of the estate. Paragraph one is by far the most comprehensive and significant. Section 541(a)(1) provides that property of the estate includes "*all* legal or equitable *interests of the debtor* in property *as of the commencement of the case*" (emphasis added).

This is a very broad statement. Note first the word "all." Property of the estate thus includes both real property (such as a company's manufacturing facility or an individual's house) and personal property (such as a store's inventory or an individual's car), both tangible (the manufacturing facility, the car, etc.) and intangible property (such as an account receivable or a patent license), both property in the debtor's possession and property in which the debtor has an interest that is held by others.[1]

The language in section 541(a)(1) raises two important litigable issues. Please reread the statutory excerpt again. Focus on the italicized phrases.

First, note the phrase "interests of the debtor in property." If the debtor has a limited interest in some

---

[1] Third parties in possession of property in which the debtor has an interest are statutorily obligated to return such property to the trustee or debtor in possession, sections 542 and 543. When we consider these sections, we will consider the obligation of a secured creditor who has seized but not yet sold property that served as its collateral to return that property to the debtor.

asset, it is that limited interest that is property of the estate. Consider the following two examples:

(1) *A* and *B* own an island as tenants in common. If *A* files a bankruptcy petition, only *A*'s limited interest in the island would be property of the estate.[2]

(2) *X* owns a new Chevrolet Silverado. He borrowed the money to buy the truck from a bank which retained a security interest in the truck. Under Article 9 of the Uniform Commercial Code, that security interest or lien is a property interest in the Silverado truck. Outside of bankruptcy then, both *X* and the bank have property interests in the Silverado. Accordingly, if *X* files a bankruptcy petition, under section 541 of the Bankruptcy Code, only *X*'s property interest in the Silverado is property of the estate.[3]

Second, consider the phrase "as of the commencement of the case" in section 541(a)(1). "Commencement of the case" is synonymous with the filing of a bankruptcy petition, sections 301, 303. Thus, assets that the debtor acquired prior to the petition become property of the estate.

Generally, property acquired after the petition generally is not property of the estate. For example,

---

[2] While only A's interest in the island is property of the estate, the entire island can be sold under section 363(h).

[3] In the specific situations described in section 363(f), X's Silverado can be sold free and clear of the Colorado bank lien.

if *D* files for Chapter 7 bankruptcy on April 5, the money *D* earns from the work that *D* does after April 5 is not property of the estate, section 541(a)(1), (6) ("earnings from services performed by an individual after the commencement of a case" excepted from property of the estate).

2. WHAT ELSE IS INCLUDED IN PROPERTY OF THE ESTATE?

While property of the estate is determined primarily by section 541(a)(1)—"the interests of the debtor in property as of the commencement of the case," property of the estate also includes some property acquired after the commencement of the case:

#1 "Any interest in property that the trustee recovers," section 541(a)(3)

As we will see in Chapter XII of this book, the bankruptcy trustee (and the debtor in possession in a Chapter 11 case) is empowered by the Bankruptcy Code to recover certain payments and other transfers of the debtor's interest in property. The trustee's use of these avoidance powers increases the property of the estate.

Assume, for example, *D* pays $1,000,000 to one of his creditors, *C*, on January 10th and *D* then files for bankruptcy on January 15th. If the bankruptcy trustee is able use her avoidance powers under sections 547 and 550 to avoid that January 10th payment, then *C* would have to return the

$1,000,000, and that $1,000,000 would become property of the estate.

#2 "Proceeds, product, offspring, rents or profits of or from property of the estate," section 541(a)(6)

Assume that Homer and Marge Simpson file a bankruptcy petition and the next day their house is destroyed by an explosion of the Springfield nuclear power plant. Any insurance proceeds would be property of the estate. Similarly, if *D* Realty Co. files for bankruptcy, both the buildings it owns as of the bankruptcy petition and the postpetition rents from the buildings would be property of the estate.

Reconsider the last sentence. The postpetition earnings of a corporation or any other "person" other than an "individual" are property of the estate under section 541(a)(6). The postpetition earnings of an individual from the services that they perform after the bankruptcy are excluded from property of the estate—unless the debtor has filed a petition for relief under Chapter 11 or 13.

#3 "Earnings from services" that an individual debtor acquires after filing a petition for relief under Chapter 11 or Chapter 13.

If an individual debtor files a petition for relief under Chapter 11 or Chapter 13, property of the estate will be determined not only by section 541 but also by section 1115 or 1306. Under these provisions, postpetition earnings are property of the estate.

#4 Property that the debtor acquires or becomes entitled to within 180 days after the filing of the petition by (a) bequest, devise, or inheritance; (b) property settlement or a divorce decree; or (c) as beneficiary of a life insurance policy, section 541(a)(5).

3. WHAT IS EXCLUDED FROM PROPERTY OF THE ESTATE?

There are some very specific exclusions from property of the estate in section 541(b) and 541(c). For example, section 541(b)(5), provides that funds placed in an educational retirement account at least 365 days prior to a bankruptcy filing, within limits established by the Internal Revenue Code and for the benefit of the debtor's children or grandchildren, are excluded from the debtor's estate.

If your professor is going to test you on insignificant stuff like that, even this book is not going to help.

The most significant section 541(b) or section 541(c) exclusion from property of the estate is section 541(c)(2). Even though neither the words "spendthrift trust" nor "ERISA" appear in section 541(c)(2), it has been read to exclude traditional spendthrift trusts and ERISA accounts from property of the estate, Patterson v. Shumate, 504 U.S. 753 (1992). Since most bankruptcy law professors do not understand ERISA, you probably do not need to understand more about section 541(b) and (c).

In both law school classes and bankruptcy cases, the most significant exclusions from property of the estate are not based on section 541(b) or (c). Rather, the most significant exclusions are exemptions which will be considered in the next chapter.

CHAPTER VII

EXEMPTIONS

Under the Bankruptcy Code, all of the interests in property that a debtor has when the debtor files a bankruptcy petition is property of the estate. An individual debtor, however, is permitted to exempt certain property from property of the estate.

A law student or lawyer needs to be able to answer two general questions about exempt property in bankruptcy: First, what property is exempt? Second what is the bankruptcy significance of exempt property status?

A. WHAT PROPERTY IS EXEMPT?

1. WHAT LAW DETERMINES WHAT PROPERTY IS EXEMPT IN BANKRUPTCY?

In bankruptcy, an individual debtor may assert the exemptions to which they are entitled under the laws of the state of their domicile and under federal laws other than title 11,[1] section 522(b)(2). Alternatively, individual debtors in a few states may claim the exemptions set out in section 522(d).

---

1 Some of the items that may be exempted under Federal laws other than title 11 include:

Social security payments, 42 USCA § 407

Civil service retirement benefits, 5 USCA §§ 729, 2265

Veterans benefits, 45 USCA § 352(E).

Section 522(d) is only available to individual debtors who reside in states that have not enacted "opt out" legislation pursuant to section 522(b)(1). Under section 522(b)(1), a state legislature can enact legislation precluding resident debtors from electing to utilize section 522(d). Most states have enacted such "opt out" legislation.

Even in states that have not "opted out" there are statutory limitations on the debtor's choice of exemption statutes. A debtor cannot select some exemptions from state law and some exemptions from section 522(d). They must choose either the nonbankruptcy exemptions or section 522(d). And, husbands and wives in joint cases filed under section 302 or in individual cases which are being jointly administered under Bankruptcy Rule 1015(b) must both elect either the nonbankruptcy exemptions or the section 522(d) exemptions.[2] While under section 522(m) each spouse will be entitled to separate exemptions, it will not be possible for one to choose section 522(d) exemptions if the other chooses nonbankruptcy exemptions.

The most significant limitation on a debtor's choice of exemption statutes is the two-year residency requirement for state exemption laws. The debtor can choose the exemption law of the state in which they were living at the time of the bankruptcy filing

---

[2] In states that have not opted out, it may be disadvantageous for a husband and wife to file a joint petition. By filing two individual petitions and paying two filing fees, a married couple may be able to increase the amount of their property that will be exempt.

only if that was the only state in which they were domiciled for the entire two years preceding bankruptcy. If the debtor has not maintained their domicile in the same state for the 730 days (two years) before their bankruptcy filing, the governing exemption law is the exemption law of the state in which the debtor lived in the 180 days before that 730 days. In other words, what is then determinative is where that debtor lived between 2 years and 2.5 years before the filing.

To illustrate, *D* files a bankruptcy petition in December 2021 In the two years before bankruptcy, she lived in Texas, California and Iowa. Now that we know that *D* did not maintain *D*'s domicile in a single state for the two years before *D*'s bankruptcy filing, we don't care where *D* lived in that two-year period. Instead, we want to know where *D* lived for most of the six-month period before that two-year period. If from June through November of 2019, *D* lived in yet another state, Minnesota, then *D*'s exemptions in bankruptcy would be determined largely by Minnesota state law.

2. WHAT IS THE EFFECT OF A DEBTOR'S CONTRACTING AWAY HER EXEMPTIONS?

The Bankruptcy Code expressly deals with the effect of a debtor's contracting away their exemptions. Such a contract has no effect. Whether an individual debtor elects to claim their exemptions under nonbankruptcy exemption law or under section 522(d), waivers of exemption are not enforceable, section 522(e).

3. WHAT IS THE EFFECT OF A DEBTOR'S CLAIMING TOO MUCH PROPERTY AS EXEMPT?

The Bankruptcy Code together with the Bankruptcy Rules also expressly deal with the situation in which the debtor claims too much property as exempt and no one makes a timely objection. Under section 522(*l*) and Rule 4003, an individual debtor files a list of the property they claim as exempt. In Taylor v. Freeland & Kronz, 503 U.S. 638 (1992), the debtor's list of exempt property included the proceeds from a pending employment discrimination action. This asset was not exempt under relevant exemption laws. Nonetheless, the Supreme Court held that it was exempt in bankruptcy because of the absence of a timely objection.

Under relevant bankruptcy laws, there is a deadline for filing objections to the debtor's claimed exemptions, section 522(*l*) and Rule 4003. In the *Taylor* case, no objection was filed until long after that deadline. Looking to the "plain meaning" of section 522(*l*) and Rule 4003, the Supreme Court concluded that the debtor was entitled to keep the proceeds from the settlement of the employment discrimination action because there was no timely objection to his claim that it was exempt.

4. WHAT IS THE EFFECT OF A DEBTOR'S CONVERTING NONEXEMPT PROPERTY TO EXEMPT PROPERTY BEFORE FILING FOR BANKRUPTCY?

Section 522(*o*) and (p) are two very specific, very limited provisions that address transfers that increase the debtor's exempt homestead. First, a state homestead exemption will be reduced by the amount that the homestead is attributable to the debtor's disposition of nonexempt property in the ten years prior to bankruptcy with the intent to hinder, delay or defraud creditors. Second, value added to the homestead within 1,215 days before the bankruptcy filing is capped at the amount set out in section 522(*o*).

The Bankruptcy Code does not otherwise expressly deal with the consequences of a debtor's converting nonexempt property into exempt property on the eve of bankruptcy. Should a debtor be permitted to convert nonexempt property into exempt property and then file for bankruptcy?

What if, before filing for bankruptcy, *D* takes funds from their bank account which is nonexempt property under relevant state law and invests the money in an annuity which is exempt under state law? *D*'s attorney can argue that *D* is simply making use of their legal rights—kind of like a taxpayer claiming every possible deduction. A Chapter 7 trustee or creditors can argue that that *D* is defrauding creditors.

A number of different reported cases have answered ruled on this fact pattern in a number of different ways. Some courts hold for *D* and sustain *D*'s exemption assertion. Some courts have used section 727 explained in Chapter XII to withhold a discharge from a Chapter 7 debtor such as *D* who converted nonexempt property into exempt property on the eve of bankruptcy. Other courts have used section 548 explained in Chapter VIII to "avoid" a debtor's conversion of nonexempt property into exempt property.

One common judicial approach is the "pig to hog analysis" in which the court compares the amount of property converted, the total amount of debt, and the total amount of other property still available to pay that debt and apply the other Southern adage that when a pig has eaten so much that it has become a hog, it is slaughtered.[3]

B. WHAT IS THE SIGNIFICANCE IN BANKRUPTCY OF EXEMPT PROPERTY?

1. GENERAL

Generally, an individual debtor is able to retain their exempt property. Exempt property is not distributed to creditors in the bankruptcy case and is

---

[3] Surprisingly, this approach is not limited to judges in the South. Not surprisingly, this approach seems limited to gentile judges.

protected from the claims of *most* prepetition[4] creditors after the bankruptcy case.

Note the italicized qualifier "most." Section 522(c) identifies the prepetition claims that are, in essence, "exempt" from the exemptions. After bankruptcy, there are basically four groups of prepetition creditors who have recourse to property set aside as exempt in a bankruptcy case:

(1) Creditors with tax claims excepted from discharge by section 523(a)(1);

(2) Spouses, former spouses and children of the debtor with domestic claims excepted from discharge by section 523(a)(5);

(3) Creditors whose claims arise from the debtor's fraud in obtaining funding for higher education;

(4) Creditors with liens on exempt property that are neither avoided nor extinguished through redemption.

2. SECTION 522(f)

As #4 suggests, some liens on exempt property that are valid outside of bankruptcy can be invalidated because of bankruptcy. The general invalidation provisions, discussed infra in Chapter VIII, are applicable to liens on exempt property. And section 522(f) empowers the debtor to avoid judicial liens

---

4 If the debtor chooses the set of exemptions set out in section 522(d), postpetition creditors will be able to reach items not exempted under relevant state law.

that impair exemptions and to avoid security interests that are both nonpurchase money and nonpossessory on certain household goods, tools of the trade, and health aids.

The most important thing for you to understand about section 522(f) is that it is not very important in the "real world." Again, it only affects (a) judicial liens and (b) certain kinds of consensual liens on certain kinds of exempt property.

Because of increases in the costs of obtaining a judicial lien and increases in bankruptcy filing, creditors' use of judicial liens has decreased significantly. If a creditor does obtain a judicial lien on exempt property, the debtor can invoke section 522(f)(1)(A) to avoid that judicial lien "to the extent that such lien impairs an exemption."

Section 522(f)(2) explains the quoted phrase "to the extent that . . . ." The following examples "explain" section 522(f)(2).

#1 Assume D's house is worth $100,000 and F has a $40,000 first mortgage on the house and J has a $50,000 judicial lien on the house and the relevant exemption lien permits D a $15,000 homestead. Add (a) the amount of the exemption—$15,000, plus (b) the amount of the judicial lien—$50,000 and (c) the amount of all other liens on the homestead—$40,000. The total in this hypothetical is $105,000. Subtract from that the value of the house—$100,000. Under these facts, the amount of impairment is $5,000 and so the debtor could use 522(f) to avoid $5,000 of J's judicial lien—to reduce that lien from $50,000 to $45,000.

#2 Now increase the amount of F's first mortgage by $50,000 to $90,000. This increases the amount of the impairment to $55,000 and so the debtor could use 522(f) to avoid all of J's $50,000 judicial lien.[5]

I have used the example of a "judicial lien" to illustrate the application of section 522(f) because that is when you will use section 522(f)—if you ever use section 522(f). Recall that section 522(f) also applies to certain kinds of consensual liens on certain kinds of exempt property. In particular, recall my limiting phrase "certain kinds of."

Section 522(f)(1) does not apply to purchase money liens.[6] It does not affect Best Buy's lien on the home entertainment center that it sold the debtor on credit; it does not apply to First Bank's lien on the dental equipment it financed. More limiting, section 522(f)(1) does not apply to any consensual lien on houses and cars—the two most valuable exempt assets of most individuals. Section 522(f)(1)(B) only applies to nonpurchase money security interests in

---

5 If class or a case requires you to look at harder problems (or if these problems look hard), look at *David Gray Carlson, Security Interests on Exempt Property After the 1994 Amendments to the Bankruptcy Code*, 4 Am.Bankr.Inst.L.Rev. 57, 64–68 (1996).

6 Section 522(f)(1)(B) also is limited to consensual liens that are nonpossessory. "Nonpossessory" simply means that the creditor with a lien is not in possession of the property subject to his lien. Except for pawn shops, creditors with nonpurchase money liens on exempt personal property are rarely in possession of that property.

the kinds of exempt property described in section 522(f)(1)(B)(i), (ii) or (iii).

The use of section 522(f) to avoid consensual liens on exemptions is further limited by section 522(f)(3). Even if the consensual lien is nonpurchase money and even if the exempt assets subject to the lien come within one of the categories described in section 522(f)(1)(B), the debtor may be precluded from avoiding the lien by section 522(f)(3). In general, you will look at section 522(f)(3) only if the debtor has job-related or farm-related exempt property that is worth more the dollar amount in section 522(f)(3) and that exempt property is subject to nonpurchase money consensual liens.

3. SECTION 722

Possessory security interests in exempt personal property, purchase money security interests in exempt personal property, and any security interests on exempt personal property not covered by section 522(f) may be extinguished through "redemption." Section 722 authorizes an individual debtor to redeem or extinguish a lien on exempt personal property by paying the lienor in cash the replacement value of the encumbered property. To illustrate, assume that *D* owes *C* $3,000. *C* has a security interest in *D*'s Subaru. If *D* files a bankruptcy petition *and* the value of the Subaru is only $1,200,[7] *D* can eliminate *C*'s lien by paying *C* $1,200 in cash.[8]

---

7 Look to section 506(a)(2) which looks to replacement value.

8 Cash! That is what the section 722 language "paying . . . in full at the time of redemption" means.

D will still owe *C* $1,800 but *C*'s $1,800 claim will be an unsecured claim that can be discharged.

Section 722 applies to all liens on "tangible personal property intended for personal, family or household use" that secures a "dischargeable consumer debt."

So, in theory, there is some[9] overlap between section 522(f) and section 722. Is there any real overlap? If you understand what happens under section 522(f) and what happens under section 722, you understand that there is no practical overlap. A debtor will not invoke 722 to redeem property from liens by paying cash if they can invoke 522(f) to avoid such liens without paying the value of the property in cash.

---

[9] The overlap is not complete. For example, section 722, unlike section 522(f) applies to purchase money security interests in a debtor's personal cars and other consumer goods.

CHAPTER VIII

AVOIDANCE OF PREBANKRUPTCY TRANSFERS

In the absence of bankruptcy, some transfers of a debtor's property can be invalidated under state laws, such as state fraudulent conveyance laws. The Bankruptcy Code incorporates these state laws in section 544(b) so that a transfer of a debtor's property that can be invalidated under state law in the absence of bankruptcy can be invalidated under section 544(b) in the event of bankruptcy.

Chapter 5 of the Bankruptcy Code also contains several other "avoidance" provisions that are unique to bankruptcy. Accordingly, some payments, sales, exchanges, judicial liens, security interests and other transfers that are valid under state law can be avoided in bankruptcy.

The Bankruptcy Code's avoidance provisions reach both "voluntary" transfers such as a debtor's making a gift to a relative or granting a mortgage to a creditor and "involuntary" transfers such as a creditor's garnishing the debtor's bank account or subjecting the debtor's real property to a judgment lien. Note also that the Bankruptcy Code's avoidance provisions reach both "absolute" transfers such as gifts, payments and sales, and "security transfers" such as mortgages and judgment liens.

In working with these avoidance provisions, law students and lawyers are called on to answer two basic questions: (1) what are the consequences of avoiding a debtor's prebankruptcy transfer and (2) which such transfers can be avoided. Law students are called on to answer these questions both in class and on exams. Lawyers are called upon to answer these questions not only in negotiating and litigating in bankruptcy cases but also in structuring transactions outside of bankruptcy. The answers to the questions of what are the consequences of avoiding a prebankruptcy transfers and which transfers can be avoided can be found in Chapter 5 of the Bankruptcy Code and this chapter of this book.

To illustrate, assume that your client *C* buys a business from *D* for $2,000,000 and pays your firm $100,000 for your legal work on the transaction. If *D* later files for bankruptcy, you do not want to be in the awkward position of having to call *C* to tell *C* that *D*'s bankruptcy trustee has been able to invoke the Bankruptcy's Code avoidance power to recover all of the assets that *C* purchased from *D*.

Understanding the Bankruptcy Code avoidance power provisions and the materials on these provisions set out below can be hard. But not as hard as calling *C*.

To understand the avoidance provisions, remember that avoidance does not occur by operation of law. Avoidance in bankruptcy of a prebankruptcy transfer requires litigation and raises all of the usual litigation questions:

1. Who can initiate avoidance litigation?
2. Where do I bring the action?

3. What are the time limitations on initiating an avoidance action?

4. Who can I sue and what can I recover?

The answer to the first question is the "Chapter 7 trustee, the Chapter 11 trustee, and the Chapter 13 trustee and . . . ." The avoidance provisions in Chapter 5 of the Bankruptcy Code generally use the phrase "the trustee may avoid." Accordingly, the trustee in a Chapter 7, 11, or 13 case can initiate avoidance litigation.

Recall that in Chapter 11 cases without a trustee, the debtor-in-possession has the rights of a trustee. Thus the Chapter 11 debtor-in-possession, and in some instances a Chapter 11 creditors' committee, can initiate avoidance litigation. The cases are divided as to whether a Chapter 13 debtor can bring an avoidance action.

The second question relating to where bankruptcy-related litigation can be brought is explained in Chapter XVI of this book dealing with allocation of judicial power over bankruptcy and bankruptcy-related litigation. Avoidance actions are brought in bankruptcy court.

Section 546 deals with the third question of when an avoidance action must be brought. Section 546 is in essence a statute of limitations that generally requires litigation be initiated within two years after the "order for relief", i.e., within two years after the bankruptcy petition.

Section 550 and the next part of this book cover the last questions of who can be sued and what recovery can be had, i.e., the consequences of avoiding a transfer.

A. WHAT ARE THE CONSEQUENCES OF AVOIDING A TRANSFER?

Think Robin Hood. Think of the Chapter 7 trustee (or the debtor in possession in a Chapter 11 case) as a person in green tights who takes from the "rich" (i.e., the transferee) to give to the "poor" (i.e., all the holders of unsecured claims).

When the bankruptcy trustee avoids an absolute transfer of property, that property then becomes property of the estate. Assume that *D* owes *C* $25,000 on an unsecured debt. *D* repays *C* $12,000 of that debt. *D* later files for bankruptcy. At the time of *D*'s bankruptcy filing, the $12,000 paid to *C* is not property of the estate. If the bankruptcy trustee is able to invoke one of the Bankruptcy Code's avoidance provisions to avoid the $12,000 payment, the $12,000 will then become property of the estate, sections 541(a)(3), 550.

The avoidance of an absolute transfer can also affect the amount of a creditor's claim. In the above hypothetical, *C* had a $13,000 claim at the time of *D*'s bankruptcy filing. Again,[1] if the bankruptcy trustee

---

[1] If the trustee is able to establish that the $13,000 payment is avoidable under some section of the Bankruptcy Code but has not been able to recover the $13,000, then section 502(d) provides that the court shall "disallow" *C*'s claim for the remaining $12,000 of debt. Disallowance of claims is covered in Chapter XV.

is able to recover the $12,000 *D* paid *C* from *C* by avoiding the payment, then *C* will have a $25,000 claim against *D*, section 502(h). *C* will then have the same claim it had before the transfer.

The consequences of avoiding a security transfer are similar. Assume, for example, that *D* borrows $77,000 from *C* and grants *C* a mortgage on Redacre which is worth $120,000. *D* later files for bankruptcy. Absent the trustee's use of one of the avoidance powers, *C* has a $77,000 secured claim. Recall that under section 541, Redacre is itself not property of the estate; rather the estate's interest in Redacre is only *D*'s limited equity and other rights in Redacre. If, however, the bankruptcy trustee is able to avoid the grant of the mortgage on Redacre, then *C* will have a $77,000 unsecured claim, and Redacre without any encumbrance will be property of the estate.

In the two examples, the consequences of avoidance were the recovery of the property interest transferred from the party to whom it had been transferred. Under section 550, the consequences of avoidance are not limited to recovery of the property transferred, are not limited to the person to whom the transfer was made.

Under section 550(a), the court can order the recovery of the "value of the property" transferred, rather than the property. Assume, for example, that the property transferred from D to T was worth $100,000 at the time of the transfer but is only worth $40,000 at the time of the avoidance litigation. The court can award the recovery of $100,000, instead of the recovery of the property.

And, under section 550(a), the recovery can be sought not only from the initial transferee but either later transferees or a person who benefitted from the transfer. Assume, for example, that *D* is indebted to both *F* and *S* and that *F* has a $100,000 first mortgage and *S* has a $200,000 second mortgage on Greenacre which is worth $150,000. If *D* makes a payment of $50,000 to *F*, that transfer to *F* has the effect of providing a $50,000 benefit to *S*. Prior to transfer, there was only $50,000 of collateral available to satisfy *S*'s claim. After the transfer, there is $100,000 of collateral available to satisfy *S*'s claim.

Now that you have considered the consequences of avoiding a transfer, let's focus on which transfers can be avoided.

B. WHICH TRANSFERS CAN BE AVOIDED—PREFERENCES

Under common law, a debtor—even an insolvent debtor—may treat certain creditors more favorably than other similar creditors. Although *D* owes *X*, *Y* and *Z* $1,000 each, *D* may pay *X*'s claim in full before paying any part of *Y*'s claim or *Z*'s claim. Common law does not condemn a preference.

Bankruptcy law does condemn certain preferences. A House report that accompanied a draft of the Code explained the rationale for such a bankruptcy policy as follows:

"The purpose of the preference section is twofold. First, by permitting the trustee to avoid prebankruptcy transfers that occur within a short period before bankruptcy, creditors are discouraged from racing to the courthouse to dismember the debtor during his slide into bankruptcy. The protection thus afforded the debtor often enables him to work his way out of a difficult financial situation through cooperation with all of his creditors. Second, and more important, the preference provisions facilitate the prime bankruptcy policy of equality of distribution among creditors of the debtor. Any creditor that received a greater payment than others of his class is required to disgorge so that all may share equally." House Report 95–595 at 117–78.

1. ELEMENTS OF A PREFERENCE

Section 547(b) sets out the elements of a preference; the bankruptcy trustee may void any *transfer of property of the debtor* if the trustee can establish

(1) the transfer was "to or for the benefit of a creditor"; and

(2) the transfer was made for or on account of an "antecedent debt," i.e., a debt owed prior to the time of the transfer; and

(3) the debtor was insolvent at the time of the transfer; and

(4) the transfer was made within 90 days before the date of the filing of the bankruptcy petition, or, was made between 90 days and 1 year before the date of the filing of the petition to an "insider";[2] and

(5) the transfer has the effect of increasing the amount that the transferee would receive in a Chapter 7 case.

Don't miss the first element of a preference which comes before any of the numbered elements: "transfer of an interest of the debtor in property." Payments and other transfers by people other than the person who is later the debtor in the bankruptcy case are never section 547 preferences.

Assume for example, *D* owes $100 to *A*, *B* and *C*. *M*, *D*'s momma, pays *A* but not *B* and *C*. *D* later files for bankruptcy. In a real sense, *M*'s payment to *A* but not *B* or *C* treated *A* more favorably than *B* or *C*—preferred *A* over *B* or *C*. In a bankruptcy sense, *M*'s payment is not a preference because it was not a "transfer of an interest of the debtor in property", not a diminution of property of *D*'s estate—*A* of course benefitted from being paid by *M*, but not to the detriment of *D*'s other creditors.

Now assume *M* gave the $100 to *D* who then used that $100 to pay *A*. Is *D*'s payment to *A* a "transfer of interest an interest of the debtor in property"? In answering that question, most courts would look to

---

[2] "Insider" is explained in section 101. An insider includes relatives of an individual debtor and directors of a corporate debtor.

the "earmarking doctrine." Under this court-created concept, if an insolvent debtor pays one of her creditors with funds from a third party that were clearly earmarked to pay a specific antecedent debt, there is no section 547 preference. Again, *A* benefitted, but not to the detriment of other creditors. Generally, the pivotal questions in cases in which the earmarking doctrine is an issue is whether the debtor had any control over how the funds from the third party could be used.

The first three numbered requirements of section 547(b) will usually be easy to apply. To illustrate, a true gift is not a preference—not to or for the benefit of a creditor. A mortgage to secure a new loan is not a preferential transfer—not for or on account of antecedent debt. The third requirement—insolvency of the debtor at the time of transfer—is made easy by section 547(f)'s creation of a rebuttable presumption of insolvency for the 90 days immediately preceding the filing of the bankruptcy petition.

In applying the fourth requirement of section 547(b), time of transfer, it may be necessary to look to section 547(e) and section 101. If under state law, a transfer is not fully effective against third parties until recordation or other public notice of the transfer has been timely given and the transfer was not timely recorded, then section 547(e) [considered later in this chapter] deems the transfer to have occurred at the time of recordation.

To illustrate, assume that on January 15, *D* borrows $100,000 from *S* and grants *S* a security interest on a piece of equipment. Under relevant nonbankruptcy state law, *S*'s security interest is not effective against other creditors who might claim a lien on that same equipment unless a financing statement was filed. *S* delays filing its financing statement until April 5. *D* then files for bankruptcy on July 1. By reason of section 547(e), the transfer from *D* to *S* creating *S*'s security interest is regarded as occurring on April 5, not January 15. And since the debt was incurred on January 15 and the transfer is not deemed to have occurred until April 5, the security interest was a transfer for an antecedent debt within 90 days of the July 1 bankruptcy.

Section 101's explanation of "insider" becomes a part of the fourth requirement of section 547(b) in determining whether the transfer was made to an "insider" so that the relevant period is one year, rather than 90 days. Remember that the presumption of insolvency is limited to the 90 days immediately preceding the bankruptcy petition. Accordingly, in order to invalidate a transfer that occurred more than 90 days before the filing of the bankruptcy petition the trustee must establish that (i) the transferee was an "insider"; and (ii) the debtor was insolvent at the time of the transfer.

The fifth element essentially tests whether the transfer enabled the creditor/transferee to get *more* than the transferee would have received if (a) the transfer had not taken place and (b) the case was a Chapter 7 case. While your prof will expect you to discuss this fifth element in any preference exam question, it is generally satisfied.

This fifth element is satisfied unless (i) the transferee has a claim secured by property worth more than the amount of its claim or (ii) the transferee has a secured claim and all that is transferred to the transferee is part or all of the collateral that secured the claim or (iii) the estate is sufficiently large to pay all unsecured claims in full. In (i), (ii) and (iii), a prebankruptcy transfer does not result in the creditor/transferee's receiving more than what they would receive in a Chapter 7 case if the transfer had not been made. Under these facts, the transferee is simply receiving earlier all or part of what they would have ultimately received in the Chapter 7 case.

Section 547 is concerned with a creditor's receiving more, not a creditor's receiving earlier. And, except for (i), (ii) or (iii) above, a transfer that satisfies sections 547(b)(1)–(4) will result in the creditor's receiving more, i.e., will also satisfy section 547(b)(5). Assume, for example, that *D* makes a $1,000 payment to *C*, a creditor with a $10,000 unsecured claim, on January 10. On February 20, *D* files a bankruptcy petition. The property of the estate is sufficient to pay each unsecured creditor 50% of its claim. An unsecured creditor with a $10,000 claim will thus receive $5,000. *S*, however, will receive a total of $5,500 from *D* and *D*'s bankruptcy unless the January 10th transfer is avoided. ($1,000 + 50% × (10,000 – 1,000)) Accordingly, the bankruptcy trustee may *avoid* the January 10th transfer under section 547(b) to "facilitate the prime bankruptcy policy of equality of distribution among creditors."

The favorite exam question on section 547(b)(5) is a prebankruptcy payment to an undersecured creditor. For example, *D* owes *U* $1M and *U* has a first mortgage on Redacre which is worth $600,000. *D* pays *U* $300,000 and days later *D* files a bankruptcy petition. Before the $300,000 payment, *U* had a $600,000 secured claim and a $400,000 unsecured claim. Nothing in the facts indicate that *U* released all or part of its mortgage. Thus, *U* still a $600,000 secured claim. Because of the payment, *U* has $300,000 in cash and an unsecured claim of $100,000 instead of no cash an unsecured claim of $400,000. You need to understand that a payment to an undersecured claim is preferential under section 547(b)(5) unless there has been a release of collateral.

2. APPLYING SECTION 547(b)

To review, the following hypotheticals illustrate the application of section 547(b).

(1) On February 2, *D* borrows $7,000 from *C* and promises to repay the $7,000 on March 2. *D* repays *C* on March 2 as promised. On May 24, *D* files a bankruptcy petition.

The bankruptcy trustee can recover the $7,000 payment from *C*. See section 547(b); see also section 550.

(2) On February 2, *D* borrows $7,000 from *C*. *D* repays *C* on March 2. On June 6, *D* files a bankruptcy petition.

The bankruptcy trustee *cannot* recover the $7,000 from *C* under section 547(b). Section 547(b)(4) is not satisfied—more than 90 days.

(3) On February 2, *D* borrows $7,000 from *C*. On March 2, *X*, a friend of *D*'s, pays *C* the $7,000 *D* owed. On May 24, *D* files a bankruptcy petition.

The bankruptcy trustee *cannot* recover the $7,000 from *C* under section 547(b). The payment was not a "transfer of an interest of the debtor in property."

(4) On January 10, *D* borrows $10,000 from *C* and grants *C* a security interest in its equipment. At all relevant times, the equipment has a value of $20,000. On March 3, *D* repays *C* $3,000 of the $10,000. On April 4, *D* files a bankruptcy petition.

The bankruptcy trustee *cannot* avoid the March 3 payment under section 547(b). Section 547(b)(5) is not satisfied. Note that *C* had a security interest. Note also that the value of the collateral securing *C*'s claim was greater than the amount of the claim.[3] In a Chapter 7 case, the holder of a secured claim will receive either its collateral or its value up to the amount of the

---

[3] See section 506. Under this provision, the amount of a secured claim is limited by the value of the collateral. Assume for example that *D* borrows $100,000 from *S* and grants *S* a security interest in equipment. One debt, one transaction, one note. *D* later files for bankruptcy still owing S $100,000. If the bankruptcy court values the equipment at $40,000, *S* has a $40,000 secured claim and a $60,000 unsecured claim.

debt. Accordingly, even if the payment had not been made, *S* as a fully secured creditor would have been paid in full. A prebankruptcy payment to a fully secured creditor is not a preference.

(5) On February 2, *D* borrows $200,000 from *S* and *S* records a mortgage on Redacre, real property of *D*'s. At all relevant times, Redacre has a value of $100,000. On April 5, *D* repays $20,000 of the loan. On May 6, *D* files a bankruptcy petition. The property of the estate is sufficient to pay each unsecured creditor 10% of its claim.

The April 5 payment is a preference. All of the elements of section 547(b) including section 547(b)(5) are satisfied. If the transfer had not been made, S would have received $110,000 ($100,000 secured claim × $10,000 on the $100,000 unsecured claim). If the transfer is not avoided, *S* will receive $119,000 ($100,000 on the secured claim $10,000, April 5 payment + 10% of $90,000 unsecured claim.)

(6) On March 3, *D* borrows $300,000 from *S*. On April 4, *S* demands security for the loan and *D* gives *S* a mortgage on Redacre. Redacre has a fair market value of $400,000. On May 5, *D* files a bankruptcy petition. The property of the estate is sufficient to pay each unsecured creditor 20% of its claim.

The trustee may avoid the April 4 mortgage so that Redacre is property of the estate free and clear of *S*' lien. Again all of the elements of section 547(b) are satisfied. The transfer would enable *S* to receive $300,000. If the transfer had not been made, *S* would receive only $60,000. [Section 547(b) avoids liens to secure past debts.]

(7) On April 4, *D* borrows $40,000 from *S* and gives *S* a security interest in equipment. The equipment has a fair market value of $60,000. On June 6, *D* files a bankruptcy petition.

The trustee may not avoid the April 4 security interest. The April 4 transfer was for present consideration, not "for or on account of an antecedent debt." Element #2 is not satisfied. [Section 547 does not avoid liens to secure new debts.]

3. INDIRECT PREFERENCES

All of the above examples illustrations involve two parties: the debtor transferor and the creditor transferee. The following language in section 547(b) contemplates three party transactions in which *D* makes a transfer to *C* that is preferential as to *X*: "to OR FOR THE BENEFIT OF a creditor," section 547(b)(1).

Assume, for example, that *C* makes a loan to *D*, and *X* guarantees payment of the loan. It is obvious from reading the hypothetical that *C* is a creditor of *D*. And, it should be obvious from reading the definitions of "creditor" and "claim" in section 101 that *X* is also a creditor of *D* for purposes of section 547.

What if *D* pays *C* on January 15 and then files for bankruptcy on January 17? *D*'s payment to *C* is a transfer "TO a creditor," C. The payment is also "FOR THE BENEFIT OF a creditor," both C and X.

As explained above, *X* is a creditor. *X* benefits from *D*'s payment to *C*: *D*'s payment to *C* frees *X* from her obligations under the guarantee. Accordingly, the payment to one creditor, *C*, can be an indirect preference to another creditor, *X*, if the other elements of section 547(b) are satisfied.

Finding such an indirect preference can be important to *D*'s bankruptcy trustee where the transferee, *C*, is also insolvent or otherwise unable to pay. Recovering from *X* is possible because section 550 allows the trustee to recover a preference from either the actual transferee or "the entity for whose benefit the transfer was made."

Finding such an indirect preference can also be important where the transfer is not avoidable as to the actual transferee. Assume, for example, that *D* pays *C* on January 15 and then files for bankruptcy on July 13. *C* is not an "insider," but *X* is. The payment to *C* is not a preference as to *C*. Since *C* is not an insider, the relevant section 547(b) time period is 90 days. The payment of *C* is a preference as to *X*. Since *X* (like most guarantors) is an insider, the relevant time period is one year. Obviously, the trustee could recover from *X*. Until the 1994 amendments, every circuit court that considered these facts held that the trustee could also recover from *C*.

Levit v. Ingersoll Rand Financial Corp., 874 F.2d 1186 (7th Cir. 1989) (more commonly referred as the *Deprizio* case) was the first circuit court case to hold that a payment to a noninsider creditor where there was an insider guarantor could be recovered from that noninsider creditor even though it occurred more than 90 days before the bankruptcy filing. In so holding, the court relied primarily on the language of section 547 and 550.

The *Levit* decision and the several other circuit court decisions following it look at section 547 and 550 as independent, unrelated provisions. The methodology of these decisions can be outlined as follows. First, look at section 547(b) and determine if there has been a preference as to anyone. Second, if there is a preference as to anyone under section 547(b), look at section 550 and determine the possible responsible parties. The party responsible under section 550 does not have to be the same party as to whom the transfer was preferential. In application, even though the payment to *C* was only preferential as to *X*, the trustee can still recover from *C* since section 550 permits recovery from the actual transferee.

Amendments to sections 547 and 550 changed the result in *Levit*. These amendments preclude recovery from a creditor that is not an insider for preferences made more than 90 days before the bankruptcy filing.

While these amendment changes the *Levit* result in situations involving a guarantor, it does not change the *Levit* reasoning. The significance of the *Levit* approach to sections 547 and 550 is not limited to guaranteed loans.

Assume, for example, that both *F* and *S* are creditors of *D* with a lien on Redacre. *F* is owed $100,000 and has a first lien. *S* is owed $200,000 and has a second lien. The value of Redacre is $150,000. Consider the consequences of *D*'s paying *F* $30,000. If you remember what you have read, you will remember that a payment to a fully secured creditor is not preferential, section 547(b)(5). Accordingly, the payment to *F* cannot be a section 547 preference as to *F*. And, if you understand what you have read, you will understand that this payment to *F* is preferential as to *S*. By paying *F* $30,000 and reducing *F*'s secured claim on Redacre to $70,000, *D* has indirectly benefited *S* by increasing *S*'s secured claim on Redacre to $80,000. Accordingly, the payment to *F* can be a section 547 preference as to *S*. And, under *Levit* and its progeny, the trustee arguably can use section 550 to recover from either *S* or *F*.

4. EXCEPTIONS (SECTION 547(c))

Section 547(b) sets out the elements of a voidable preference. Section 547(c) excepts certain prepetition transfers from the operation of section 547(b).

Apply paragraph (b) of section 547 first. Only if a transfer is a preference under section 547(b), is it necessary to do paragraph (c). If a transfer comes within one of section 547(c)'s nine exceptions, the bankruptcy trustee will not be able to invalidate the transfer even though the trustee can establish all of the requirements of section 547(b). While section 547(c) contains nine numbered exceptions and this nutshell will explain all nine, Section 547(c)(2)("ordinary course") and 547(c)(4)("new value") are the exceptions most frequently tested in law school and at issue in practice

The first paragraph (c) exception is for a transfer that

(i) was intended to be for new value, not an antecedent debt

(ii) did in fact occur at a time "substantially contemporaneous" with the time that the debt arose, section 547(c)(1).

For example, *D* borrows $50,000 from *C* on April 5. Both parties then intend the loan to be a secured loan, secured by a pledge of *D*'s *X* Corp. stock. On April 6, *D* pledges her *X* Corp. stock by delivering the certificates to *C*. On May 7, *D* files a bankruptcy petition. The bankruptcy trustee will not be able to void the April 6 pledge under section 547. The transfer for an antecedent debt is protected by section 547(c)(1).

Note that section 547(c)(1) requires both that the transfer actually be a "substantially contemporaneous exchange" and that the parties so intended. Assume that *C* makes a loan to *D* that both *C* and *D* intend to be a 180-day loan. Later that same day *C* first learns that *D* is in financial difficulty and so demands and obtains repayment. Section 547(c)(1) could not protect the repayment. While the transfer actually was a "substantially contemporaneous exchange," it was not so intended. If bankruptcy occurs within 90 days, the trustee can avoid the payment under section 547(b).

While section 547(c)(1) can apply either to an absolute transfer such as a payment or a security transfer such as a mortgage, section 547(c)(2) protects only payments. Section 547(c)(2) looks to both (1) the nature of the debt and (2) the nature of the payment.

First, the nature of the debt. The debt must be in the ordinary course of business (business debtor) or financial affairs (consumer debtor) of both the debtor/payor and the creditor/payee.

Second, the nature of the payment. The payment must be in the ordinary course of both this debtor and creditor (a subjective test) or according to ordinary business terms (an objective test).

To illustrate, *D* receives *D's* water bill for January water use on February 2. *D* and most water customers regularly pay their water bills by check before the end of the month. *D* pays *D*'s water bill by check on February 14. *D*'s payment of *D*'s water bill is a section 547(b) preference, but it is not avoidable. Section 547(c)(2) applies.

The third exception protects "enabling loans." Section 547(c)(3) requires that:

(1) the creditor gives the debtor "new value" to acquire certain real or personal property;

(2) the debtor signs a security agreement giving the creditor a security interest in the property;

(3) the debtor in fact uses the "new value" supplied by the creditor to acquire the property; and

(4) the creditor perfects its security interest no later than 30 days after the debtor receives possession.

For example, on April 4, *F* borrows $34,000 from *S* to buy a new tractor and signs a security agreement that describes the tractor. *S* files a financing statement. On April 20, *F* uses *S*'s $34,000 to buy a new tractor. On May 5, *F* files a bankruptcy petition.

F's bankruptcy trustee may *not* avoid *S*'s security interest. While all of the elements of section 547(b) are satisfied,[4] all of the elements of section 547(c)(3) are also satisfied.

Section 547(c)(4) provides a measure of protection for a creditor who receives a preference and "after such transfer" extends further unsecured credit. For example, on June 6, *C* lends *D* $60,000. On July 7, *D* repays $40,000. On August 8, *C* lends *D* an additional $30,000. On September 9, *D* files a bankruptcy petition. The bankruptcy trustee can recover only $10,000. The July 7 payment of $40,000 was a

---

4 The creation of a lien is a transfer of property of the debtor. It was, of course, "to or for the benefit of a creditor." And, it was "for or on account of an antecedent debt." "For purposes of this section, a transfer is not made until the debtor has acquired rights in the property transferred," section 547(e)(3). The other elements of section 547(b) are discussed earlier in this chapter.

preference under section 547(b). The trustee's recovery, however, is reduced by the amount of the August 8 unsecured advance of $30,000, section 547(c)(4).

Note that under section 547(c)(4), the sequence of events is of critical significance. The additional extension of credit must occur after the preferential transfer. If on June 6, *C* lends *D* $60,000; on July 7, *C* lends *D* an additional $30,000; on August 8, *D* repays $40,000, and on September 9, *D* files a bankruptcy petition, the trustee could recover $40,000 under section 547.

Section 547(c)(5) creates a limited exception from preference attack for certain Article 9 floating liens. Article 9 provides a mechanism for establishing a "floating lien." Such liens are most commonly used in financing accounts or inventory which normally "turn-over" in the ordinary course of the debtor's business. For example, on January 10 Credit Co., *C*, lends Department Store, *D*, $800,000 and takes a security interest in the store's inventory. Obviously, *C* wants *D* to sell its inventory so that it can repay the loan. It is equally obvious that as inventory is sold, the collateral securing *C* loan decreases unless *C*'s lien "floats" to cover the proceeds from the sale of the inventory and/or cover new inventory that *D* later acquires. Accordingly, the security agreement that *D* signs on January 10 will probably contain an after-acquired property clause that grants *C* a security interest not only in the inventory that *D* now owns but also in the inventory that *D* later acquires.

Even though *D* only signs this one security agreement, section 547 views *D* as making numerous different transfers of security interests. Under section 547(e)(3), "For purposes of this section, a transfer is not made until the debtor has acquired rights in the property transferred." This means that every time *D* acquires additional inventory there is a new transfer for purposes of section 547. Thus, if *D* acquires new inventory on March 3 and files for bankruptcy within the next 90 days, it would *seem* that the trustee can invalidate *C*'s security interest in the March 3 inventory because there was

1. a transfer of property of the debtor to a creditor
2. for an antecedent debt

[The debt was incurred on January 10. As noted above, section 547(e)(3) dates the transfer of the security interest in the March 3 inventory as March 3.]

3. presumption of insolvency

[Remember section 547(f).]

4. transfer made within 90 days of the bankruptcy petition
5. transfer increased bankruptcy distribution to *C* (unless *C* was already fully secured.)

Section 547(c)(5), however, will usually protect *C*. Under this provision, a creditor with a security interest in inventory or accounts receivable is subject to a preference attack only to the extent that it improves its position during the 90-day period before bankruptcy. The test is a two-point test and requires a comparison of the secured creditor's position 90 days before the petition and on the date of the petition. [If new value was first given after 90 days before the case, the date on which it was first given substitutes for the 90-day point.]

There are seven steps involved in applying section 547(c)(5)'s "two-step" test:

1. Determine the amount of debt on the date of the bankruptcy petition;
2. Determine the value of the debtor's accounts and/or inventory encumbered by the secured creditor's lien on the date of the petition;
3. Subtract #2 from #1;
4. Determine the amount of debt 90 days before the petition;
5. Determine the value of the debtor's accounts and/or inventory encumbered by the secured creditor's lien 90 days before the petition;
6. Subtract #5 from #4;
7. Subtract the answer in #3 from the answer in #6.

This is the amount of the preference.

The following hypotheticals illustrate the application of section 547(c)(5).

(1) At the time of its bankruptcy petition, *D* owes *C* $100,000 and has inventory with a

value of $60,000. *C* has a security interest in all of *D*'s inventory. Ninety days before bankruptcy, *D* owed *C* $90,000 and had inventory with a value of $70,000. All of *D*'s inventory was acquired within the last 90 days. Under these facts, *C* has not improved its position. Under these facts, *C*'s security interest will be protected by section 547(c)(5).

(2) At the time of its bankruptcy petition, *D* owes *C* $100,000 and has inventory with a value of $75,000. *C* has a security interest in all of *D*'s inventory. Ninety days before bankruptcy, *D* owed *C* $90,000 and had inventory with a value of $30,000. All of *D*'s inventory was acquired within the last 90 days. Under these facts, the bankruptcy trustee may reduce *C*'s secured claim from $75,000 to $40,000.[5]

Compare the facts of (1) with (2). Which fact situation is more common? How often in the "real world" will a debtor in financial difficulty acquire additional inventory or generate an increased amount of accounts? Not often. In the usual situation section 547(c)(5) completely protects a security interest in after-acquired inventory or accounts—

(3) *D* files a bankruptcy petition on April 22. At the time of the bankruptcy petition, *D* owes

---

[5] There was a $35,000 reduction in the amount by which the claim exceeded the collateral. (90 – 30) – (100 – 75). The $75,000 secured claim is thus reduced by this $35,000 improvement in position.

S $200,000. *S* has a security interest in *D*'s inventory of Oriental rugs which then have a value of $200,000. On January 22, 90 days before the bankruptcy petition was filed, *D* owed *S* $200,000, and the rugs had a fair market value of $150,000. *D* did not acquire any additional rugs after January 22; the value of *D*'s rugs increased because of market considerations. The trustee has no section 547 rights against *S*. There is no transfer to invalidate. *S*'s improvement in position was not from a transfer, not "to the prejudice of other creditors holding an unsecured claim."

(4) *D* Manufacturing Co., *D*, files a bankruptcy petition on April 4. At the time of the filing of the bankruptcy, *D* owes *C* Credit Corp., *C*, $400,000. *C* has a valid in bankruptcy security interest in all of *D*'s equipment. The *D–C* security agreement has an after-acquired property clause. On the date of the filing of the petition, *D*'s equipment has a fair market value of $310,000. On January 4, 90 days before the filing of the bankruptcy petition, *D* owed *C* $400,000 and *D*'s equipment had a fair market value of $320,000. On February 2, *D* sold a piece of equipment for $60,000. (*D* used the $60,000 to pay taxes.) On March 3, *D* bought other equipment for $50,000. The trustee can limit *C*'s security interest to the equipment owned on January 4. The March 3 "transfer" is a preference under section

547(b).[6] The March 3 "transfer" of a security interest in equipment is not protected by section 547(c)(5) because it only applies to security interests in inventory or accounts.

Section 547(c)(6) exempts "statutory liens" from the scope of section 547. Statutory liens are covered by section 545; section 545 is covered infra.

"Statutory lien" is defined in section 101(45) as a lien "arising *solely* by force of statute." Section 101(45) expressly provides that neither a security interest nor a judicial lien is a "statutory lien." While there are statutes providing for security interests and judicial liens, neither a security interest nor a judicial lien arises "*solely* by force of statute." A security interest will always require an agreement; a judicial lien will always require court action.

The following hypothetical illustrates the operation of section 547(c)(6). *C* Construction Co. is building a warehouse for *D*. Under relevant state statutes, a builder can obtain a mechanics lien. *C* takes the steps required by the state law and obtains a mechanics lien on the warehouse to secure payment for the work that it has done. If *D* files for bankruptcy, the bankruptcy trustee will not be able to attack the mechanics lien under section 547.

Section 547(c)(7) protects bona fide payments of a "domestic support obligation" from avoidance as a preference. For example, *D* makes a $22,500 payment to cover five missed child support payments.

---

[6] Remember, that March 3 is the date that the transfer is deemed made for purposes of section 547, section 547(e)(3).

Two weeks later *D* files a bankruptcy petition. Even though the $22,500 payment was for an antecedent debt, it cannot be recovered as a preference.

Section 547(c)(8) is also relevant only in cases in which the debtor is an individual. It applies only if

1. the debtor is an individual and
2. the debts are "primarily" consumer debts and
3. the aggregate value of all property covered by the transfer is less than $600

If, for example, *D* owes *C* $11,200 and pays *C* $400 four days before filing for bankruptcy, the bankruptcy trustee will not be able to recover the $400 from *C* under section 547.

Similarly, section 547(c)(9) creates another de minimus exception. There are two important differences between section 547(c)(8) and (9). First, the nature of the debtor's debts. Section 547(c)(8) applies only if the debts are "primarily consumer debts." Section 547(c)(9) applies only if the debts are "not primarily consumer debts", section 547(c)(9) applies to debtors who are not consumer debtors, section 547(c)(8) applies to consumer debtors. Second, the amount: of the preferential transfer. The section 547(c)(9) amount is "less than $6,825[7] the section 547(c)(8) amount is less than $600."

---

7 The dollar amount fluctuates pursuant to section 104.

C. WHICH TRANSFERS CAN BE AVOIDED—SETOFFS

Setoff possibilities arise when a person is both a debtor to and creditor of another person. Assume, for example, that *B* buys goods from *S* each month on credit. *B* owes *S* $100,000 on the December shipment, and *S* owes *B* $20,000 because of problems with the November shipment. *B* is both a debtor and a creditor of *S*, and *S* is both a debtor and a creditor of *B*.

The most common setoff situation involves a bank and its customer.[8] Assume, for example, that *W* has a checking account at Bank *B*, *B*, with a $10,000 balance. *W* borrows $20,200 from *B*. *B* is *W*'s creditor on the loan; *B*, however, is also *W*'s debtor on the checking account. *B* is thus both *W*'s creditor and *W*'s debtor.

In attempting to collect the $20,200 loan from *W*, *B* may assert its right of setoff. To explain by illustration, if Bank *B* asserts its right of setoff against *W*, it will reduce *W*'s checking account balance from $10,000 to 0 and reduce the amount owed by *W* on the $20,200 loan to $10,200.

What if *W* files a bankruptcy petition one day after the setoff? Can the bankruptcy trustee recover the $10,000 from *B*? If one day before the filing of a bankruptcy petition, *W* withdraws $10,000 from *W's*

---

[8] 2001 changes in Article 9 may diminish the importance of bank setoffs. The 2001 amendments enable a bank to obtain a security interest in its customers' bank accounts. Banks may rely more on their security interests in bank accounts and less on their rights of setoff.

savings account and uses that $10,000 to reduce *W*'s indebtedness to *B*, the trustee can recover the $1,000 under section 547. Is there any reason to treat *B*'s setoff differently?

Two reasons.

First, section 506 expressly makes a right of setoff a secured claim. A secured claimant's taking its collateral is not a section 547 preference—it does not "enable such creditor to receive more." Similarly, a secured claimant's exercising its right of setoff does not receive more.

Second, section 553 expressly provides that section 547 does not apply to setoffs. Section 553 is the only provision of the Bankruptcy Code that limits prepetition setoffs.

Section 553 contains a number of limitations on setoffs:

(1) "Mutual Debt"

The debts must be between the same parties in the same right or capacity. For example, a claim against a "bankrupt"[9] as an administratrix cannot be set off against a debt owed to the "bankrupt" as an individual.

---

[9] The Bankruptcy Code uses the term "debtor," not the term "bankrupt." Nevertheless, in discussing setoffs in which each party is the debtor of the other, it seems less confusing to use the term "bankrupt" to identify the party that filed a voluntary bankruptcy petition (or the party whose creditors filed an involuntary bankruptcy petition).

(2) "Arose before the commencement of the case"

Both the debt owed to the "bankrupt" and the claim against the "bankrupt" must have preceded the filing of the bankruptcy petition. A creditor cannot setoff its prepetition claim against a debtor against its postpetition obligation to the debtor.

(3) "Disallowed," section 553(a)(1)

Certain claims against a "bankrupt" are disallowed. See section 502 considered in Chapter XV. A claim that is disallowed under section 502 may not be used as the basis for a setoff. To illustrate, *A* owes *B* $40,000. *B* files a bankruptcy petition. The debt from *A* to *B* is property of the estate. The trustee attempts to collect the $40,000 from *A*. *A* only pays the trustee $30,000. *A* alleges that it had set off a $10,000 claim it had against *B* prior to the bankruptcy filing. If that $10,000 claim would be barred by the statute of limitations in a state collection action, it would be disallowed under section 502(b)(1) and the setoff would be disallowed under 553(a)(1).

(4) "Acquired" Claims, section 553(a)(2)

Certain acquired claims cannot be setoff. Assume for example, that *B* is insolvent; *A* owes *B* $40,000; *B* owes *C* $10,000. Because *B* is insolvent, *C*'s $10,000 claim is of little value to *C*. *C* would be willing to sell its claim against *B* to *A* for less than $1,000. *A* would be willing to buy *C*'s claim for less than $10,000 if it could then assert that claim as a $10,000 setoff to reduce its debt to *B* from $40,000 to $30,000.

Under section 553(a)(2) claims against the "bankrupt" acquired from a third party may *not* be set off against a debt owed to the "bankrupt" if:

a. the claim was acquired within 90 days before the bankruptcy petition or after the bankruptcy petition, *and*

b. the "bankrupt" was insolvent when the claim was acquired. [Section 553(c) creates a rebuttable presumption of insolvency.]

(5) Build-ups, section 553(a)(3)

Section 553(a)(3) precludes a setoff by a bank[10] if:

a. money was deposited by the "bankrupt" within 90 days of the bankruptcy petition,[11] and

b. the "bankrupt" was insolvent at the time of the setoff (remember section 553(c)'s presumption of insolvency), and

c. the purpose of the deposit was to create or increase the right of setoff.

For example, *X* Bank makes a loan to *D* Corp. Payment of the loan is guaranteed by *P*, the president of *D* Corp. *D* Corp. suffers financial reverses. *X* Bank pressures *D* Corp. and *P* to increase the balance of the corporation's general bank account. *D* Corp. moves $100,000 from other banks to its *X* Bank

10 Again, section 553(a)(3) is not expressly limited to bank setoffs.

11 A bank deposit is the most common example of a "debt owed to the debtor by such creditor" for purposes of section 553(a)(3).

account before filing its bankruptcy petition. Section 553(a)(3) would preclude *X* Bank from taking the $100,000 by way of setoff.

(6) Improvement in Position, section 553(b)

Section 553(b) is similar to section 547(c)(5), considered supra. Both are designed to prevent an improvement in position within 90 days of bankruptcy. Application of section 553(b) requires the following simple computations:

1. Determine the amount of the claim against the debtor 90 days before the date of the filing of the petition;[12]
2. Determine the "mutual debt" owing to the "bankrupt" by the holder of such claim 90 days before the filing of the petition;
3. Subtract #2 from #1 to determine the "insufficiency;
4. Determine the amount of the debt on the date that the right of setoff was asserted;
5. Determine the amount of the setoff;
6. Subtract #5 from #4 to determine the insufficiency;
7. Subtract the answer in #6 from the answer in #3, to determine what part, if any, of the amount of setoff the trustee may recover.

---

[12] If there is no "insufficiency" (as defined in section 553(b)(2)) 90 days before the petition, examine the 89th day, then the 88th day, etc. until a day is found that has an "insufficiency." Computations 1–3 will then focus on that day.

The following problems illustrate the application of section 553(b):

(1) *D* files a Chapter 13 petition.

90 days before the petition, *D* owes *B* Bank $100,000 and has $40,000 on deposit.

10 days before the petition, *B* exercises its right of setoff. At that time, *D* owes *B* Bank $70,000 and the account has $60,000 balance.

The trustee may recover $50,000 from *B* Bank.[13]

(2) *D* files a Chapter 7 petition.

90 days before the petition, *D* owes $200,000 to *B* Bank and has $200,000 on deposit at *B* Bank.

88 days before the petition, *D* withdraws $80,000 from the account; 5 days before the petition, *B* exercises its right of setoff. At that time, *D* owes *B* $70,000 and has $60,000 on deposit in *B* Bank.

The trustee may recover $60,000 from *B* Bank.[14]

---

[13] There was a $60,000 ($100,000 – $40,000) "insufficiency" 90 days before the bankruptcy petition was filed. At the time of the setoff, the "insufficiency" was only $10,000 ($70,000 – $60,000). There was a $50,000 improvement in position ($60,000 – $10,000). The bankruptcy trustee may recover $50,000 of the amount of offset under section 553(b).

[14] On the first date within the 90 day period that there was an "insufficiency," it was an insufficiency of $80,000. At the time of the setoff, the "insufficiency" was only $10,000 ($70,000 – $60,000). There was an improvement in position of $70,000 ($80,000 – $10,000). Nevertheless, the trustee may recover only $60,000 under section 553(b). "The amount so offset" establishes the ceiling for recovery under section 553(b).

In summary, a bankruptcy trustee will apply the above seven steps to any setoff that has occurred prior to the filing of the bankruptcy petition.

The filing of a bankruptcy petition automatically stays any further setoffs. Section 553 subjects the right of setoff to limitations provided in sections 362 and 363. Section 362(a)(7) stays setoffs. Thus, in order, to exercise a right of setoff after the filing of the bankruptcy petition it is necessary to obtain relief from the stay. Section 362(d), considered supra, governs relief from the stay. If a stay is terminated or modified to permit a postpetition setoff, the setoff will be limited by section 553(a)—requirements 1–5, discussed supra. Section 553(b) does not apply to postpetition setoffs.

None of section 553 applies to "recoupment." Recoupment is like setoff, only different. In recoupment, the claim that each party has against the other must arise from the same transaction.

This difference is especially important in bankruptcy. Neither section 553 nor any other section of the Bankruptcy Code mentions recoupment.

Bankruptcy courts hold that a creditor's exercise of the right of recoupment is not affected by limitations of section 553 such as the requirement that the debts owing by and to the debtor both arose before the commencement of the case. For example, prepetition Medicare overpayments for nursing services made to the debtor in one fiscal year before bankruptcy and Medicare payment obligations for debtor's postpetition services made in a later fiscal year have been held to be part of the same "transaction" for purposes of equitable recoupment. Thus the government could, on grounds of equitable recoupment, deduct prepetition overpayments from the sums that the government owed to the debtor for postpetition services, without violating section 553 (or the automatic stay).

D. WHICH TRANSFERS CAN BE AVOIDED—FRAUDULENT TRANSFERS AND OBLIGATIONS

1. SECTION 548

The Bankruptcy Code, like nonbankruptcy law, invalidates transfers that are fraudulently made and obligations that are fraudulently incurred. The Bankruptcy Code fraudulent conveyance provisions are very much like the nonbankruptcy fraudulent conveyance statutes considered infra. Section 548 is based on the Uniform Fraudulent Conveyances Act (UFCA).[15]

---

[15] Section 548(a)(1)(A) corresponds to section 7 of the UFCA; it empowers the trustee to invalidate transfers made with actual intent to hinder, delay or defraud creditors. Transfers by a partnership to a non-partner are governed by section 548(a). And section 548(a)(1)(B) resembles UFCA sections 4–7; it provides for avoidance of transfers where the debtor received less than a "reasonably equivalent value" and (i) was insolvent or became insolvent as a result of the transaction, or (ii) was engaged in business or was about to engage in a business transaction for which his remaining property was unreasonably small capital; or (iii) intended to incur or believed that he would incur debts beyond his ability to pay.

In 2014, the Uniform Law Commission adopted the Uniform Voidable Transactions Act which amends the UFCA and makes it even more like section 548.

Section 548(a) reaches transfers that are actually fraudulent, i.e., made by the debtor with the actual, subjective intention of defrauding creditors, section 548(a)(1)(A). There is almost never any direct evidence of actual fraudulent intent. Establishing actual fraudulent intent is usually established through circumstantial evidence such as a close relationship between the transferor and the transferee. Reade v. Livingston, 8 Am. Dec. 520 (N.Y. Ch. 1818) involving a husband's gift to his wife of all of his real estate after a creditor won a judgment against him remains the classic example of a conveyance made with actual fraudulent intent.

Of far greater, current practical significance are conveyances that are constructively fraudulent. Section 548(a)(1)(B), like state fraudulent conveyance laws, also makes some transfers constructively fraudulent. Establishing a constructively fraudulent conveyance turns on the adequacy of consideration for the transfer and the financial position of the debtor, rather than the intention of the debtor. If the debtor is able to pay its debts, creditors (or at least the bankruptcy courts) are not concerned with what the debtor receives when it transfers property. On the other hand, if the debtor is in financial trouble as described by either section 548(a)(1)(B)(ii)(I) or (II) or (III), then bankruptcy courts are concerned with the adequacy of the consideration that the debtor receives for the transfer.

The easiest example of a transfer that is constructively fraudulent under section 548(a)(1)(B) is a gift by a person who is insolvent [16] to a friend or relative.[17] Increasingly, in bankruptcy courtrooms and law school classrooms, section 548(a)(1)(B) and the concept of constructively fraudulent conveyance are being applied to common business transactions such as asset sales, foreclosure sales, intercorporate guarantees, and leveraged buyouts.

a. Asset Sales

D Inc. owns three convenience stores and is in financial distress. *D Inc.* sells one of its three stores to *X* for $100,000; Less than two years later, *D Inc.* files for Chapter 7

D's *Inc.* sale of the convenience store to *X* is a section 548 fraudulent transfer if *D Inc.* at the time of the sale was in financial trouble as described

---

[16] No surprise that the term "insolvent" is used in section 548 and throughout the Bankruptcy Code. The Bankruptcy Code's definition of "insolvent" in section 101(32) is somewhat surprising. It looks to the amount of the debtor's debts and the value of the debtor's nonexempt property rather than to the debtor's record of paying debts or the debtor's present ability to pay debts as they come due.

[17] I have used the example of a gift to a friend or relative to make the explanation of section 548(a)(1)(B) constructive fraudulent transfers as easy as possible. Your teacher or client can make this more difficult by changing the donee to a "qualified religious or charitable entity or organization. Some such contributions are protected by section 548(a)(2) from avoidance as a fraudulent transfer.

548(a)(1)(B)(ii) and the $100,000 that *D Inc* received was less than "reasonably equivalent value" for the store. If the sale is a section 548 fraudulent transfer then under section 550, the trustee can recover the convenience store or "the value of such property" at the time of the sale from *X*, and, under section 502(h), *X* would have an unsecured claim.

b. Foreclosure Sales

Assume, for example, that *D* borrowed $180,000 from *M*. The debt was secured by a deed of trust. *D* defaulted. *M* foreclosed on the realty and sold the property for $115,400, the amount of *D*'s outstanding debt. *M*'s foreclosure and sale completely complied with state law. A few days later, *D* filed for bankruptcy.

Do you see any possible fraudulent conveyance argument? What if *D* found an appraiser who was willing to testify that the value of the realty at the time of the foreclosure sale was $200,000? Can it be argued that the foreclosure sale was a fraudulent conveyance since it was a transfer for less than reasonably equivalent value while the debtor was insolvent?

Such an argument was made in various cases with varying degrees of success until the Supreme Court in BFP v. RTC, 511 U.S. 531 (1994) held that " 'reasonably equivalent value' is the price received at the foreclosure sale so long as all the requirements of the state's foreclosure law have been complied with."

c. Intercorporate Guarantees

Intercorporate guarantees present even more challenging section 548(a)(1)(B) problems. In an intercorporate guarantee, the creditor generally is providing an appropriate amount of consideration, but is providing the consideration to a person other than the guarantor.

Assume, for example, that *C* lends $900,000 to *X*, Inc., *D* Corp., a subsidiary of *X*, Inc., guarantees repayment. A few months later *D* Corp. files for bankruptcy. Can the trustee use section 548(a)(1)(B) to avoid *D* Corp.'s guarantee to *C* as a constructively fraudulent obligation?

Note that *C* provided a sufficient amount of consideration—*C* is trying to collect $900,000 from *D* Corp. because it loaned $900,000. Note also that *C* provided that consideration to someone other than *D* Corp.—someone other than the transferor was debtor in this bankruptcy case.

Recall that section 548(a)(1)(B) does not ask whether the creditor/transferee *gave* reasonably equivalent consideration to someone but rather whether the debtor "*received*" reasonably equivalent value. Do you now understand why a bankruptcy trustee for the guarantor can challenge an intercorporate guarantee as a fraudulent obligation under section 548(a)(1)(B)? Do you also understand why such challenges will not always be successful?

Recall also that section 548(a)(1)(B) inquires not only into the adequacy of consideration to the debtor but also the financial condition of the debtor? If *D*

Corp. was clearly solvent at the time of the guarantee, then section 548 cannot be used to void the guarantee.

Additionally, a loan to one corporation can benefit related entities. Conceivably, *C*'s loan to *X*, Inc., *D* Corp.'s parent, did indirectly benefit *D* Corp. Maybe *X* Inc as parent of *D* Corp was devoting a part of the loan proceeds to benefit *D* Corp. Accordingly, the appropriate inquiry is to compare what *D* Corp. gave and what *D* Corp. got from the loan to *X*, Inc. And, part of that inquiry into what *D* Corp. "gave" depends on a determination of the probability that *X* Inc will itself pay *C*.

d. Leveraged Buyouts

In essence, a leveraged buyout (LBO) involves a person's buying the stock of a corporation from its shareholders and paying those shareholders with the proceeds of a loan secured by the corporation's assets. Assume, for example, that *C* makes a loan to *X* to enable *X* to buy all of the stock of *D* Corp. from its shareholders. and *C* obtains a lien on the assets of *D* Corp., as collateral for the loan. Shortly after the LBO is completed, *D* Corp. files for bankruptcy.

Do you see that the net effects of an LBO are that (1) debt is substituted for equity and (2) assets which were unencumbered before the LBO and thus available to pay the company's unsecured debt are now subject to a the LOB lender's lien?

Do you see the trustee's possible section 548(a)(1)(B) argument to avoid the lien on *D* Corp.'s assets?? First, the trustee must show that D Corp was insolvent as a result of the transfers. Second, the trustee must show that the D Corp. did not receive reasonably equivalent value.

What consideration did *D* Corp. receive for the transfer? *C* gave value to someone; it made the loan to *X* that made the LBO possible but what is the "reasonably equivalent value" that *D* Corp received from a loan to *X*? Was the change in ownership of value to *D* Corp.? Was it of a value reasonably equivalent to what *D* Corp. transferred?

e. Remember Insolvency or . . .

As the above LBO hypothetical reminds us, proof of a constructive fraudulent transfer under section 548(a)(1)(B) requires not only proof of the absence of reasonably equivalent value but also proof of the existence or insolvency or one of the other forms of financial distress described in section 548(a)(B)(ii) If *D* Corp. was not in financial distress at the time of the LBO or as result of the LBO, then there is no fraudulent transfer.

f. Comparison of Fraudulent Transfers and Preferential Transfers

Assume that *D* has $100,000 of assets and owes $70,000 to *A*, $80,000 to *B* and $90,000 to *C*. *D* transfers $60,000 of asset

If *D* transferred the $60,000 to *A*, B, or *C*—one of *D*'s creditors, then the transfer will be scrutinized as a section 547 preference. but not a 548 fraudulent transfer. "Satisfying or securing" an antecedent debt is reasonably equivalent value under section 548. See section 548(d)(2).

If *D* transferred the $60,000 of assets to someone other than *A*, *B* or *C* and then files for bankruptcy, the transfer will be scrutinized only as a section 548 fraudulent conveyance. Section 547 only applies to transfers to creditors.

To summarize and simplify, section 547 focuses on who the transferee was: section 547 is the statutory basis for avoiding transfers to people who were creditors of the debtor. Section 548 focuses on what the debtor received for the transfer: section 548 is the statutory basis for avoiding transfers in which the debtor received less than reasonably equivalent value for what the debtor transferred.

g. Comparison of Section 548 and State Law

Section 548 differs from state fraudulent conveyance law in a couple of significant respects:

1. Section 548 eliminates the requirement of actual unpaid creditors as to whom the transfer was fraudulent. Under state fraudulent conveyance law a transfer by an insolvent not for fair consideration may be set aside only by creditors who were creditors at the time of the transfer. Under section 548(a)(1)(B) such a transfer may be avoided even though all who were creditors at the time of the transfer have been paid.

2. Under section 548, the bankruptcy trustee may only reach transfers made[18] within two years of the filing of the bankruptcy petition.[19] To illustrate, assume that in June of 2020, Marge Simpson gave her daughter Lisa a new piano as a birthday present. Mrs. Simpson was insolvent at the time of the gift. On August 1, 2022, Mrs. Simpson files a bankruptcy petition. By the date of bankruptcy, Mrs. Simpson has repaid all of her June, 2020 creditors except Mr. Burns whom she owed $10. Mrs. Simpson's bankruptcy trustee will not be able to recover the piano under section 548. The transfer was a fraudulent conveyance (a transfer for less than "reasonably equivalent value" while insolvent) but it was made more than two years prior to the bankruptcy petition.

States generally have a three- to six-year reach-back period for actions to invalidate fraudulent

---

[18] For purposes of section 548, a transfer will be deemed made when it becomes so far perfected that a bona fide purchaser from the debtor could not acquire an interest in the property transferred superior to the interest of the transferor, section 548(d). The problems of determining the date that a transfer will be deemed made are considered later in this chapter.

[19] The two-year period of section 548 is a true statute of limitations. It does not require that the trustee's action to invalidate the transfer be commenced within one year of the time the transfer was made. If the transfer was made within two years of the date of the filing of the bankruptcy petition, the bankruptcy trustee has up until the closing or dismissal of the case or two years after their appointment, whichever first occurs, to commence the invalidation action, section 546.

conveyances. Mrs. Simpson's trustee can use state fraudulent conveyance law with its longer reach-back period to recover the piano under section 544(b).

2. SECTION 544(b)

Section 548's two-year reach back significantly limits the use of section 548. Section 548 is not, however, the only provision in the Bankruptcy Code that invalidates fraudulent conveyances. The trustee may also use section 544(b) to invalidate fraudulent conveyances.

Section 544(b) does not specifically provide for the invalidation of fraudulent conveyances. Rather it empowers the bankruptcy trustee to avoid any prebankruptcy transfer that is "voidable under applicable law by a creditor holding an unsecured claim that is allowable."[20]

Section 544(b) incorporates state fraudulent conveyance law into the Bankruptcy Code. Section 544(b) in essence incorporate state reach back periods [21] for fraudulent conveyances.

---

20 Section 502 governs allowance of claims. Section 502 is considered in Chapter XI.

21 The state limitations period determines which transfers may be challenged, not when the challenge must be made. Section 546 again gives the trustee time after his or her appointment to commence the action. To illustrate, *D* makes a fraudulent conveyance in January of 2020. State law imposes a five-year limitation period on fraudulent conveyance actions. If *D* files a bankruptcy petition in December of 2024, that satisfies or tolls the state law limitations period, *D*'s bankruptcy trustee will have the additional section 546 period to commence a fraudulent conveyance action.

In the Simpson problem, the June gift of a piano would be a fraudulent conveyance under nonbankruptcy law, Statute of Elizabeth, UFCA, or UFTA as to Mr. Burns. Burns was a creditor holding an unsecured claim that is allowable. Accordingly, the bankruptcy trustee may use section 544(b) to recover the piano.

While the existence of the trustee's section 544(b) avoiding powers depends upon the existence of an avoiding power held by an actual creditor, the extent of the trustee's section 544(b) avoidance powers is greater than the power of the actual creditor. In the Simpson problem, under state fraudulent conveyance law, if Lisa Simpson paid Mr. Burns $10, she could keep the piano. Under section 544(b), Lisa is not so fortunate. Legislative history clearly indicates that section 544(b) retains the rule of Moore v. Bay, 284 U.S. 4 (1931).

Under the rule of Moore v. Bay, the trustee is not limited in his recovery by the amount of the claim of the actual creditor. A transfer which is voidable by a single, actual creditor, may be avoided entirely by the trustee, regardless of the size of the actual creditor's claim. Thus Lisa may not keep the piano by simply paying the bankruptcy trustee $10.

3. COMPARISON OF SECTIONS 548 AND 544(b)

The Simpson hypothetical points up the similarities and differences of sections 548 and 544(b).

These provisions are also compared in the following chart:

548	544(b)
1. Essentially UFCA	1. UFCA, UFTA or Statute of Elizabeth, which is the state law
2. Reaches transfers made within two years of bankruptcy petition [reach-back period is measured from the time the transfer is deemed made]	2. Reaches all transfers made with state limitations period [reach-back period is generally measured from the time the transfer was actually made]
3. Elements of fraudulent conveyance tested at the time that transfer was deemed made under section 548(d)	3. Elements of fraudulent conveyance tested as of time that the fraudulent conveyance was actually made
4. Transferee that takes for value and in good faith protected	4. Transfer that takes for value and in good faith protected
5. No requirement of actual creditor as to whom conveyance is fraudulent	5. Voidable only if transfer is fraudulent as to an actual creditor with an unsecured allowable claim
6. Complete invalidation	6. Complete invalidation

E. WHICH TRANSFERS CAN BE AVOIDED—TRANSFERS NOT RECORDED OR OTHERWISE PERFECTED

State law requires recordation or other public notice of a number of transfers. Real estate recording statutes require the recording of deeds and real property mortgages. And, Article 9 of the Uniform Commercial Code calls for public notice (perfection) of most security interests in personal property. A bankruptcy trustee may avoid these prepetition transfers that are not recorded or perfected before bankruptcy.

A failure to record can adversely affect other creditors. If creditor *X* does not record its lien on *D*'s property, creditor *Y* might not know that *D*'s property is encumbered. Relying on the mistaken belief that *D* holds his property free from liens, *Y* might extend credit, refrain from obtaining a lien, or forebear from instituting collection proceedings.

The Bankruptcy Code does not have its own public notice requirements. Rather, the Bankruptcy Code makes use of the recording requirements of state law in section 544(a) which some courts call the "strong arm clause."

Section 544(a) empowers the bankruptcy trustee to invalidate any unrecorded transfer that under nonbankruptcy law is voidable as to a creditor who extended credit and obtained a lien on the date of the filing of the bankruptcy petition or is voidable as to a bona fide purchaser of real property whether or not such a creditor or purchaser actually exists. In applying section 544(a), it is thus necessary to determine whether:

(1) nonbankruptcy law public notice requirements have been satisfied as of date of the filing of the bankruptcy petition;

(2) a creditor who extended credit and obtained a lien on the date that the bankruptcy petition was filed or a bona fide purchaser of real property on the date of the bankruptcy petition comes within the class of persons protected by such state law.

The following hypotheticals illustrate the application of section 544(a):

(1) On January 10, *D* borrows $10,000 from *M* and gives *M* a mortgage on Redacre. On February 2, *D* files a bankruptcy petition. As of the date of the petition, *M* had not recorded its mortgage.

In #1, the bankruptcy trustee may invalidate *M*'s mortgage under section 544(a).

The public notice requirements of the state real property recording statutes were not satisfied. Real property recording statutes typically protect bona fide purchasers. Since the mortgage was unrecorded on the date that the bankruptcy petition was filed, M's mortgage would be ineffective as against a bona fide purchaser of Redacre on the date that the petition was filed. Section 544(a) gives the bankruptcy trustee the same powers as a person who was a bona fide purchaser on the date that the bankruptcy petition was filed.

(2) On January 10, *D* borrows $10,000 from *S* and gives *S* a security interest in equipment. On February 22, *D* files a bankruptcy petition. *S* fails to perfect its security interest prior to February 22.

In #2, the bankruptcy trustee will be able to invalidate *S*'s security interest under section 544(a).

Again, the applicable public notice requirement was not satisfied. Article 9 of the Uniform Commercial Code requires that a security interest be perfected in order to be effective against a lien creditor, section 9–317(a)(2). Since the security interest was unperfected on the date that the bankruptcy petition was filed, *S*'s security interest would be subordinate[22] to the claim of a creditor who obtained a judicial lien on the date that the petition was filed. Section 544(a) gives *S* the same invalidation powers as a person who extended credit and obtained a judicial lien on the date that the bankruptcy petition was filed.

(3) On January 10, *D* borrows $10,000 from *S* to buy equipment and gives *S* a purchase money security interest in the equipment.[23] On January 28,

---

[22] Even though the Uniform Commercial Code uses the term "subordinate" instead of "voidable," a security interest that would be "subordinate" to a creditor that obtained a judicial lien on the date of the filing of the bankruptcy petition is "voidable" by the bankruptcy trustee.

[23] *S*'s security interest is "purchase money" since this extension of credit enabled *D* to obtain the property that is the collateral for the extension of credit. See section 9–103.

D files a bankruptcy petition. On January 29, *S* perfects its security interest.[24]

In #3, the bankruptcy trustee may not invalidate *S*'s security interest.

Section 544(a) empowers the bankruptcy trustee to invalidate security interests that would be subordinate to the claims of a creditor who obtained a judicial lien on the date that the petition was filed, January 28. *S* did not perfect its security interest until January 29. Recall the general rule of section 9–317(a)(2), that an unperfected security interest is subordinate to a lien creditor. This general rule is subject to section 9–317(e)'s exception for purchase money security interests. Purchase money security interest perfected within 20 days prevails over a gap lien creditor. By reason of section 9–317(e),[25] *S*'s *purchase money* security interest perfected on January 28 (within the requisite 20 days) would be effective as against a creditor who obtained a lien on January 28, the date that the bankruptcy petition

[24] The filing of a bankruptcy petition stays or stops most creditor collection efforts. Section 362(a), considered infra, defines the scope of the stay, by listing the acts that are stayed by the commencement of the bankruptcy case. Section 362(a)(4) stays lien perfection. Section 362(b) lists exceptions to the automatic stay. Section 362(b)(3) read together with section 546(b) excepts perfection of purchase money security interests.

[25] Section 9–317(e) provides: "[I]f a person files a financing statement with respect to a purchase money security interest before or within 20 days after the debtor receives delivery of the collateral, the security interest takes priority over the rights of a . . . lien creditor which arise between the time the security interest attaches and the time of filing."

was filed. Accordingly, *S*'s *purchase money* security interest is effective against the bankruptcy trustee.

(4) On January 10, Dudley Doright, D, borrows $10,000 from Snidely Whiplash, S, and gives S a security interest in equipment. On December 29, S properly files his financing statement. On December 30, D files a bankruptcy petition.

In #4, the bankruptcy trustee may not invalidate *S*'s security interest under section 544(a).[26]

The public notice requirements of Article 9 were not timely satisfied; *S* delayed in perfecting its security interest for almost a year. Article 9's perfection requirements protect "gap" lien creditors and buyers. In this hypothetical, the bankruptcy trustee has the right of a lien creditor, but not a gap lien creditor. Section 544(a) gives the bankruptcy trustee the invalidation powers of a creditor who obtained a judicial lien as of the date of the bankruptcy petition. On the date of the bankruptcy petition, December 30, *S*'s security interest was perfected. A perfected security interest is effective against lien creditors, cf. sections 9–201, 9–301. Accordingly, *S*'s security interest may not be invalidated under section 544(a).

---

[26] The bankruptcy trustee will probably be able to invalidate *S*'s security interest under some other provision of the Bankruptcy Code. If *D* was insolvent on December 29, the bankruptcy trustee may invalidate *S*'s security interest under section 547. The applicability of section 547 to transfers not timely perfected or recorded is considered later in this chapter.

The above hypotheticals suggest three general rules for the use of section 544(a) in invalidating transfers:

(1) If the transfer has been recorded or otherwise perfected prior to the date that the bankruptcy petition was filed, the trustee will not be able to invalidate the transfer under section 544(a).

(2) Except as noted in (3) below, if the transfer was not recorded or otherwise perfected by the date that the bankruptcy petition was filed, the bankruptcy trustee will be able to invalidate the transfer under section 544(a).

(3) The bankruptcy trustee will not be able to invalidate a purchase money security interest perfected within 20 days after the delivery of the collateral to the debtor even if the debtor files a bankruptcy petition in the gap between the creation of the security interest and perfection.

F. WHICH TRANSFERS CAN BE AVOIDED—TRANSFERS NOT TIMELY RECORDED OR OTHERWISE PERFECTED

Section 544(a) can only be used to avoid transfers that are not recorded as of the date of the bankruptcy petition, In the Dudley Doright/Snidely Whiplash hypothetical on page 140, the bankruptcy trustee was not able to invalidate Snidely's security interest under section 544(a) notwithstanding Snidely's long delay in giving public notice of his lien. Should Doright's bankruptcy trustee be able to invalidate Snidely's lien?

As noted earlier, there are a number of reasons for invalidating such "secret liens." Creditors of Doright may have been misled by Snidely's failure to record or a delay in recording. Unaware of this "secret," unrecorded lien, Nell Fenwick might extend credit to Doright she would not extend if aware of the lien. Unaware of a "secret," unrecorded lien, Mr. Peabody might delay in collecting a delinquent debt from Doright he would try to collect if aware of the lien. The Bankruptcy Code should provide for invalidation of transfers that are not timely recorded. And it does. In section 547.

1. SECTION 547(e)

Although it is easy to see the reason for invalidating liens that are not timely perfected, it is difficult to understand why section 547 should be the mechanism for invalidating such liens. The easy way to invalidate such secret liens would be to add a section to the Bankruptcy Code to the effect that any lien that can be recorded or otherwise perfected under state law must be recorded within 30 days after it is obtained in order to be valid in bankruptcy. While that is the "easy way," it is not the way of the Bankruptcy Code. Basically, the Bankruptcy Code's method is to "deem" that for purposes of applying the requirements of section 547(b)[27] the date of transfers

[27] The elements of section 547(b) are considered earlier in this chapter.

not timely recorded is the date of perfection,[28] not the actual date of transfer.

The Doright/Whiplash hypothetical illustrates the practical significance of the statutory delay of the effective date of the transfer until public notice of the transfer has been given. Remember, Doright borrowed $10,000 from Snidely on January 10 and gave Snidely a security interest in equipment which Snidely perfected on December 29. Doright filed a bankruptcy petition on December 30. At first, it might seem that section 547 is not applicable—that the security transfer from Doright to Snidely was not

---

[28] Section 547 does not specify the means of perfection. Rather, section 547(e)(1) provides that for purposes of section 547, transfers shall be perfected when effective under nonbankruptcy law against certain specified third parties. In a transfer of real property other than fixtures, the third parties are bona fide purchasers, i.e., the date of perfection is the date that the transfer is effective against bona fide purchasers. Nonbankruptcy law generally requires that transfers of interests in real property other than fixtures be recorded in order to be effective against bona fide purchasers.

A transfer of personal property or fixtures is perfected for purposes of section 547 when it is effective against a creditor with a judicial lien. Absolute transfers of personal property are generally effective against subsequent lien creditors of the transferor without any recording. For example, *A* pays *B* $1,000. This transfer is effective against subsequent lien creditors of *A* without any recording. *X* delivers 200 widgets to *Y*. Again, the transfer is effective as against subsequent lien creditors of the transferor without recordation.

Security transfers of liens in personal property or fixtures are not effective against subsequent judicial lien creditors of the transferor without recordation or other perfection. For example, *D* gives *S* a security interest in equipment to secure a debt. Under UCC § 9–317(a)(2), *S*'s security interest is not superior to the rights of a subsequent judicial lien creditor of *D* unless *S* had perfected its security interest before the judicial lien.

for an antecedent indebtedness and did not occur within 90 days of the bankruptcy petition. For purposes of section 547, however, the transfer will be *deemed made on December 29, not* January 10. [Under section 9–301, Snidely's security interest would not be effective as against subsequent judicial lien creditors until that date. Accordingly, by reason of section 547(e), the transfer will not be deemed made until that date.] Thus, the "December 29 transfer" would be within 90 days of the bankruptcy petition. Thus, the "December 29 transfer" would be for an antecedent indebtedness, i.e., the $10,000 loaned on January 10. Thus, the trustee would be able to invalidate S's security interest under section 547 if D was insolvent on December 29. [Remember section 547(f) creates a rebuttable presumption of insolvency.]

The above hypothetical illustrates that a delay in perfection can result in a security interest actually given for present consideration being deemed made for an antecedent indebtedness and thus a section 547 preference.

In the Dudley Doright hypothetical, over 11 months elapsed between the granting of the security interest and the perfecting of the security interest. What if the delay was eleven weeks? Eleven days? Eleven hours? Is there some sort of "grace period" in section 547?

Section 547(e) does provide a "grace period" for perfection.

Section 547(e)(2) describes three situations. First, section 547(e)(2)(A) deals with transfers perfected within 30 days. Such a transfer will be deemed made at the time of the transfer. A transfer deemed made at the time of the transfer is not vulnerable to attack by the bankruptcy trustee under section 547.

Second, section 547(e)(2)(B) deals with transfers not perfected within the 30 day grace period. Such a transfer will be deemed made at the time of perfection. A transfer deemed made at a point in time later than the time of the transfer is vulnerable to attack by the bankruptcy trustee under section 547.

Third, section 547(e)(2)(C) deals with the effect of filing a bankruptcy petition during the "grace period." Under such facts, the transfer will be deemed made at the time of the transfer if it is perfected within 30 days of the transfer or will be deemed made at the time of the filing of the bankruptcy petition if it is not perfected within 30 days.

The operation of section 547(e) is illustrated in the following four hypotheticals:

(1) On January 10, *S* lends *D* $10,000 and obtains a nonpurchase money security interest in *D*'s equipment. *S* perfects this security interest on January 19. For purposes of section 547, the security transfer will be deemed to have occurred on January 10, section 547(e)(2)(A). *S* perfected within 30 days after the transfer so the transfer is deemed made when it was actually made, January 10. Not a transfer

for an antecedent debt—January 10 transfer for a January 10 debt. Not a preference.

(2) On January 10, *D* borrows $10,000 from *S* and grants *S* a security interest in its equipment. *S* perfects its security interest on February 22. *S* did not perfect within 30 days so that for purposes of the elements of section 547(b), the transfer will be deemed to have occurred when it was finally perfected, February 22. A transfer for an antecedent debt—a February 22 transfer for a January 10 debt. Possibly a preference.

(3) On January 10, *S* lends *D* $10,000 and obtains a security interest in *D*'s equipment. *D* files a bankruptcy petition on January 15. *S* perfects its security interest on January 19.[29] For purposes of section 547, the security transfer will be deemed to have occurred on January 10, section 547(e)(2)(A), section 547(e)(2)(C)(ii). [Same facts as #1 except that *D* filed a bankruptcy

---

[29] This hypothetical raises not only section 547(e) issues but also issues under section 362 and section 544. Section 362(a)(4) bars the perfection of liens after the filing of a bankruptcy petition. Section 362(b)(3), however, creates an exception for perfection "accomplished within the period provided under section 547(e)(2)(A)." Accordingly, it would seem that the perfection in problem #3 did not violate the automatic stay. Accordingly, it would seem that the bankruptcy trustee will not be able to avoid the security interest under section 547.

petition before the security interest was perfected.]

(4) On January 10, *S* lends *D* $10,000 and obtains a security interest in *D*'s equipment. *D* files a bankruptcy petition on January 15. *S* perfects its security interest on February 22. For purposes of section 547, the security transfer will be deemed to have occurred on January 15, section 547(e)(2)(C). Transfers not perfected within 30 days are deemed made at the date of the bankruptcy petition if the filing of the petition preceded perfection. [Same facts as (2) except that *D* filed a bankruptcy petition before the security interest was filed.]

2. SECTION 548(d)

Section 548(d) is similar to section 547(e). Section 547(e) fixes the time when a transfer is deemed made for purposes of the preference invalidation provisions of section 547. Section 548(d) fixes the time when a transfer is deemed made for purposes of the fraudulent conveyance invalidation provisions of section 548: when the transfer is so far perfected that no subsequent bona fide purchaser of the property from the debtor can acquire rights in the property superior to those of the transferee.

The purpose of section 548(d) is to prevent a fraudulent conveyance from escaping invalidation by being kept secret for over a year. For example, on January 10, 2021, *D*, who is insolvent, gives Redacre to *X*. *X* does not record the deed until November 11,

2021. On October 10, 2023, *D* files a bankruptcy petition. Remember, section 548 has a two-year reach back period.[30] The transfer of Redacre was actually made more than two years before the bankruptcy petition was filed. The transfer, however, was not effective against a subsequent bona fide purchaser until it was recorded on November 11. Accordingly, under section 548(d), the transfer is deemed made on November 11, 2021. Without section 548(d), the bankruptcy trustee could not invalidate the gift by an insolvent under section 548.

The transfer from *D* to *X* in the preceding paragraph was a "true" fraudulent conveyance: a transfer by an insolvent without "reasonably equivalent value." Action 548(d), however, also may enable the bankruptcy trustee to invalidate some transfers that are not "true" fraudulent conveyances—transfers in which there has been merely a delay in recordation or perfection. Consider the following illustration.

Wallace, *W*, gives Redacre to his brother Theodore, *T*, in December of 2020. *W* is solvent at that time. *T*, however, does not record the transfer until June of 2021. At that time, *W* is insolvent. In May of 2023, *W* files a bankruptcy petition. The bankruptcy trustee will be able to avoid the 2020 gift because, for purposes of section 548, it will be treated as a June 2021 gift.

---

[30] This two-year reach back period and the other requirements of section 548 are considered earlier in this chapter.

Note that *T*'s delay in recordation is crucial to the bankruptcy trustee's section 548 case. At the time that the gift is actually made, the donor, *W*, is solvent. There are no legal problems with people who are solvent making gifts. This happens every Chanukah and Christmas. Gifts are fraudulent conveyances when made by people who are insolvent.

While the donor, *W*, was solvent when the gift was actually made, *W* is insolvent when the gift is deemed made under section 548(d) the time the transfer is perfected against bona fide purchasers from the transferor. Section 548(d), like section 547(e), enables the trustee to test all aspects of the transaction as of the time of recordation rather than as of the time of the actual transfer. Since W was insolvent when the transfer is deemed made at the time of recordation, the transfer was fraudulent as a transfer by an insolvent without reasonably equivalent value.

G. WHICH TRANSFERS CAN BE AVOIDED—LANDLORDS' LIENS

Sections 545(3) and 545(4) are the easiest invalidation provisions to read, understand and apply. "The trustee may avoid the fixing of a statutory lien on the property of the debtor to the extent that such lien . . .

(3) is for rent

(4) is a lien of distress for rent."

Note that the provisions only invalidate STATUTORY landlord liens, i.e., liens for rent arising "solely by force of a statute." If the lease agreement creates a security deposit or other Article 9 security interest in property of the lessee, this contractual lien is not affected by section 545.[31]

H. WHICH TRANSFERS CAN BE AVOIDED—STATUTORY LIENS THAT ARE DISGUISED PRIORITIES

Section 507 of the Bankruptcy Code is a priority provision;[32] it sets out the order in which the various unsecured claims against the debtor are to be satisfied. It displaces any state priority statutes.

Section 545 protects this federal priority scheme from disruption by state priority provisions that are "disguised" as statutory liens. Section 545 reaches spurious statutory liens which are in reality merely priorities.

When is a statutory lien more like a priority than a lien? Recall that a priority does not arise until distribution of a debtor's assets on insolvency. Accordingly, section 545(1) provides for invalidation of a statutory lien which first become effective on the bankruptcy or insolvency of the debtor.

---

[31] When a landlord requires its tenant to sign a security agreement giving the landlord a security interest in property of the tenant to secure rental payments, the landlord has, of course, obtained a lien. This lien held by the landlord is not however, a "landlord's lien"; it is a security interest. Not all liens securing claims by landlords are "landlord's liens." Only Chuck Berry would be inclined to call a security interest obtained by Mabel a "Mabel lien." https://www.youtube.com/watch?v=v124f0i0Xh4[ ]

[32] Section 507 is considered in Chapter XV.

I. SELLER'S RECLAMATION AND RETURN RIGHTS

When a buyer fails to pay for goods it accepts, the seller has a legal right to recover the contract price, UCC § 2–709. This legal right to be paid is of limited practical significance if the buyer is insolvent. Accordingly, the Uniform Commercial Code grants certain unpaid sellers a right to recover the goods. Section 2–702 of the Uniform Commercial Code empowers a seller to "reclaim" (recover) the goods if:

(1) the seller sold the goods on credit; credit sale, *and*

(2) the buyer was insolvent when the goods were received, *and*

(3) the buyer made a written misrepresentation of solvency within 3 months before the goods were delivered, or the demand for reclamation is made within 10 days of the buyer's receipt of the goods.

Article 2's right of reclamation is not a "lien" and is not a prebankruptcy transfer avoidable by a provision in Chapter 5 of the Bankruptcy Code. Instead, the Bankruptcy Code recognizes and alters a nonbankruptcy right of reclamation.

In bankruptcy, section 546(c) governs the right of reclamation in bankruptcy. Section 546(c), unlike 2–702, requires that the reclamation demand be in writing. And section 546(c) has a longer time period than the UCC's 10-day period.

More specifically, a seller has 45 days after the debtor's receipt of the goods on credit to make a written reclamation demand. If, however, the 45-day period expires after the commencement of the case, the seller has 20 days after the date of commencement to make the reclamation demand. To illustrate, if *D* received goods on credit from *S* and then filed for bankruptcy 44 days later, *S* would have 20 days after the bankruptcy filing to make its written reclamation demand.

Legally, the seller's right of reclamation turns on the seller's satisfaction of the various requirements in section 2–702 and section 546 discussed above. Practically, the seller's right of reclamation also turns on what the debtor has and has not done prior to the seller's reclamation demand. If the debtor has disposed of the goods prior to the seller's reclamation demand, then there is nothing to reclaim—under nonbankruptcy law, the reclamation remedy is limited to the goods that the seller delivered. Similarly, if the debtor has granted another creditor a security interest that covers all of its inventory, there is nothing to reclaim—under nonbankruptcy law and under section 546(c) of the Bankruptcy Code, a security interest has priority over a right of reclamation. To illustrate, if *D* is indebted to *B* Bank which has a security interest in *D*'s inventory and *D*'s inventory includes goods sold by *C* on credit, all of *D*'s inventory, including the goods delivered by *C*, must be used to satisfy *B* Bank's security interest before *C* is able to reclaim anything under section 546(c).

Section 546(c) needs to be read together with 503(b)(9). Even if an unpaid credit seller is not able to recover goods delivered on credit within 45 days before bankruptcy, such an unpaid seller can recover the value of any goods the debtor received from that seller within 20 days before filing for bankruptcy.

And both section 546(c) and section 503(b)(9) need to be read together with section 546(h). While section 546(c) creates a right in the seller to recover goods not yet paid for, section 546(h) creates a right in the buyer to return goods for credit.

The express limitations on this section 546(h) right include (1) Chapter 11 cases only, (2) within 120 days after the case was commenced, (3) consent of both the debtor and the seller, (4) return for full credit of the purchase price, and (5) court determination that the return is "in the best interests of the debtor."

This right of return is subject to an additional limitation not mentioned in section 546—the rights of a secured party with a security interest on the debtor's inventory. Assume that *X* has a valid security interest in all of *D*'s inventory, including after-acquired property. *Y* delivers goods to *D* on credit. Those goods would be subject to *X*'s security interest—would be a part of *X*'s collateral. *D* later files for bankruptcy. Can *D* now take a part of *X*'s collateral and "return" it to *Y*? Amended section 546 does not expressly address this question. Courts will and should be reluctant to take away a part of a secured creditors collateral, i.e., its property interest, without a more express statutory direction.

CHAPTER IX

POSTBANKRUPTCY TRANSFERS

A. WHEN DO POSTBANKRUPTCY TRANSFERS HAPPEN?

The prior chapter dealt with avoidance of transfers that occurred prior to the time that the bankruptcy petition was filed. Sections 544, 545, 547 and 548 apply only to prebankruptcy transfers. None of these provisions can be used to avoid an unauthorized transfer of property of the estate that occurs after the bankruptcy petition is filed. Section 549 applies to postbankruptcy transfers.

Postbankruptcy transfers of property of the estate present problems primarily in Chapter 7 cases. Only in Chapter 7 cases does the right of possession of property of the estate pass to the trustee; only in Chapter 7 cases are the proceeds from the trustee's liquidation of property of the estate what is distributed to creditors. In Chapter 11 and Chapter 13 cases, the debtor continues to possess property of the estate postpetition and creditors are paid under a plan that is generally based on the debtor's future earnings. And, in Chapter 11 and Chapter 13 cases, most postpetition transfers of property of the estate are permitted by section 363(c)(1).

Accordingly, section 549 is much more important to Chapter 7 cases than to Chapter 11 cases or Chapter 13 cases. And, section 549 is much more important to Chapter 7 cases in law school than to

Chapter 7 cases in the "real world." Most Chapter 7 debtors do not have significant assets to transfer postbankruptcy; and most Chapter 7 debtors do not make improper postbankruptcy transfers; and most Chapter 7 trustees are able to recover property of the estate that was transferred postbankruptcy without litigation. So, if your prof spent any meaningful time in the "real world," you will not have to spend any time on this Chapter.

B. HOW DOES A POSTBANKRUPTCY TRANSFER HAPPEN?

For most purposes, the date of the filing of the bankruptcy petition is the critical date in a Chapter 7 case. Subject to limited exceptions, only the property of the debtor as of the date of the filing of the petition becomes property of the estate. Generally, property acquired by the debtor after the bankruptcy petition has been filed remains property of the debtor.

The date of the filing of the petition is significant not only in determining what property becomes property of the estate but also in determining when the property becomes property of the estate. The filing of a bankruptcy petition—voluntary or involuntary—creates the estate.

The date of the filing of the bankruptcy petition is not, however, the date that the debtor loses possession of her property. Even in Chapter 7 cases. While section 701 provides for the appointment of an interim trustee in Chapter 7 cases "promptly after the order for relief," there will be some delay before the trustee takes possession of the property.

During the hiatus between the filing of the bankruptcy petition and the bankruptcy trustee's taking possession of the property of the estate, the debtor will usually have possession and control of the property of the estate. At times, the debtor will, after the filing of the petition, transfer property of the estate to some third party. Assume, for example, that *B* files a Chapter 7 petition on January 10. On January 12, *B* sells their summer home to *X*. On January 13, *B* sells their boat to *Y*. Obviously, *B* should not have made these postbankruptcy transfers. Obviously, the trustee has a cause of action against *B* for conversion. Obviously, the trustee can claim any proceeds from the postbankruptcy transfers as property of the estate. And, obviously the claim against the debtor *B* and the right to remaining proceeds will usually be of limited practical significance. The significant inquiry is whether the trustee can recover the summer house from *X* and/or the boat from *Y*? Should the bankruptcy laws protect transferees *X* and/or *Y*?

C. HOW DOES SECTION 549 AFFECT POSTBANKRUPTCY TRANSFERS OF PROPERTY OF THE ESTATE BY THE DEBTOR?

Section 549 protects *X* and *Y* in certain circumstances. Before considering these circumstances, remember that section 549 protects only the *transferee*, not the debtor-transferor.

Generally, section 549 protects the *transferee* if

(1) the transfer was authorized by the Bankruptcy Code or by the bankruptcy court; or

(2) the transfer was after an involuntary petition for postbankruptcy consideration; or

(3) the transfer was a real property transfer that was recorded before the bankruptcy was noted in the real property records.

The first of the three situations in which a transferee is entitled to retain property of the estate transferred by the debtor after the bankruptcy filing is the easiest to understand and apply. Obviously, a postbankruptcy transfer will be effective against the bankruptcy trustee if the transfer was authorized by the Bankruptcy Code or the bankruptcy court. See section 549(a)(2)(B). Most of the postbankruptcy transfers by a Chapter 11 debtor will be authorized under section 363(c)(1).

Second, section 549(b) validates transfers by the debtor that occur after the filing of an *involuntary* bankruptcy petition and before the order for relief to the extent that the transferee gave value to the debtor after the filing of the bankruptcy petition. To illustrate,

(1) On February 22, *D*'s creditors file an involuntary petition. On February 25, *D* sells their boat to *X* for $30,000. The trustee

may *not* recover the boat from *X*. *X* is protected by section 549(b).

(2) Same facts as #1 except that *X* knew of the involuntary petition. Same result. Section 549(b) protects postpetition transfers "notwithstanding any notice or knowledge of the case that the transferee has."

(3) On January 10, *C* lends *D* $30,000. On February 2, *D*'s creditors file an involuntary petition. On February 15, *D* transfers their boat to *C* in satisfaction of the January 10 debt. The trustee can recover the boat from *C*. The boat was transferred to satisfy a debt that arose before the petition. The transferee did not give value to the debtor after the filing of the bankruptcy petition. The transferee is not protected by section 549(b).

(4) On April 4, the creditors of *D* file an involuntary petition. On April 14, *D* sells Greenacre to *Y* for $40,000. The trustee may not recover Greenacre from *Y*. Section 549(b) protects transferees of both personalty and realty.

Third, section 549(c) protects certain postpetition transfers of *realty* from trustee avoidance. A transfer of real property by the debtor after the filing of a voluntary petition or after an order for relief in an involuntary case will be effective against the bankruptcy trustee if:

(1) the transfer occurs and is properly recorded before a copy of the bankruptcy petition is filed in the real estate records for the county where the land is located; and

(2) the transferee is a buyer or lienor for fair equivalent value without knowledge of the petition.

Consider the following hypothetical illustrating the operation of section 549(c):

On February 2, *B* files a voluntary petition. On February 3, *B* sells land in White County to *Y* for $10,000, the "fair equivalent value" of the land. *Y* has no "knowledge of the commencement of the case." *Y* properly files the transfer in the White County real estate records on February 4. A copy of the bankruptcy petition is filed in the real estate records for White County on February 5. The trustee *cannot* avoid the transfer. *Y* is protected by section 549(c).

There is no personal property counterpart of section 549(c). Personal property of the debtor transferred by the debtor after the filing of a voluntary petition can be recovered from the transferee unless the transfer was authorized by the Bankruptcy Code or by the bankruptcy court.

D. HOW DOES SECTION 542 AFFECT POSTBANKRUPTCY TRANSFERS OF PROPERTY OF THE ESTATE BY THIRD PARTIES?

Some postpetition transfers of property of the estate are made by persons holding property of the debtor, not the debtor. For example, on January 15, *D* files a voluntary bankruptcy petition. As of that date, *D* has $30,000 in its checking account at *B* Bank. This checking account becomes property of the estate on January 15. On January 17, *B* Bank honors a $5,000 check issued by *D* to *X* on January 13 and charges *D*'s account. Can *D*'s bankruptcy trustee recover the $5,000 from *B* Bank?

Section 542 protects *B* Bank. Under section 542(c), a third party who in good faith transfers property of the estate after the filing of the petition is protected from the bankruptcy trustee if the third party had "neither notice nor actual knowledge of the commencement of the case." Accordingly, if *B* Bank has neither actual knowledge or notice of *D*'s petition, *B* Bank will not be liable to the bankruptcy trustee. Note that section 542(c) only protects *B* Bank, the party that transfers the property of the estate; it does not protect *X*, the transferee. The trustee has a right to recover the $5,000, property of the estate, from *X*.[1]

---

[1] This is the point of the reference to section 542(c) in section 549(a)(2)(A). Even though section 542(c) protects the person who transfers property of the estate postpetition, section 549 empowers the trustee to recover the property from the transferee.

CHAPTER X

EFFECT OF BANKRUPTCY ON SECURED CLAIMS

A. WHAT IS A SECURED CLAIM?

The Bankruptcy Code deals with "claims," not creditors. Accordingly, under the Bankruptcy Code there will be creditors with secured claims, not secured creditors.

A creditor has a secured claim if it (1) has a right of setoff or (2) holds a lien on property of the estate. The claim is secured only to the extent of the value of "such creditor's interest in the estate's interest in such property," section 506(a).

The phrase "such creditor's interest" becomes important if more than one creditor has a lien on the same property. The phrase "estate's interest" becomes important if the debtor is a co-owner or has an otherwise limited interest in the encumbered property. To illustrate,

(1) owes *X* $100,000 and *Y* $200,000.

Both *X* and *Y* have mortgages on *D*'s building. *X*'s mortgage has priority over *Y*'s under state law.

D files for bankruptcy. The building has a value of $160,000.

Under these facts, *X* would have a $100,000 secured claim; *Y* would have a secured claim of $60,000 and an unsecured claim of $140,000.

(2) Same facts as (1) except that *D* only has a 50% ownership interest in the $160,000 building. Under these facts, *X* would have an $80,000 secured claim and a $20,000 unsecured claim. *Y* would have a $200,000 unsecured claim.

(3) *J* obtains a $2,000 judgment against *D* and causes the sheriff to execute on personal property belonging to *D*.

The personal property subject to *J*'s execution lien has a value of $800.

J has a $800 secured claim and a $1,200 unsecured claim.

(4) *D* owes *B* Bank $30,000 on an unsecured loan.

D has $9,000 on deposit in *B* Bank.

B Bank has a $9,000 secured claim and a $21,000 unsecured claim.

The answer to problem #4 assumes that *B* Bank has a right of setoff under state law. The answers to problems #1, #2 and #3 assume that the liens are valid in bankruptcy.

And all of the questions assume the value of the collateral. In law school hypotheticals, the teacher gets to decide what the value of the collateral is. "Real lawyers" do not enjoy that luxury. The question of the value of the collateral is a difficult and important one. The last sentence of section 506(a)(1) states that the value of the collateral (and accordingly the amount of the secured claim) is to be determined by the court on a case-by-case basis in light of the purpose of the valuation and the proposed disposition of the property. This last sentence of section 506(a) needs to be read together with (i) a 1997 Supreme Court decision and (ii) the 2005 addition of section 506(a)(2).

The leading case on determining the value of a secured creditor's collateral for purposes of section 506(a) is the Supreme Court's decision in Associates Commercial Corp. v. Rash, 520 U.S. 953 (1997). *Rash* is a Chapter 13 case in which the debtor wanted to retain his tractor truck and pay off the secured claim under the plan. In setting the amount of that secured claim, the debtor looked to the foreclosure value of the truck. The holder of the secured claim objected, contending that the replacement value of the truck should determine the amount of the secured claim.

The Court looked to the phrase "disposition or use" in section 506 and looked to the "disposition or use" in the debtor's Chapter 13 plan. Since the debtor's plan proposed that he retain the truck rather than the secured creditor foreclose on the truck, the Court concluded that the "value of the property retained * * * is the cost the debtor would incur to obtain a like asset."

Note that *Rash* does not hold that replacement value is always the appropriate way of measuring the secured claim. The *Rash* opinion repeatedly emphasizes the section 506 phrase "disposition or use" and the *Rash* fact that the debtor was using a Chapter 13 "cramdown" to retain the tractor truck.

Section 506(a)(2), like *Rash*, looks to replacement value in determining the amount of the secured claim. Unlike *Rash*, section 506(a)(2) only applies if the following three factual requirements are met:

(1) The debtor must be an individual; and

(2) The encumbered property must be personal property; and

(3) The case must be a 7 case or a 13 case.

While the *Rash* facts meet these three requirements, the *Rash* rule is not limited to cases with these three factual requirements.

B. INVALIDATION OF LIENS

Some liens that are valid outside of bankruptcy can be invalidated in a bankruptcy case. Section 522(f) considered supra, empowers the debtor to invalidate certain liens on certain exempt property. Sections 544, 545, 547, 548 and 549, considered supra, empower the bankruptcy trustee to invalidate certain transfers that create liens.

To illustrate, assume that *S* lends *D* $10,000 and obtains a security interest in *D*'s inventory. *S* does not file a financing statement or otherwise perfect its security interest. Under section 9–201, this unperfected security interest is effective between *S* and *D* and is effective against most third parties. For example, *S*'s right to *D*'s inventory is superior to the rights of any of *D*'s unsecured creditors. If, however, *D* files a bankruptcy petition, *S*'s unperfected security interest may be invalidated by the trustee under section 544(a)[1] so that *S* will simply have an unsecured claim for $10,000.

Note the effect of lien invalidation. All that is eliminated is the lien. The creditor's claim remains. Lien invalidation converts a secured claim into an unsecured claim.

C. OVERVIEW OF IMPACT OF BANKRUPTCY ON SECURED CLAIMS

In thinking about the impact of bankruptcy on secured claims, a law student or lawyer should focus on two questions:

(1) How can the debtor's bankruptcy filing adversely affect the holder of a secured claim?

(2) How can a secured claim be satisfied when the debtor is in bankruptcy?

D. WHAT CAN HAPPEN TO SECURED CLAIMS DURING BANKRUPTCY?

Most liens cannot be avoided under sections 522(f), 544, 545, 547, 548 or 549. What effect does bankruptcy have on a creditor that holds a valid in bankruptcy lien? [This question is particularly

---

1 Section 544(a) gives the bankruptcy trustee the rights and powers of a creditor who obtains a judicial lien at the time the bankruptcy petition was filed. At the time the bankruptcy petition was filed, *S*'s security interest was unperfected. An unperfected security interest is ineffective as against a creditor with a judicial lien, UCC § 9–317. Accordingly, S's unperfected security interest is ineffective as against the bankruptcy trustee.

important in Chapter 11 cases and Chapter 13 cases for two reasons:

(1) A Chapter 11 or Chapter 13 case can last three years or more;

(2) In Chapter 13 cases and in most Chapter 11 cases, the debtor remains in possession of encumbered property.]

1. DELAY IN REALIZING ON COLLATERAL

Recall that the automatic stay of section 362 prevents a creditor from enforcing its lien against property of the estate or property of the debtor. Accordingly, a creditor will not be able to sell or even seize encumbered property from a debtor who is in bankruptcy without obtaining relief from the automatic stay.

2. DEBTOR'S USE, LEASE OR SALE OF COLLATERAL

Not only does the Bankruptcy Code bar the secured creditor from recovering its collateral, the Bankruptcy Code also empowers the debtor to continue using the collateral. More specifically, section 363 provides for continued use, lease, or sale of encumbered property during bankruptcy. The lien holder is protected by section 363's adequate protection requirements. Section 363 is considered infra.

3. NON-ACCRUAL OF INTEREST

Recall that generally the amount of a claim is fixed by the amount that is owed at the date of the filing of the petition. If *D* borrows $10,000 from *C* at 10% and then files for bankruptcy, section 502 limits the amount of *C*'s claim in bankruptcy to the unpaid loan balance and the interest accrued "as of the date of the filing of the petition." Interest that has not accrued ("matured") as of the date of the filing of the petition is not generally allowable as part of *C*'s claim in the bankruptcy case, section 502(b)(2).

The general rule that a creditor does not earn interest after the bankruptcy petition is filed also applies to secured creditors with one exception. Section 506(b) provides for postpetition interest for over-secured creditors. If, and only if, the amount that is owed on a secured claim is less than the value of the collateral securing the claim, "there shall be allowed to the holder of such claim, interest on such claim."

Test your understanding of the above two paragraphs with the two problems below:

#1 *D* borrows $10,000 from *S* at 10% interest. The note is secured by a first mortgage on Whiteacre. *D* files for bankruptcy. As of the time of the filing of the bankruptcy case, *D* owes *S* $10,000 plus $222 in accrued unpaid interest, and Whiteacre is worth $8,000. *S* will have a $8,000 secured claim and a $ 2,222 unsecured claim. The amount of S's claim, will not increase during the bankruptcy case. No increase in the allowed claim for postpetition interest.

#2 Same facts as #1 except that Whiteacre is worth $13,000. *S* will have a $10,222 secured claim that will increase during the bankruptcy case as interest accrues.

While section 506(b) provides for interest on over-secured claims, it does not provide an interest rate. The reported cases are divided as to the appropriate rate of interest under section 506(b).

4. LOSS OF PRIORITY

Section 364(d) empowers the bankruptcy court to allow debtor's granting a postpetition creditor a lien on encumbered property that has priority over all prepetition liens. To illustrate, *X* makes a $600,000 construction loan to *D* and obtains and records a first mortgage on the project. *D* is unable to complete the building with the $600,000 provided by *X*. *D* is unable to obtain additional financing. *D* is able to file for Chapter 11. *Y* is willing to loan *D* the $200,000 needed to finish the building if its mortgage has priority over *X*'s. Under section 364(d), the bankruptcy court can authorize *D*'s granting *Y*, the later-in-time postpetition lender, a lien that has priority over *X*'s.

Section 364(d) imposes three requirements on the granting of such a "super-priority": (i) there must be "notice and a hearing," (ii) the debtor in possession or trustee is unable to obtain credit otherwise, and (iii) the "interest" of the holder of the prepetition lien is adequately protected.

Think about the third requirement. If you understand the third requirement, you will understand why prepetition creditors such as *X* are generally successful in opposing court approval of a section 364(d) priming lien for a postpetition creditor such as *Y*.

In essence, a creditor such as *Y* seeking a priming lien will have to convince the court that either (i) there is an equity cushion—the collateral is worth more than amounts due to *X* and *Y* or (ii) the amount of the increase in the value of the collateral as a result of *Y*'s loan is greater than the amount of *Y*'s loan.

For example, if the bankruptcy judge concludes that *Y*'s $200,000 loan to complete the building will increase the value of the building by $500,000 then *X*'s "interest" is adequately protected even though *Y* gets a priming lien.

5. LIMITATIONS ON FLOATING LIENS

In commercial credit transactions, security agreements usually provide that the collateral includes property that the debtor later acquires. Such after-acquired property clauses are expressly permitted by section 9–204 of the UCC; such after-acquired property clauses are expressly cut off in bankruptcy by section 552(a).

The following example illustrates the operation of section 552(a):

On January 10, *S* extends credit to *D* and obtains and perfects a security interest in all of *D*'s inventory, now owned or later acquired.

On March 3, *D* acquires additional inventory.

On March 4, *D* files a Chapter 11 petition and continues operating its business.

On April 7, *D* acquires additional inventory.

In bankruptcy, *S*'s claim would be secured by the January 10 inventory and by the March 3 inventory. It would not be secured by the April 7 inventory.[2] Section 552(a) states that a security agreement entered into before the commencement of the case does not reach property acquired after the commencement of the case except as provided in section 552(b).

Section 552(b) generally permits a prepetition lien to reach proceeds and other specified forms of earnings from and product of prepetition collateral. If in the above example *D* sold inventory on March 5, the "proceeds" from this postpetition sale of prepetition collateral would be subject to *S*'s security interest. Similarly, if *X* had a prepetition lien on *Y*'s apartment buildings and the rents therefrom, *X*'s lien would reach the postpetition rents as "profits of such property."

While the Bankruptcy Code provides that the secured claim in bankruptcy includes postpetition

---

[2] Section 552(a) thus needs to be read together with section 506. Section 552(a) has the effect of limiting a section 506 secured claim.

proceeds, the Bankruptcy Code does not provide a definition of the term "proceeds." Obviously, the term "proceeds" in section 552(b) is a term in a federal statute and so its definition is a matter of federal law. Nonetheless, courts have generally looked to state law, more specifically to Article 9 of the Uniform Commercial Code, to determine what constitutes "proceeds."

6. RETURN OF REPOSSESSED PROPERTY

Section 542(a) compels the holder of a secured claim that has taken possession of its collateral prior to bankruptcy to return it to the debtor when she files a bankruptcy petition. Assume, for example, that *S* extended credit to *D* and obtained and perfected a security interest in *D*'s inventory. *D* defaulted. *S* repossessed the inventory. *D* then filed for Chapter 11 relief. Reading section 362(a)(4) should leave you convinced that *S* cannot sell the inventory without obtaining relief from the stay. Reading section 542 should leave you confused.

Section 542(a) compels the turnover of "property that the trustee may use, sell, or lease under section 363" "unless *such property* is of inconsequential value or benefit to the estate." What is the antecedent of the pronoun "such"? If it is "property that the trustee may use, sell, or lease under section 363," then it is necessary to look at section 363. Section 363 provides for the use, sale, or lease of "property of the estate."[3]

---

[3] Section 363's use of the term "property of the estate" is probably misleading. Section 363 does more than just authorize the use, sale, or lease of property of the estate, i.e., the debtor's

It is thus necessary to look at section 541 which describes property of the estate in terms of the "interest of the debtor in property." What is the interest of the debtor in inventory that has been repossessed? A right of redemption under section 9–506? A right to any surplus produced by a forced sale under 9–504? Are these rights of "inconsequential value" for purposes of section 542?

The Supreme Court worked through these questions in United States v. Whiting Pools, Inc., 462 U.S. 198 (1983), and concluded that section 542 requires that a creditor that seized its collateral prior to bankruptcy turn over the property to a Chapter 11 debtor. *Whiting Pools* involved a seizure by the IRS of property subject to a tax lien. It seems clear from dicta in *Whiting Pools* that the Court would reach a similar result if a private creditor seized property subject to its security interest, and courts have so held.

More recently, the Supreme Court in *City of Chicago, Illinois v. Fulton* (2021), reversed a Seventh Circuit decision that a creditor's retaining property it had seized prepetition violated section 362(a)(3) which stays "any act" "to exercise control" over property of the estate. The Court reasoned that "reading section 362(a)(3)[4] to cover mere retention of

---

interest in property. Instead, section 363 authorizes the use, sale, or lease of property in which the debtor has an interest.

[4] If your prof covered this case in class you probably should know that the majority opinion expressly limited the holding to section 362(a)(3) and a concurring opinion suggested that a creditor's retaining possession might violate section 362(a)(4) and (6).

property . . . would render the central command of section 542 largely superfluous."

7. EFFECT OF DISCHARGE ON SECURED CLAIMS

Most individuals and many businesses that file voluntary bankruptcy petitions expect to receive a bankruptcy discharge. Discharge is considered in Chapter XIII supra.

A bankruptcy discharge simply relieves the debtor from any further personal liability for the debts covered by the discharge. A bankruptcy discharge does not wipe out the debts: the ability of creditors to look to other parties such as guarantors and insurers is unaffected. And, a bankruptcy discharge does not wipe out liens: the ability of secured creditors to look to their collateral is unaffected.

Assume, for example, that *D* owes *M* $100,000 and *M* has a mortgage on *D*'s house. *D* is in default on *D*'s mortgage obligations. *D* files for bankruptcy and receives a discharge. The discharge means that *M* is barred from attempting to collect the $100,000 from *D* personally. The discharge does not mean that *M* is barred from enforcing its lien by seizing and selling its collateral, *D*'s house.

What if the foreclosure sale of *D*'s house only results in net proceeds of $70,000? The discharge would then preclude *M* from taking actions or acts to collect the $30,000 deficiency from *D*, section 524(a).

E. SATISFACTION OF SECURED CLAIMS

1. RECOVERY OF COLLATERAL

If the holder of a secured claim recovers its collateral, the secured claim is extinguished. Assume, for example, that *D* owes *S* $22,000 and *S* has a security interest on equipment worth $10,000. *D* files a Chapter 7 bankruptcy petition. If the trustee turns over the equipment to *S*, *S* no longer has a secured claim. *S* still has a $12,000 claim, but the claim is an unsecured claim.

Chapters 7, 11 and 13 all *permit* satisfaction of a secured claim by surrender of the collateral. Neither Chapter 7, nor Chapter 11, nor Chapter 13 *requires* the satisfaction of a secured claim by surrender of the collateral.

In Chapter 7, 11 or 13, a holder of a secured claim can recover its collateral by obtaining relief from the stay under section 362(d) and foreclosing on its lien.

A Chapter 7 trustee can voluntarily turn over encumbered property to a lien holder under section 725. Similarly, a plan of reorganization under Chapter 11, 12 or 13 can provide for the surrender of encumbered property to the lienholder.

A holder of a secured claim cannot recover its collateral by abandonment. Section 554 permits a bankruptcy trustee to abandon any property that is burdensome to the estate or of inconsequential value to the estate. Assume, for example, that James Kirk, *K*, files a Chapter 7 petition. Mr. Spock is appointed trustee. *K* owes Federation Bank, *F*, $100,000. *F* has a properly perfected security interest in *K*'s ship. The ship has a value of $80,000. Because the amount of *F*'s secured claim is greater than the value of the ship, the ship is of inconsequential value to the estate. Thus, Spock can abandon the ship to Kirk, the debtor. Courts have looked to legislative history to hold that encumbered property must be abandoned to the debtor, not to a creditor with a lien on the property. If Spock abandons the ship to *K*, *K* can then release the ship to *F*.

2. PAYMENTS OF AMOUNT EQUAL TO THE VALUE OF THE COLLATERAL IN CHAPTER 7 CASES AND CHAPTER 11 CASES

If the holder of a secured claim does not recover its collateral, it should receive a payment at least equal to the value of the collateral.

a. Chapter 7

In a Chapter 7 case, this payment to the holder of a secured claim can come from the trustee's sale of the collateral, or this payment can come from the debtor.

In certain limited situations, the trustee has the power to sell encumbered property free and clear of all liens and pay holders of secured claims with the proceeds from such sales. See section 363(f). For example, Mr. Spock can sell *K*'s ship free and clear if the sale yields more than *F*'s $100,000 secured claim, section 363(f)(3). The proceeds of any such sale will first be used to cover the costs of the sale; the remaining net proceeds will be first used to pay *F*.

In certain limited situations, the Chapter 7 debtor will want to pay holders of secured claims from postpetition borrowings and/or earnings. Recall that (i) most of the debtor's interests in property as of the date of the filing of the bankruptcy petition becomes property of the estate, (ii) the debtor can retain property that is either exempt under section 522 or abandoned to him, and (iii) if such property is encumbered by liens, the liens remain enforceable after a discharge.

Accordingly, if K's ship is exempt property, *K* keeps the ship and *F* keeps its lien on the ship. Because *F* retains its lien notwithstanding the discharge, *F* can seize and sell the ship after *K*'s discharge if *K* is in default. *K* may be willing to pay *F* from postpetition earnings or borrowings in order to retain the ship. If so, *K* should look to section 524 reaffirmation agreement and section 722 redemption.[5]

Paragraphs (c) and (d) of section 524 deal with reaffirmation agreements. [This book deals with section 524(c) and 524(d) in Chapter XIII.] A reaffirmation agreement is a postbankruptcy agreement for the repayment of a prebankruptcy debt. For example, *K* and *F* might agree that *K* will pay *F X* dollars over *Y* months.

Note that section 524 does not require the payment of any particular amount. Note also that section 524

---

[5] Under nonbankruptcy law, section 9–623 provides a different, more limited form of redemption. Section 9–623 only applies if (i) the debtor is not in bankruptcy and (ii) the secured party has repossessed the collateral. Section 722 is not limited to situations in which the secured party has repossessed.

does require an agreement: the debtor and creditor must agree as to the amount that is to be paid and other terms.

Section 722, on the other hand, does not require any agreement, but does require the payment of a particular amount. Section 722 empowers Chapter 7 debtors to extinguish liens on certain property by paying the holder of the secured claim an amount equal to the "amount of the allowed secured claim," i.e., an amount measured by the value of the collateral not the amount of the debt.

If section 722 applies to the Kirk/Federation loan, *K* can extinguish *F*'s lien by paying *F* $80,000 in cash. Note that section 722 would apply to the Federation lien only if (1) the ship was "intended for personal, family, or household use" (i.e., not an enterprise), (2) the debt was a "dischargeable consumer debt," and (3) the ship had been exempted or abandoned.

Think through the Kirk example again. Particularly the payment of $80,000 in cash.

Under the last clause of section 722, the amount of the section 722 redemption payment depends upon the "amount of the allowed secured claim." Under the first sentence of section 506(a)(1), the amount of the allowed secured claim depends on the value of the collateral. And, under section 506(a)(2) added in 2005, that depends on the replacement price.

The following chart compares the debtor's payment of a secured claim under section 524 reaffirmation with the debtor's payment of a secured claim under section 722 redemption.

	524	722
1. Reason for debtor's payment	Prevent holder of secured claim from selling property exempted by or abandoned to the debtor	Prevent holder of secured claim from selling property exempted by or abandoned to the debtor
2. Amount of payment	Determined by agreement between debtor and creditor	Determined by the value of the collateral which is fixed at the replacement price
3. Form of payment	Determined by agreement between debtor and creditor	Cash

	524	722
4. Availability	a. Chapter 7, 11, 12 or 13	a. Chapter 7 only
	b. All kinds of collateral	b. Only collateral that is exempt or abandoned, only collateral that is tangible personal property, only collateral that is intended primarily for personal, family or household use

b. Chapter 11

What the holder of a secured claim receives in a Chapter 11 case (or a Chapter 13 case) depends on the provisions of the court-approved plan. And, the Bankruptcy Code sets some parameters on such plan provisions. Consider the following example to understand these statutory parameters.

D owes *S* $700,000 and that amount is secured by a mortgage on Greenacre. The mortgage contract provides for 10% interest and 36 equal monthly payments. *D*'s Chapter 11 plan can modify *S*'s contract rights. It can reduce the total amount to be paid to *S*, change the interest rate, change the number of payments, and/or provide for payments in varying amounts.

In some situations, the holder of the secured claim consents to these modifications. In other situations, the holder of the secured claim objects to the Chapter 11 plan's modifications of its rights. Notwithstanding such an objection, the court can still approve the plan. Lawyers, judges and law professors commonly call such court approval of a plan that changes a creditor's rights over that creditor's objection a "cram down" or a "cramdown." And, so cramdown (or cram down) needs to be a part of your bankruptcy vocabulary, even though the term does not appear in the Bankruptcy Code.

Limitations on the cram down of a secured claim do appear in the Bankruptcy Code. And these limitations are so important that they appear three times in this book: (1) in the next few paragraphs of this chapter, (2) in the chapter on Chapter 11 and in the chapter on Chapter 13.

Section 1129(b)(2)(A)(i)(II) limits a bankruptcy court's confirmation of a cram down of a secured claim to a plan that provides for distributions to the holder of that claim that have a present value[6] at least equal to the value of the collateral.[7] Accordingly, a Chapter 11 cram down requires a court to answer two separate questions:

(1) What is the amount of the value of the collateral?

(2) How much more than that amount has to be paid if the amount is paid in installments over the life of the plan instead of in cash on the effective date of the plan?

The first question is answered in the second sentence of section 506(a), the Supreme Court's decision in *Rash* and an earlier part of this chapter. The Supreme Court later considered the second question in the *Till* case that we will consider on the next page.

Assume again that *D* owes *S* $700,000, secured by a first mortgage on Greenacre. If, applying *Rash*, the court determines that the value of Greenacre is only $600,000, then $600,000 is the amount of *S*'s secured claim. Or, as bankruptcy lawyers and judges put it, *S*'s secured claim can be "stripped down" to $600,000. That $600,000 then becomes the amount by which

---

[6] The Bankruptcy Code provisions use the phrase "value as of the effective date of the plan" instead of the phrase "present value."

[7] And, the Bankruptcy Code uses the phrase "allowed amount of such claim" rather than the phrase "value of the collateral." The antecedent of the adjective "such" is "secured" claim; and, the amount of a secured claim is based on the "value of the collateral." Remember 506 and *Rash* earlier in this chapter.

the present value of the plan payments on the secured claim are to be measured.[8]

Obviously if *D*'s Chapter 11 plan provides for a $600,000 cash payment to *S* on the effective date of the plan, that payment will meet the present value test. Obviously, most Chapter 11 plans provide for payments in installments. And, obviously, a plan provision for 60 monthly payments of $10,000 has a value significantly less than $600,000 in cash, right now. What is not obvious is how much more than $600,000 the debtor must pay under a plan that pays over 60 months.

The Bankruptcy Code nowhere addresses this question. The Supreme Court addressed the question in Till v. SCS Credit Corp., 541 U.S. 465 (2004) and adopted a "formula approach": "The approach begins by looking at the national prime rate. . . . Because bankrupt debtors typically pose a greater risk of nonpayment than solvent commercial borrowers, the approach then requires the bankruptcy court to adjust the prime rate accordingly."

What does "accordingly" mean? The appropriate risk adjustment remains a litigable issue.[9]

You can't confuse cram down "interest" under section 1129 (and section 1325) with interest on over-

---

8 The other $100,000 of *D*'s debt to *S* would be treated as an unsecured claim. Unsecured claims are treated differently than secured claims.

9 While what the appropriate interest rate is a "litigable issue," it is not an issue that is frequently litigated. More judges have their own rule of thumb as to appropriate risk adjustment.

secured claims under section 506. The following hypothetical and then the chart should help you see the differences in the two.

To illustrate, in January of 2021, *D* borrows $10,000 from *C* and offers to pay 10% interest on the debt until it is repaid. *D* grants *C* a mortgage on Blueacre. In February 2022, *D* files a Chapter 11 petition. At the time of the bankruptcy filing, *D* owes *C* $12,000 in principal and unpaid, accrued interest, and Blueacre has a value of $8,000. Accordingly, *C* has an $8,000 secured claim and a $4,000 unsecured claim, section 506(a).

D's Chapter 11 plan is confirmed in March 2023. *C*'s $8,000 secured claim does not accrue interest from the date of bankruptcy filing in February 2022 until the time of confirmation in March 2023. Only a claim that is fully secured draws interest from the time of the filing of the petition to the date of confirmation of the plan, section 506(b). *C*'s $8,000 secured claim will, however, draw interest from the time of confirmation of the plan until it is fully satisfied. It is not clear whether this interest will be 10% or some other rate.

To summarize, (1) only a claim that is fully secured will draw interest from the time of the bankruptcy filing until the confirmation of a plan; and (2) any claim that is paid in installments under a Chapter 11 plan will draw interest from the time of the confirmation of the plan until the time of the last plan payment.

	506(b)	1129(b)(2)(A)(i)(II) and 1325(a)(5)(b)(ii)
Which chapter?	Applies in all cases—Chapter 7, 11, 12, 13	Not Chapter 7
Which secured claims?	Applies only to over-secured claims, i.e., amount of debt is less than value of collateral	All secured claims
When?	Interest from the time of the petition to the time of the Chapter 7 distribution or the time of confirmation of the Chapter 11 or Chapter 13 plan	Interest from the time of the confirmation of the Chapter 11 or Chapter 13 plan through the entire period of plan payments

3. CARS AND HOUSES IN CHAPTER 13 CASES AND CHAPTER 11 CASES WITH INDIVIDUAL DEBTORS

In Chapter 13 cases, like Chapter 11 cases, the payments on a secured claim are determined by a court-approved plan. In Chapter 13, the debtor's ability to cram down changes on certain secured claims is severely limited. More specifically,

(1) For claims secured by purchase money security interests in motor vehicles the debtor purchased within 910 days of bankruptcy, changes in number of payments, interest rate, and amount of each payment can be imposed (i.e., cram downed) on a creditor with a secured claim. The Chapter 13 plan cannot, however, change the total amount to be paid—cannot

strip down the secured debt to the value of the collateral under section 506.

(2) Similarly, for all secured debt incurred within one year of bankruptcy, changes in number of payments, interest rate, and amount of each payment can be imposed (i.e., cram downed) on a creditor with a secured claim. The Chapter 13 plan cannot, however, change the total amount to be paid—cannot strip down the secured debt to the value of the collateral under section 506.

(3) And for claims secured "only by a security interest in real property that is the debtor's principal residence" (i.e., home mortgages), no cram down at all—no court-imposed changes in the number of payments, interest rate or any other terms.[10]

We will cover Chapter 13 treatment of secured claims in more detail later in Chapter XIV. And, we will also later cover individual Chapter 11 cases and learn that individual Chapter 11 cases, in many respects, look more like Chapter 13 cases than like Chapter 11 cases. For example, an individual debtor cannot use either Chapter 11 or Chapter 13 to cram down changes in their home mortgage obligations, section 1123(b)(5).

Individual Chapter 11 cases are not, however, identical to Chapter 13 cases in all respects. For

---

[10] There is a limited exception in Subchapter V which is explained in Chapter XVI of the book.

example, an individual debtor could use Chapter 11 but not Chapter 13 to strip down the amount of a loan secured by their automobile. As we later learn more about other differences between individual Chapter 11 cases and Chapter 13, we will see that it is highly unlikely that an individual who meets the debt limits of Chapter 13 would choose to file Chapter 11 instead just to force changes in their car loan.

CHAPTER XI

CLAIMS

A. WHY IS "CLAIM" AN IMPORTANT BANKRUPTCY CONCEPT?

The word "claim" appears throughout the Bankruptcy Code, throughout a bankruptcy case. For example,

(1) an involuntary petition can be filed only by holders of claims;

(2) the automatic stay that is triggered by the filing of an involuntary or voluntary petition bars actions by holders of claims to collect on their claims from the debtor or property of the estate;

(3) a discharge bars further efforts by holders of claims to collect their claims from the debtor;

(4) distributions in a Chapter 7 case are made to holders of claims;

(5) payments under a Chapter 13 plan go to holders of claims;

(6) holders of claims vote on filed Chapter 11 plans and payments under an approved Chapter 11 plan go to holders of claims.

B. WHAT IS A CLAIM? (AND, WHO CARES?)

The term "claim" is defined in section 101: "right to payment, whether or not such right is reduced to judgment, liquidated, unliquidated, fixed, contingent, matured, unmatured, disputed, undisputed, legal, equitable or unsecured." Both legislative history and case law describe the definition as an effort to be as comprehensive and inclusive as possible.

For example, *D*'s car runs into *C*. *C* contends that *D* was negligent and that her negligence caused *C* substantial damages. Before *C* files a law suit against *D*, *D* files for bankruptcy. Under these facts, *C* has a "claim" even though *D* disputes *C*'s allegations of negligence and even though the amount of any liability has not yet been liquidated.

Similarly, on December 7, 2020, *D* borrows $100,000 from *C*. The loan provides for repayment on April 5, 2024. The loan also includes *X*'s guarantee of repayment if *D* fails to pay. *D* files for bankruptcy on January 15, 2022. Under these facts, *C* has a claim even though her right to payment had not yet matured. And *X* who would have a right of reimbursement from *D* if he has to pay the debt would also have a claim even though its right to payment was still contingent.

While the Bankruptcy Code concept of claim is comprehensive, there are two significant limitations on what is a claim. The first limitation is based on the language of section 101's definition of claim. "Claim" requires a right to payment. Obligations of the debtor that cannot be satisfied by payment are not within the definition of claim. This can be an issue in situations involving injunctions and specific performance.

Assume, for example, that (i) *D* sells their business to *C* and, as part of the sale, contracts not to start a competing business for 5 years, (ii) under state law, *C* could enjoin *D* from opening a competing business, (iii) *D* files for bankruptcy a year later, and (iv) it appears that *D*'s creditors will only receive 25% on their claims. Under these facts, *C* might contend that their right to enforce the covenant to compete through injunction is not a "right to payment" and so is not a section 101(5) "claim" and so is not affected by the discharge which protects the debtor from any further personal liability on claims. Most courts have dealt with this contention by looking to state law to determine whether *C* could be compelled to take a money judgment instead of injunctive relief—whether, in the language of section 101(5), *C* has a "right to payment."

The second limitation on what is a claim—a limitation based on when the claim and claimant are identifiable—is not based on the language of section 101(5) but rather the language of various court decisions.

This timing issue has arisen with respect both to products liability matters and environmental cases.

The cases differ as to whether future, unknown and unidentifiable victims of a prebankruptcy act of the debtor have section 101(5) claims. And, in different cases, lawyers for different parties are contending that these "future claimants" have a section 101(5) claim.

If, for example, the debtor company is liquidating in Chapter 7 or is selling all of its assets in a Chapter 11 sale that provides protection for the purchaser from successor liability, then the lawyer representing the future claimants is likely to argue that their clients have section 101(5) claims and so should share in the sale proceeds.

That same lawyer will make the different argument that their future claimant clients do not have a section 101(5) claim and so should not be subject to the discharge which only affects claims if the debtor company is reorganizing in Chapter 11 and that lawyer and their financial adviser are optimistic the debtor company's ability to make meaningful payments from postbankruptcy earnings

Again, there is no language in the Bankruptcy Code that expressly addresses these timing issues. And the language in the reported cases as to when a claim arises is not consistent.

C. WHAT IS AN UNSECURED CLAIM?

A claim is unsecured if the creditor has not obtained a consensual, judicial, or statutory lien or if the value of the property subject to the lien is less than the amount of the creditors claim. Consider the following examples of unsecured claims:

(1) *D* buys airline tickets using their American Express card and *D* files a bankruptcy

petition. At the time of the bankruptcy petition, *D* owes American Express $1,000 for airline tickets. American Express has an unsecured claim.

(2) *D* Corp. borrows $2,000,000 from *C* and grants *C* a mortgage on Redacre. At the time of *D* Corp.'s bankruptcy it still owes *C* $2,000,000 and the encumbered property has a value of $800,000. *S* is a creditor with a $1,200,000 unsecured claim. [*S* is also a creditor with an $800,000 secured claim.][1]

D. COLLECTION OF UNSECURED CLAIMS FROM THE DEBTOR

Under section 362, the filing of a Chapter 7 petition operates as a "stay." This automatic stay prevents a creditor from collecting its unsecured claim from the debtor until the bankruptcy case is closed. The automatic stay and relief therefrom is considered in Chapter V.

Under section 727, the bankruptcy court generally grants a Chapter 7 debtor a "discharge." This discharge prevents a creditor from collecting its claim from the debtor after the bankruptcy case is closed. The discharge and exceptions thereto is considered in Chapter XVII.

The section 362 stay coupled with the section 727 discharge makes it necessary for most holders of

---

1 The rights of holders of secured claims are considered supra in Chapter X.

unsecured claims to look to the "property of the estate" for the satisfaction of their claims.

Now that we know

(1) what an unsecured claim is; and

(2) that the automatic stay generally precludes collection of unsecured claims from the debtor during the bankruptcy case; and

(3) that the discharge generally bars collection of unsecured claims from the debtor after the bankruptcy case, we need to determine how to collect on unsecured claims in a Chapter 7 bankruptcy case.

It thus becomes necessary to learn

(1) what property is distributed to unsecured claims; and

(2) which holders of unsecured claims are eligible to participate in the distribution of this property; and

(3) what is the order of distribution, i.e., which claims are paid first.

E. WHAT PROPERTY IS DISTRIBUTED TO HOLDERS OF UNSECURED CLAIMS?

1. WHAT PROPERTY IS DISTRIBUTED TO HOLDERS OF UNSECURED CLAIMS IN CHAPTER 7 CASES?

The bankruptcy trustee has a statutory duty to sell the "property of the estate," section 704(1). The net proceeds received from the liquidation of the "property of the estate" are to be distributed to the holders of unsecured or general claims. Such claimants do not, however, receive the net proceeds from the sale of all of the "property of the estate":

(1) Some "property of the estate" will be turned over to the debtor as exempt property, section 522.

(2) Some "property of the estate" will be validly transferred after the filing of the bankruptcy petition to third parties, section 549.

(3) Some "property of the estate" will be subject to liens that are valid in bankruptcy. Encumbered property or the proceeds thereof must be first used to satisfy the holders of secured claims, cf. section 725.

(4) Some "property of the estate" must be used to satisfy the administrative expenses of the bankruptcy case.

Subject to these four exceptions, holders of unsecured claims in Chapter 7 cases receive the net proceeds from the bankruptcy trustee's sale of the "property of the estate." The great majority of Chapter 7 cases are "no asset" cases, at least in the sense that there are no assets available to pay unsecured claims.

2. WHAT PROPERTY IS DISTRIBUTED TO HOLDERS OF UNSECURED CLAIMS IN CHAPTER 13 CASES AND INDIVIDUAL CHAPTER 11 CASES?

In Chapter 13 cases, the plan controls the payment to holders of unsecured claims. Only the debtor can file the plan.

Section 1322 governs the contents of a chapter 13 plan. In section 1322, paragraph (a) governs what the plan *must* provide; paragraph (b) governs what the plan *may* provide.

In Chapter 13 cases, creditors do not vote on the plan. Both chapters require the bankruptcy judge to confirm (approve) the plan, and creditors may object to the confirmation. Section 1325 sets out the standards for confirmation of a plan.

It would be helpful to read section 1325. Especially section 1325(b). Note that in Chapter 13, the debtor must commit all "disposable income" to the repayment plan.

There is a similar disposable income requirement commitment for individual debtors in Chapter 11 cases. Unless no holder of an unsecured claim objects, an individual debtor's Chapter 11 plan must have a minimum payment from the debtor measured by five years of disposable income, section 1129(a)(15).

3. WHAT PROPERTY IS DISTRIBUTED TO HOLDERS OF UNSECURED CLAIMS IN OTHER CHAPTER 11 CASES?[2]

In Chapter 11 cases, like Chapter 13 cases, the plan controls the payment to holders of unsecured claims. Chapter 11's treatment of holders of unsecured claims is significantly different from Chapter 12's or 13's in that

(1) Chapter 11 generally does *not* require that all of the debtor's "disposable income" be used to make payments under the plan. Only in Subchapter V cases in which the requisite majorities of holders of unsecured claims fail to vote for (accept) a plan will there be a possible need to use all of the debtor's "disposable income" for payments under the plan.

(2) In Chapter 11, the holders of unsecured claims can file a plan, section 1121(c).

(3) In Chapter 11, holders of unsecured claims vote on the proposed plan. If the requisite majorities fail to vote for (accept) a plan, the standards for court approval (confirmation) are more onerous, cf. section 1129(a) and 1129(b).

The formulation, acceptance, and confirmation of Chapter 11 plans are considered later.

---

[2] Since 2020, Subchapter V is available for certain Chapter 11 debtors. Subchapter V is explained in Chapter XVI of this book.

F. WHICH HOLDERS OF UNSECURED CLAIMS ARE ELIGIBLE TO PARTICIPATE IN THE BANKRUPTCY DISTRIBUTION?

1. PROOF OF CLAIM

The debtor will file a list of creditors, section 521. The court will then send notice of the bankruptcy case to the listed creditors, section 342. The creditors that wish to participate in the distribution of the proceeds of the liquidation of the "property of the estate" must file a proof of claim, sections 501, 726. In Chapter 11 cases, a creditor is required to file a proof of claim only if its claim is scheduled as disputed, contingent, or unliquidated, section 1111(a); Rule 3003(b)(1).

Most of the requirements as to form, content, and procedure for proofs of claim are found in the Bankruptcy Rules. For example, there is no statutory language governing the time for filing a proof of claim. Section 501 simply speaks of "timely filing." Rule 3002(c) governs the time for filing a proof of claim in a Chapter 7 case or a Chapter 13 case.

Section 501(c) authorizes the debtor to file a proof of claim for a creditor who does not timely file. This provision is primarily intended to protect the debtor if the claim of the creditor is nondischargeable. When no proof of claim is filed, there will be no bankruptcy distribution to the holder of the claim. If no bankruptcy distribution is made to the holder of a claim excepted from discharge, the debtor will have to pay the claim in full after the bankruptcy case is closed. If, however, the debtor files a proof of claim, the holder of the nondischargeable claim will participate in the bankruptcy distribution and the postbankruptcy liability of the debtor to the creditor will be reduced by the amount of distribution.

To illustrate, assume that *D* files a Chapter 7 petition. He owes *C* $10,000. *C* made the loan to *D* because of a false financial statement; its claim against *D* is excepted from discharge.[3] If no proof of claim is filed by or for *C*, it will have a $10,000 claim against *D* after the close of the Chapter 7 case. If, however, *D* files a proof of claim for *C* Bank, *C's* postbankruptcy claim against *D* will be reduced by the amount it receives in the bankruptcy distribution.

2. ALLOWANCE

In a Chapter 7 case, the proceeds of the liquidation of the property of the estate is not distributed to all holders of unsecured claims against the debtor. Rather, the distribution is only made to unsecured creditors whose claims are "allowed," section 726.

If a proof of claim has been filed, the claim is deemed allowed "unless a party in interest objects," section 502(a). The statute does not define "party in interest"; clearly, another creditor or the bankruptcy trustee is a "party in interest" for purposes of objections to allowance of a claim.

---

[3] Section 523(a)(2) excepts from discharge claims based on credit extended in reliance on a false financial statement. Section 523(a)(2) is explained in Chapter XIII.

a. Grounds for Disallowance in 502(b) and 502(d)

The statute does set out nine grounds for disallowing claims in section 502(b):

1. If the claim is unenforceable against the debtor or the property of the debtor by reason of any agreement or applicable law, it will not be allowed, section 502(b)(1).

[A nonrecourse loan is an example of an agreement which makes a claim unenforceable; UCC § 2–302 is an example of a law which makes a claim unenforceable.]

2. A claim for "unmatured" interest will be disallowed, section 502(b)(2).

[Generally, interest stops accruing when a bankruptcy petition is filed.[4] Assume, for example, that *D* borrows $100,000 from *C*; the loan agreement provides for 8% interest. At the time of the bankruptcy filing, *D* owes $110,00. *C*'s allowable claim will be $110,000 that amount will not continue to draw the 8% interest after the bankruptcy filing.]

3. If a claim is for an ad valorem property tax, it will not be allowed to the extent that the claim exceeds the value of the estate's interest in the property, section 502(b)(3).

---

[4] Only claims that are secured by collateral that has a value greater than the amount of the claim will accrue interest after the filing of a bankruptcy petition, section 506(b).

4. If the claim is for the services of the debtor's attorney or an "insider,"[5] it will be disallowed to the extent the claim exceeds the reasonable value of such services, section 502(b)(4).

5. If the claim is for postpetition alimony or child support, it will not be allowed, section 502(b)(5).[6]

6. If the claim is that of a landlord for future rent, it will be limited to the greater of one year's payments or 15% of the payments for the balance of the lease, not to exceed three years' payments in total, section 502(b)(6).

[Note that section 502(b)(6) only limits the allowance of claims for *future* rentals by a lessor of

---

[5] "Insider" is defined in section 101(28). "Insider" includes the relatives of an individual debtor; the partners of a partnership debtor; and the officers, directors, and other control persons of a corporate debtor.

[6] These claims are excepted from discharge under section 523(a)(5). The following hypothetical illustrates the application of sections 502(b)(5) and 523(a)(5).

H and *W* are divorced in January 2022. The divorce decree orders *H* to pay alimony of $1,000 a month. *H* files a bankruptcy petition on December 31, 2022. He owes *W* $2,000 for November and December alimony.

W's claims for $2,000 of unpaid 2022 alimony is allowable. Section 502(b)(5) only disallows a claim for alimony that is "unmatured on the date of the filing of the petition." Accordingly, *W*'s claim for postpetition alimony is disallowed.

If *W*'s claim for $2,000 of unpaid 2022 alimony is not fully satisfied by the bankruptcy distribution, *W* may attempt to collect any deficiency from *H* personally. Section 523(a)(5) excepts alimony claims from the bankruptcy discharge. Accordingly, *H*'s bankruptcy discharge will not affect *W*'s right to collect postpetition alimony from *H* personally.

real property.[7] It does not affect a claim for rentals due on or before the filing of the bankruptcy petition. It does not affect a claim for rentals under a lease of personal property.]

[Note also that section 502(b)(6) does not guarantee an allowable claim for back rent plus a minimum of one year's rent; rather, it places a ceiling on the allowance of rent claims. Assume, for example, that *D* rents a building from *C* and signs a 20-year lease at a monthly rental rate of $50,000. At the time that *D* files its bankruptcy petition, *D* owes *C* $100,000 in back rent. If *D* immediately rejects the lease and *C* then relets the building to *X* for $60,000 a month, *C*'s allowable claim will be limited to the $100,000 in back rent.]

7. Section 502(b)(7) imposes a similar limitation on the allowable claim for termination of an employment contract—no more than back wages due at the time of the bankruptcy filing and one year's future compensation.

8. If the claim is a federal tax claim which arises because the state unemployment tax is paid late and so no federal tax credit is allowed, the federal claim will be treated the same as if the credit had been allowed in full in the federal return, which means the

---

[7] Section 502(b)(6) does not limit the amount of a claim for future rents of personal property. Section 547(e) suggests that the Bankruptcy Code considers "fixtures" to be real property. If so, section 502(b)(6) would apply to a claim by a lessor of equipment that was installed in such a manner as to become a fixture under state law.

federal tax claim would be disallowed, section 502(b)(8).

9. Section 502(b)(9) deals with disallowance of claims that are not timely filed. In reading and applying section 502(b)(9), law students and lawyers need to understand section 726 discussed infra. Section 726 provides that late-filed claims will be paid in Chapter 7 but will be paid after claims that are timely filed. The reference to section 726 in section 502(b)(9) means that tardily filed claims will not be disallowed in a Chapter 7 case; instead their priority of distribution will be governed by section 726. Section 502(b)(9) will result in the disallowance of claims only in cases under Chapter 11, 12, or 13. Generally, the question of what constitutes a timely filing is left to the Rules; section 502(b)(9) does, however, give a governmental creditor at least 180 days from the order for relief for filing its claim.

Section 502(d) provides for the disallowance of a claim held by a creditor who received a voidable transfer and has not surrendered the property so transferred or its value. For example, *C*'s $100,000 claim can be disallowed under section 502(d) if the debtor made a$200,000 fraudulent transfer to *C* that has not been turned over by *C*.

b. Contingent Claims and 502(c) and 502(e)

With a limited exception, the fact that a claim is contingent or unliquidated at the time that the bankruptcy petition is filed does not affect its allowance. The court may either delay bankruptcy distribution until the claim is fixed in amount, or, if liquidation of the claim would "unduly delay the administration of the case," estimate the amount of the claim, section 502(c). Assume, for example, that *V* files a $100,000 tort suit against *T*. *T* immediately files a bankruptcy petition. *V* then files a proof of claim. *V*'s claim is allowable. The court may either delay distribution to *T*'s creditors and the closing of *T*'s bankruptcy case until *V*'s tort claim has been litigated or estimate the amount of *V*'s claim.[8]

Section 502 does not dictate or even indicate how the bankruptcy court should estimate the claim. Most of the relatively few reported cases involve estimation of claims for the limited purpose of Chapter 11 plan voting. Cf. section 1126(c).

Section 502(e) provides for the disallowance of a claim for contribution or indemnity that is still contingent. Assume, for example, that *D* and *X* are both companies that "dumped waste" at the same site. The EPA investigates the site and notifies *D* and *X* that they are liable for cleanup costs. [Under the relevant law, CERCLA, the EPA can collect the cleanup costs from either or both. If the EPA collects the entire cleanup costs from *X*, then *X* has a right to contribution from *D*.] *D* immediately files for bankruptcy before the EPA takes any action. *X*'s right of contribution, while contingent and

---

[8] 28 USCA § 157(b)(2)(B) states that "estimation of contingent or unliquidated personal injury tort or wrongful death claims against the estate for the purposes of distribution" is not a "core proceeding."

This provision is considered in the chapter on allocation of judicial power over bankruptcy, Chapter XVIII.

unmatured, is a section 101(5) claim. But if *X* files a proof of claim, its claim will be disallowed under section 502(e). The rationale is that (i) since the EPA claim is allowable, then (ii) allowance of both the EPA claim and *X*'s contingent contribution claim would result in the bankruptcy estate's paying twice for a single wrong.

c. Time of Claim

Generally, only claims that arise before the bankruptcy petition are allowable in Chapter 7 cases. If, for example, *D* files a voluntary bankruptcy petition on January 11, and *C* lends *D* $100 on February 2, *C*'s claim is not allowable.

There are four exceptions to the rule that only claims that predate the bankruptcy petition are allowable in Chapter 7:[9]

(1) In an involuntary case, claims arising in the ordinary course of the debtor's business after the commencement of the case but before the earlier of the appointment of a trustee or the order for relief will be allowed as if the claim had arisen before the bankruptcy petition, section 502(f).

(2) Claims arising from the rejection of an executory contract or unexpired lease of the debtor are allowed as if the claim had arisen

---

[9] In Chapter 13 cases, certain postpetition taxes and consumer debts are allowable, section 1305(a).

before the date of the filing of the petition, section 502(g).

(3) A claim arising from the recovery of property because of a voidable transfer will be determined and allowed as though it were a prepetition claim, section 502(h).[10]

(4) A claim that does not arise until after the commencement of the case for a tax entitled to the seventh priority shall be treated as if the claim had arisen before the date of the filing of the petition, section 502(i).

Before a case is closed, a claim that has been allowed may be reconsidered for cause and disallowed according to the equities of the case, section 502(j).

G. WHAT IS THE ORDER OF DISTRIBUTION?

There are a number of statements in reported cases, law review articles, and legal texts praising the theme of equality of distribution to creditors in bankruptcy proceedings. Such statements must be using the term "equality" in the *Animal Farm* sense; in bankruptcy, some creditors are clearly "more equal" than others. Some unsecured claims must be

---

[10] To illustrate, assume that on January 11, *D* repays *C* the $1,000 he owes her. On February 2, *D* files a bankruptcy petition. On May 5, *D*'s bankruptcy trustee recovers the $1,000 from *C* as a section 547 preference. Under section 502(h), *C* has an allowable claim for $1,000.

fully satisfied before any distribution is made to other unsecured claims.

In a bankruptcy case, certain allowed unsecured claims are entitled to priority in distribution over other unsecured claims. Section 507(a) sets out the levels of priorities. In its proof of claim form, a creditor can assert a priority and state the amount and basis therefore. Most of the litigation over whether a claim is entitled to a priority involve assertions of section 507(a)(1) administrative expense status.

1. TREATMENT OF PRIORITY CLAIMS IN 7

Chapter 7 requires that the various priority classes are paid in the order in which they are listed in section 507, section 726(a)(1). In other words, each first priority claim is to be paid in full before any second priority claim is paid at all. If there are not sufficient funds to pay all claims within a particular class, then generally all claims entitled to that priority are paid pro rata.

Section 726 establishes the rules for distribution in a Chapter 7 case to the holders of unsecured claims. Basically, the distribution is to be as follows:

(1) priorities under section 507 (section 507 is considered below);

(2) allowed unsecured claims which were either timely filed or tardily filed by a creditor who did not know of the bankruptcy;

(3) allowed unsecured claims which were tardily filed by creditors with notice or actual knowledge of the bankruptcy;

(4) fines and punitive damages;

(5) postpetition interest on prepetition claims.

Each claim of each of the five categories must be paid in full before any claim in the next category receives any distribution. Each claim within a particular category shares pro rata if the proceeds from the liquidation of the property of the estate is insufficient to satisfy all claims in that category.

Assume, for example, that there is $20,000 available to pay to holders of unsecured claims and the following unsecured claims:

$11,000 claims entitled to priority under section 507

$4,800 claim by *X* that was timely filed

$7,200 claim by *Y* that was timely filed

$3,000 claim by *Z* that was not timely filed even though *Z* knew of the bankruptcy proceedings.

The distribution would be:

$11,000 to holders of priority claims

$3,600 to *X*[11]

---

[11] The first $11,000 must be used to pay priority claims. The remaining $9,000 ($20,000 – $11,000) must be distributed pro rata to $12,000 ($4,800 + $7,200) of timely filed claims. Accordingly, each timely filed claim will be paid at the rate of 75¢ on the dollar.

$5,400 to *Y*.

In the very unlikely event that the sale of the "property of the estate" yields enough to satisfy each claim in each of the five "classes" listed above, the surplus is paid to the debtor.

2. TREATMENT OF PRIORITY CLAIMS IN 11 AND 13

Chapter 11, and Chapter 13 require the plan to provide for payment in full of all priority claims, although the payments of claims within certain priority classes may be stretched over a period of time, sections 1129(a)(9), and 1322(a)(2).

3. 507 PRIORITIES

The task of distributing the proceeds from the sale of the property of the estate is complicated by the fact that claims do not come neatly labelled "claims entitled to priority under section 507." Instead, it is necessary to recognize which claims are entitled to priority under section 507.

The debtor's "domestic support obligations" as defined in section 101 have the first priority. And, then, there is a priority within this first priority. If proceeds from the trustee's sale of property of the estate are not sufficient to pay all "domestic support obligations," then support owed to children or former spouses is paid in full before any payment to a governmental unit on an assigned support obligation.

($9,000 ÷ $12,000). Accordingly, *X* will receive $3,600 for its $4,800 claim.

After payment in full of all "domestic support obligations," distributions are made to the second priority, administrative expenses allowed under section 503(b).

Administrative expenses include the costs of maintaining, repairing and restoring property of the estate; taxes and professional fees the trustee incurs in administering property of the estate; and limited expenses of certain creditors. When a nonresidential real property lease is assumed and later rejected, then up to two years of post-rejection lease payments is an administrative expense. There is also an administrative expense priority for the value of goods sold on credit to the debtor in the ordinary course of the debtor's business and received by the debtor within 20 days before the commencement of the case.

Obviously, first priority claims—domestic support obligations—only arise in bankruptcy cases in which the debtor is an individual. Second priority claim—administrative expenses—arise in all bankruptcy cases.

The third priority only applies in involuntary cases. This third priority is accorded to claims arising in the ordinary course of the debtor's business after creditors file an involuntary petition but before the earlier of an order for relief or the appointment of a trustee. For example, the creditors of a restaurant, *D*, file an involuntary petition on January 11. On January 15, *C* makes its usual weekly delivery of grits to *D*. *C*'s claim will be entitled to a third priority under section 507(a)(3).

Section 507(a)(4) grants a fourth priority to wage claims. This fourth priority includes claims for sales commissions, vacation pay, severance pay and sick leave pay. It is subject to two limitations:

(1) Timely—compensation earned within 180 days before the bankruptcy petition. (If the debtor's business ceased operations before the bankruptcy petition, the 180-day period is measured from the cessation of business operations.)

(2) Amount—which was $12,850 in 2021[12].

Claims for contributions to employee benefit plans receive a fifth priority under section 507(a)(5). This priority for fringe benefits is also subject to time and amount limitations:

(1) Time—only for services rendered within 180 days of the bankruptcy petition. (If the debtor's business ceased operations before the bankruptcy petition, the 180 days is measured from the cessation of business operation.)

(2) Amount—[$12,850 × number of employees] – total payment to employees under section 507(a)(4) + total payments to other employee benefit plans.

Note that payments under section 507(a)(5) will be made to the benefit plan, not directly to individual employees. Note also that section 507(a)(5) focuses on

---

[12] The amount is inflation indexed pursuant to section 104.

the aggregate of other payments to all employees covered by the plan, not the payments to an individual employee.

Section 507(a)(6) grants farmers a sixth priority for claims against grain storage facilities and fishermen a sixth priority against fish processing facilities. This priority is subject to a dollar limit.

Section 507(a)(7) grants a seventh priority to consumers who made a money deposit for property or services that were never provided. This priority is also subject to a dollar limit.

Certain specified tax claims enjoy an eighth priority.[13] Taxes subject to this eighth priority include:

(1) income taxes for the three tax years immediately preceding the filing of the bankruptcy petition;[14] and

(2) property taxes assessed before the filing of the bankruptcy petition and last payable

---

[13] Please remember that (1) section 507 affords priority to certain unsecured claims, (2) because of the Federal Tax Lien Act and various state statutes, many tax claims are secured claims and (3) section 724 subordinates certain secured tax claims to certain priority claims.

[14] The three-year period is measured from the last date including extensions for filing a return to the date of the bankruptcy petition. If, for example, *D* files a bankruptcy petition on April 15, 2023, claims for taxes for 2022, 2021 and 2020 would be entitled to a priority. If, however, *D* files a bankruptcy petition on December 7, 2023, only claims for taxes for 2022 and 2021 would be entitled to a priority.

without a penalty one year before that date; and

(3) if the debtor is an employer, taxes withheld from employees' paychecks.

The ninth priority is of limited application. It applies only in bankruptcies related to insured federal depository institutions and provides a priority for claims based upon a commitment to regulatory agencies to maintain the institution's capital.

The tenth priority is for claims for personal injuries or death caused by the debtor's operation of a motor vehicle, boat or airplane while under the influence of alcohol or some other drug. There is no monetary cap on this priority.

To review, section 507 establishes ten categories of priority claims. Each claim in each category must be paid in full before any claim in the next category receives any distribution.

4. SECTION 510 TREATMENT OF SUBORDINATION

Section 507, the priority provision, has the effect of moving certain, specified claims to the head of the line. Section 510, the subordination provision, has the effect of moving some claims further back in the line.

Section 510 requires subordination in two instances:

(1) where there is a subordination agreement that would be enforceable under nonbankruptcy law, section 510(a);

(2) when a seller or purchaser of equity securities seeks damages or rescission, section 510(b).

Additionally, the court has the discretion, after notice and hearing to subordinate any claim to other claims "under principles of equitable subordination," section 510(c).

The Bankruptcy Code does not define or even describe the principles by which equitable subordination is to be applied. The reported cases on equitable subordination emphasize facts, rather than specific rules or tests. The most significant fact is whether the holder of a claim is an insider or fiduciary. If a creditor is not in control of the debtor or otherwise an insider, courts are very reluctant to use equitable subordination.

5. CLASSIFICATION OF CLAIMS

In a Chapter 7 case, the debtor has no control over how the property of the estate is to be distributed. Section 726 prescribes the scheme of distribution to unsecured creditors in a Chapter 7 case. All allowed, unsecured nonpriority claims are treated alike: a pro rata distribution will be made to the holders of such claims after all priority claims are paid in full, section 726(a)(2).

To illustrate, assume that *D* owes $90,000 to *X*, $50,000 to *Y* and $60,000 to *Z* for total debts to *X*, *Y* and *Z* of $200,000. Assume further that *X*, *Y* and *Z*'s claims are allowed, nonpriority, unsecured claims. If there is $100,000 available after satisfying secured claims and priority claims, then *X*, *Y* and *Z* will each receive 50 percent of its claim—$45,000 to *X*, $25,000 to *Y* and $30,000 to *Z*. [Total debts divided by total available funds equals percentage of each claim paid.]

In a Chapter 11 case, a Chapter 12 case or a Chapter 13 case, a debtor's plan can affect how the property of the estate is to be distributed. The plan can treat some unsecured claims differently than others: it can classify claims and provide for different treatment for each class, sections 1123(a)(1), 1222(b)(1), 1322(b)(1).

CHAPTER XII

LEASES AND EXECUTORY CONTRACTS

Bankruptcy involves both the assets and the obligations of the debtor. Bankruptcy deals with these assets and obligations through the creation of a fictional estate. The assets of the debtor become property of the estate. The estate is administered by a trustee or debtor in possession to satisfy the secured and unsecured obligations of the debtor. In the course of administration, the estate will incur its own obligations; these administrative expenses are given priority over the debtor's unsecured obligations.

Generally, the Bankruptcy Code's provisions dealing with the debtor's assets are separate from the Bankruptcy Code's provisions dealing with the debtor's obligations and the estate's obligations: property of the estate in section 541, allowable claims and administrative expenses in sections 502 and 503. A lease or executory contract involves potentially both property of the estate and a claim against the debtor or the estate.

This hybrid nature of a lease or executory contract is most apparent in lease situations in which the debtor is the lessee. Assume, for example, that D Store, Inc. (*D*) leases its store in the mall from *L*. *D* later files for bankruptcy. *D*'s rights to the use of the space in the mall is an asset of the estate. *D*'s lease, however, involves burdens as well as benefits. D has performance obligations under the lease such as paying rent. If these obligations are not performed, *L* will have a claim.

The bankruptcy treatment of a lease or executory contract can take one of three possible forms:

(1) rejection;

(2) assumption;

(3) assignment.

In comparing rejection, assumption and assignment, it is important to keep in mind that the lease or contract involves potentially both property of the estate and a claim against the estate. The following chart provides a general view of the effects of rejection, assumption and assignment on property of the estate and claims against the estate.

	Rejection	Assumption	Assignment
Property of the estate	No property of the estate	Debtor's rights under contract or lease	Proceeds, if any, from assignment of debtor's rights under contract or lease
Claims	Unsecured claim for (i) prepetition defaults and (ii) breach resulting from rejection; administrative expense priority claim for postpetition obligations, if any.	Administrative expense priority claim for all obligations under contract or lease, postpetition or prepetition.	No claim against the estate. Nondebtor party to an assigned contract or lease looks solely to the assignee.

An understanding of the bankruptcy law of leases and executory contracts requires an understanding not only of rejection, assumption and assignment, the three different elections available to the debtor under the Bankruptcy Code, but also an understanding of the election that is not available to the debtor under the Bankruptcy Code. A debtor does not have a legal right to modify or change the terms of an unexpired lease or an executory contract.

To illustrate, assume that *D* Store, Inc. (*D*) leases space in a mall from *L* for $20,000 a year. *D* owes $600,000 to unsecured trade creditors and $3,000,000 to secured lenders. *D* files a Chapter 11 petition. *D* wants to continue operating in the mall, wants to retain the leasehold. *D* will have to assume the lease, will have to assume the lease payment as is: $20,000 a year, no change. In its Chapter 11 plan, *D* will be able to alter its payment obligations to lenders and trade creditors, secured and unsecured. *D* cannot, however, use a provision of the Bankruptcy Code to effect a modification in its obligations under its leases or executory contracts. The Bankruptcy Code provides only for rejection, assumption or assignment. Not modification.

The previous statement in the text is both correct and misleading. There are only the three possible choices under the Bankruptcy Code. A debtor does not have a right under the Bankruptcy Code to change the terms of an unexpired lease or executory contract. Nonetheless, a debtor is often able to use its bargaining power and other legal rights under the Bankruptcy Code to "persuade" the other party to the lease or contract to "agree" to modifications in the lease or contract.

For example, *D* is leasing a building from *L*. *D* files for bankruptcy. *D* wants *L* to reduce its rent. *D* presents *L* with the choice that either *D* will reject the lease which will leave *L* with an empty building and a general claim in *D*'s bankruptcy case or *L* will agree to modifications in the lease. *L* will often choose to "agree" to modify the lease.

To review, look primarily to section 365 to determine the effect of bankruptcy on a debtor's leases and executory contracts. Under section 365, a bankruptcy trustee can either:

(1) reject (i.e., breach) a lease or executory contract;

(2) assume (i.e., keep) a lease or executory contract;

(3) assign (i.e. sell) a lease or executory contract.

In order to understand section 365 and assess these three options, a law student or lawyer must be able to answer the following questions:

(1) What is the effect of rejecting, assuming or assigning a lease or executory contract?

(2) What is the procedure for rejecting, assuming or assigning a lease or executory contract?

(3) What are the limitations, if any, on rejecting a lease or executory contract?

(4) What are the limitations, if any, on assuming or assigning a lease or executory contract?

(5) What is an executory contract?

A. EFFECT OF REJECTION, ASSUMPTION, ASSIGNMENT

Floyd Lawson, *L*, leases a building for a barbershop from Mayberry Realty Corp., *M*. The lease agreement provides for a ten-year term and monthly rentals of $250. *L* files a bankruptcy petition. What is the effect of the bankruptcy trustee's or debtor in possession's rejecting the lease? Assuming the lease? Assigning the lease?

If the lease is rejected, *L* has no further right to use the building. If the lease is rejected, *L* has no further personal liability on the lease. The rejection of the lease is, of course, a breach of the lease, section 365(g). *M* will have an allowable unsecured claim against the bankrupt estate for back rent and future rentals, section 502(g), 502(b)(7). The amount that *M* will receive on this unsecured claim will depend on the property of the estate in a Chapter 7 case and will depend on the provisions of the plan in a Chapter 11 or Chapter 13 case.

If the lease is assumed, the leasehold continues to be an asset of the estate. *L* can continue to operate *L*'s barbershop in the building. Assumption covers the burdens of the lease as well as the benefits. By assuming the lease, the trustee or debtor in possession is obligating the estate to make all payments under the lease.[1] This obligation is a

---

1 Compare the Bankruptcy Code's treatment of the debtor's landlord with its treatment of the debtor's secured creditor. If a Chapter 11 or Chapter 13 debtor wants to retain a building that she is leasing, the debtor must continue to make all payments called for by the lease. Section 365 does not provide for the alteration or modification of leases; under section 365, the lease is either rejected or assumed, as is.

In contrast, if a Chapter 11 or Chapter 13 debtor wants to keep a building other than an individual debtor's principal residence that is subject to a mortgage, the debtor can "impair or modify" the rights of the mortgagee in her plan, sections 1123(b)(1), 1322(b)(2).

To illustrate, *D* Corp. files a Chapter 11 petition. *D* is using two buildings. It is leasing one of the buildings from *X* at a rental of $2,000 a month. *Y* is financing *D*'s purchase of the other building. The *D*-*Y* loan agreements grant *Y* a mortgage on the building and

section 507 priority administrative expense. For example, *L* files for Chapter 11. If *L* assumes the lease, the landlord *M* will have an administrative expense priority for all unpaid rent and will be paid in full before L's other unsecured creditors are paid at all.

What if, in Floyd Lawson's bankruptcy, the trustee or debtor in possession sells the lease to Aunt Bea Taylor who wants to open an "adult" bookstore in the building? Such an assignment "relieves the trustee and the estate from any liability for any breach of such contract or lease occurring after such assignment," section 365(k). After the assignment, *M* can look only to Aunt Bea for the payment of the post-assignment obligations under the lease.

B. PROCEDURE FOR REJECTION OR ASSUMPTION

Section 365(a) contemplates court approval of rejection or assumption. Rule 6006 provides that the assumption or rejection is a contested matter governed by Rule 9014. Neither the Code nor the Rules indicate what standard the court should apply in determining whether to grant or withhold its approval.

Most, but not all, cases seem to give great deference to the "business judgment" of the debtor in possession or trustee in approving a motion to reject

call for monthly payments of $3,000. *D* can keep the leased building only if it continues to pay *X* $2,000. As Chapter X explained, *D* has greater flexibility with respect to retention of the building subject to *Y*'s mortgage.

an unexpired lease or executory contract. Because assumption of an unexpired lease or executory contract creates an administrative priority obligation that must be paid before other unsecured claims, courts give greater weight to creditors' objections to motions to assume than to creditors objections to motions to reject.

1. CHAPTER 7 (OTHER THAN NONRESIDENTIAL REAL PROPERTY LEASES)

In Chapter 7, there is a general rule that executory contracts and leases that are not assumed by the Chapter 7 trustee within 60 days after the order for relief are deemed rejected, section 365(d)(1). You should know three exceptions to this general rule.

First, section 365(d)(1) provides that the court can extend the 60-day deadline. Second, section 365(d)(1) does not apply to nonresidential real property leases. Third, section 365(p) provides a three-step process by which an individual debtor can themself assume a lease. The first step is for the debtor to make a written request; the second step is for the lessor to notify the debtor of its willingness to have the lease assumed by the debtor; the third step is for the debtor to notify the lessor that the lease is assumed. When a lease is assumed by the debtor under section 365(p), the debtor individually (and not the estate) has both the benefits and the burdens of the lease.

2. CHAPTERS 11 AND 13 (OTHER THAN NONRESIDENTIAL REAL PROPERTY LEASES)

In cases under Chapter 11 or Chapter 13, the general rule is that executory contracts and leases can be assumed or rejected any time before the confirmation of the plan, section 365(d)(2). Again, you should know two exceptions to this general rule. First, section 365(d)(2) provides that the court can order an earlier determination of whether the contract or lease is to be assumed or rejected. Second, section 365(d)(2) does not apply to nonresidential real property leases.

3. NONRESIDENTIAL REAL PROPERTY LEASES IN CHAPTERS 7, 11 AND 13 CASES

The general rule is that a lease of nonresidential real property is deemed rejected unless it has been assumed within 120 days after the order for relief, section 365(d)(4). And, this general rule is also subject to two exceptions. First, if a plan is confirmed earlier, then the deadline becomes the date of the entry of the order confirming the plan. Second, the court can extend the 120 period by 90 days. The lessor must agree to any additional extension.

C. THE GAP PERIOD

There is going to be some gap period between the filing of a bankruptcy petition and action on a contract or lease. Accordingly, it would seem necessary to consider the rights and responsibilities of the debtor and nondebtor party during the interim between the commencement of the bankruptcy case and the assumption or rejection decision.

1. NONDEBTOR'S PERFORMANCE

Section 365 does not expressly deal with the performance obligations of the nondebtor party to a lease or executory during this gap period. The few cases that have expressly dealt with the question have held that the nondebtor party is obligated to perform. Most courts seem simply to assume that the nondebtor party is so obligated. If *L* is leasing a building or machinery to *D*, *L*'s performance (providing the building or machinery) continues after *D*'s bankruptcy filing.

2. DEBTOR'S PERFORMANCE

Section 365(d)(3) expressly deals with the performance obligations of the debtor party to a nonresidential real property lease: it requires a debtor/lessee to "timely perform" all obligations under a nonresidential real property lease. Assume that dentist *D* files for Chapter 13 relief. *D* leases their office from *L*; the unexpired lease provides for rent of $2,000 per month. While it is clear that section 365(d)(3) contemplates that within 60 days of the filing, *D* will be making all postpetition rent payments to *L*, it is not clear from the cases under section 365(d)(3) what happens if *D* is unable to perform during the gap period.

Section 365(d)(5) deals with the gap period performance obligations of the debtor on its equipment leases. Section 365(d)(5) needs to be read together with and compared to section 365(d)(3). While section 365(d)(3) contemplates that a debtor will make all postpetition rent payments on commercial real estate and will start making such payments within 60 days, section 365(d)(5) contemplates that the debtor will make equipment lease payments that first arise after 60 days. And, the court can excuse equipment lease payments that first arise after 60 days "based on the equities of the case."

Section 365(d)(5) also needs to be read together with section 363(e). Under section 363(e), a lessor of personal property can request that the court prohibit or restrict the debtor's use of its property "as is necessary to protect" the lessor's interest in the leased property.

D. LIMITATIONS ON THE EFFECT OF REJECTION OF A LEASE OR EXECUTORY CONTRACT

Nothing in section 365 limits the availability of rejection. Section 365 does, however, set out four situations in which the effect of rejection is limited:

1. Section 365(h) limits the effect of rejection of a lease of real property when the debtor is the landlord. A trustee for a debtor who owns rental real property may not use section 365 to evict tenants. Even, if the trustee decides to reject the debtor/lessor's leases, the tenant has a right to remain in possession. Assume, for example, that Epstein uses some of his nutshell royalties to build an office building; your law firm rents an office in Epstein's building. If Epstein later

files for bankruptcy and rejects the lease, your firm can still remain in possession of the leasehold.

The trustee for the debtor/lessor may, however, use rejection to terminate some of the services required by the lease such as maintenance. The lessee may then offset any damages caused by such termination against its rent obligation.

2. Sections 365(h) and (i) provide similar limitations on a debtor/seller's rejection of a timeshare contract.

3. Section 365(i) provides similar limitations on the debtor/seller's rejection of an installment land sales contract.

4. Section 365(n) provides similar limitations[2] on the debtor/licensor's rejection of a lease of a patent, copyright or other "intellectual property."

There is language in Mission Product Holdings, Inc. v. Tempnology, LLC, 139 S.Ct. 1652 (2019) that suggests that 1–4 above are surplusage. In that case the debtor rejected an executory contract in which it licensed its trademark. The debtor argued that the effect of its rejection was that the licensee could no longer use the debtor's license.

---

[2] Under section 365(n), an intellectual property licensee, like a real property lessee, is granted an election with respect to the consequences of a debtor/licensor's rejection of the license agreement. The licensee may treat the rejection as a breach that terminates the lease and assert a claim for damages. Alternatively, the licensee may elect to retain its rights under license agreement "as such rights existed immediately before the case commenced."

The Bankruptcy Code's definition of "intellectual property" does not include "trademarks." The trademark licensee in *Mission Product Holdings* was not protected by section 363(n).

Nonetheless, the court held that the licensee could continue to use trademark, As Justice Kagan explained, "A rejection breaches a contract but does not rescind it. And that means that all the rights that would ordinarily survive a breach, including those conveyed here, remain in place . . .We reject the competing claim that by specifically enabling the counterparties in some contracts to retain rights after rejection, Congress showed that it wanted the counterparties in all other contracts to lose their rights."

Congress included two sections in Chapter 11 to protect employee executory contracts. Section 1113 limits the rejection of collective bargaining contracts in Chapter 11 cases. Paragraph (f) of section 1113 prohibits a debtor/employer from unilaterally changing a prebankruptcy collective bargaining agreement. Paragraph (e) provides for court approval of interim changes pending court action on a request to reject a collective bargaining agreement. Paragraph (b) requires postpetition negotiations with and disclosures to the union as a condition precedent to rejection of the collective bargaining agreement. And, paragraph (c) sets out the standard the court is to apply in ruling on a motion to reject a collective bargaining agreement.

Section 1114 limits the rejection of employee benefits contracts in Chapter 11 cases. It (1) requires

Chapter 11 debtors in possession or trustees to continue paying retiree medical and life insurance benefits at prebankruptcy levels until a modification is either agreed to by the retiree's "authorized representative" or authorized by the bankruptcy court and (2) provides that all preconfirmation retiree benefits are administrative expenses entitled to priority over other unsecured claims.

E. LIMITATIONS ON ASSUMPTION AND ASSIGNMENT

Although the Bankruptcy Code limits the possible *effects* of a debtor's rejection of a lease or executory contract, the Bankruptcy Code's only limitation on the debtor's decision to reject a lease or executory contract is the section 365(a) requirement of "subject to the court's approval." There are however some other Bankruptcy Code limitations on the debtor's decision to assume or assign a lease or executory contract. Section 365(a) and (c) indicates which leases and executory contracts cannot be assumed or assigned. And, section 365(b) sets out requirements that must be satisfied before the court will approve the assumption or assignment of a lease or executory contract.

1. CONTRACT LIMITATIONS

While the Bankruptcy Code prohibits and limits the assumption or assignment of certain leases and executory contracts, contract clauses that prohibit or limit the assumption and assignment of leases and executory contracts will not be effective in bankruptcy, section 365(e), (f). The trustee or debtor in possession can assume a lease even though the lease agreement provides for automatic termination or a right of termination because of bankruptcy or insolvency, section 365(e). Similarly, the trustee or debtor in possession can sell or otherwise assign a lease even though the lease agreement provides it is not assignable, section 365(f).

Assume, for example, that in 2021, *T* leases two floors of a building from *L* for ten years. The lease provides that it can not be assigned without *L*'s written approval and that the lease terminates *ipso facto* on *T*'s bankruptcy. In 2022, *T* files for Chapter 11 bankruptcy. *T*'s one *T* valuable asset is the lease. Because of the desirability of the location and the favorable rental rate, third parties a*re willing to pay substantial sums to acquire the lease from T. Notwithstanding the language in the lease, T can sell the lease by meeting the requirements for assignment set out in section 365(f).*

What happens to the "substantial sums" that *T* receives when *T* sells the lease? Recall that the debtor's interest in the lease was section 541(a)(1) property of the estate and that proceeds from the sale of property of the estate are property of the estate, section 541(a)(6). Accordingly, it would seem that the answer to this question is that the "substantial sums" from the sale of the lease would, like the rest of the property of the estate, be available for distribution to unsecured creditors in a Chapter 7 case and be available for the debtor's plan performance in a Chapter 11 or 13 case.

2. LEASES AND EXECUTORY CONTRACTS THAT CANNOT BE ASSUMED OR ASSUMED AND ASSIGNED

There are some leases and executory contracts that cannot be assumed and assigned. A lease or contract that has expired or been terminated before bankruptcy cannot be assumed or assigned.

For example, *D* leases Redacre from *L*. *D* defaults. *L* takes the steps required by state law to evict *D* and terminate the lease. *D* later files for bankruptcy. *D* cannot assume the lease. Regardless of religious views, there is no such thing as a born-again lease.

A loan commitment or other financing arrangement cannot be assumed, section 365(c)(2). *C* agrees to provide *D* with a $250,000 line of credit. *D* files a bankruptcy petition before drawing on this line of credit. *D* cannot assume this executory contract and compel *C* to loan the $250,000.

More generally, contracts that are not assignable under "applicable law" are not assignable in bankruptcy, section 365(c)(1). "Applicable law" can be the common law of contracts. Under the common law of contracts, for example, personal services contracts cannot be assigned and delegated. And so, under section 365(c)(1), personal services contracts cannot be assigned. If Wonder Woman contracts to defend of Richmond and Wonder Woman later files a bankruptcy petition, Wonder Woman cannot use bankruptcy to assign this personal services contract to Superman.

"Applicable law" for purposes of section 365(c) can also be a statute so long as it is a statute other than the Bankruptcy Code. Assume, for example, that state law prohibits the assignment of a car dealer franchise contract without the approval of the franchisor. *D* Ford dealer could not file for bankruptcy and then assign his franchise without the approval of the franchisor because of "applicable law."

Read literally, a contract that is not assignable under "applicable law" cannot even be assumed in bankruptcy, Section 365(c) begins "A trustee cannot *assume or assign* . . . if." (emphasis added) By its terms, section 365(c) bars a debtor from even assuming (i.e., keeping) a lease or executory contract where applicable nonbankruptcy law bars assignment (i.e. selling) of the contract to a third party,

And some circuit courts have read section 365(c) literally Most casebooks include the Ninth Circuit decision In re Catapult Entertainment, Inc., 165 F.3d 747 (9th Cir 1999). There a Chapter 11 producer of video games was not able to assume a nonexclusive patent license since patent law makes nonexclusive patent licenses not assignable.

3. REQUIREMENTS FOR ASSUMPTION

Paragraph (b) of section 365 sets out the requirements for assumption of a lease or executory contract. Note that paragraph 365(b) only applies if there has been a default other than breach of a provision relating to bankruptcy filing or insolvency.

Assume, for example, that *D* rents a building from *L*. *D* files a bankruptcy petition. At the time of the bankruptcy petition, *D* is current on all of its obligations under the lease. If *D* decides to assume the lease, section 365(b) does not apply.

If there has been a default, section 365(b) imposes requirements with respect to the past failures to perform and requirements with respect to the future performance obligations. Section 365(b)(1) requires

(1) cure of past defaults or "adequate assurance"[3] of prompt cure;

(2) compensation for "actual pecuniary loss" resulting from the default or "adequate assurance" of prompt compensation.

(3) "adequate assurance of future *performance*."

Obviously, some prebankruptcy defaults cannot be cured. Assume, for example, that *D* Tavern's lease required that it not be closed for more than 72 consecutive hours and that in the week prior to its bankruptcy filing, *D* Tavern was closed for 75 hours. Section 365(b) was amended to "clarify" that *D*

---

[3] This standard sounds similar to but is different from the standard applied in stay litigation. Section 362(d) protects the holder of secured claims by requiring "adequate protection" of the creditors interest in the collateral. Section 362(d) thus protects a creditor's property rights. Section 365(b) protects the lessor of property by requiring "adequate assurance" of the lease obligations. Section 365(b) thus protects a creditor's contract rights.

Tavern can assume this lease even though it is impossible to cure an earlier nonmonetary default[4].

Remember that a debtor who is assuming a lease or executory contract must satisfy the three requirements of section 365 only "If there has been a default."

4. REQUIREMENTS FOR ASSIGNMENT

The requirements for assigning a lease or executory contract are different from the requirements for assuming a lease or executory contract. And they should be.

Remember that after assignment, the other party to the lease or executory contract can look only to the assignee for the performance of the debtor's post-assignment obligations under the lease or contract. To protect the nonbankrupt counterparty to the lease or contract, section 365(f)(2) requires that the *assignee* provide adequate assurance of future *performance* as a condition to *any* assignment.

Note the three italicized words. First, "assignee." After assignment of a lease or executory contract, the assignee (but not the debtor) has performance obligations and so it is the assignee that provides the adequate assurance.

Second, "performance." Section 365(b) and section 365(f)(2) use the term "performance", not "payment."

---

[4] If your professor points out that section 365(b) is still not clear and makes a point of this, you might want to make a point of carefully comparing 365(b)(1)(A) with section 365(b)(2)(D).

An assignee assuming a lease or executory contract that is in default must assure its future performance of all terms of the lease or other contract, not just the payment term.

What if the lease contains a use restriction such as the premises shall only be used for "a book store" and the assignee wants to use the space for a copy center? The assignee would not be able to provide adequate assurance of its future performance of the use restriction. It would seem like the court should deny this assignment. Especially if the leased space is a part of a shopping center.

The term "adequate assurance of future performance" is not statutorily defined. However section 365(c)(3) states that if the lease covers space in a "shopping center,[5] "adequate assurance of future performance is "subject to all the provisions" including use restriction provisions.

Notwithstanding this language, there are reported decisions that approve the assignment of a shopping center lease even though the assignee will be operating in violation of a use restriction Courts so ruling compare a use restriction to a prohibition on an assignment which is invalid under section 365(f)(1).

The third word I italicized in excerpting section 365(f)(2) is "any." In assignments (unlike assumptions) adequate assurance of future

---

[5] The term "shopping center" is not statutorily defined. Because of section 365(b)(3), a lessor of a shopping center enjoys greater protection than a lessor of other real property.

performance is required for any assignment of any lease or executory contract, not just assignments of a lease or executory contract in which "there has been a default."

F. DEFINITION OF EXECUTORY CONTRACT

Section 365 applies to leases and executory contracts. The Bankruptcy Code does not define the term "lease." There is probably no need for a definition. When there is a problem as to whether a "lease" of personal property is a disguised credit sale, bankruptcy courts look to the definition of "security interest" in UCC § 1–201(35).

Similarly, the Bankruptcy Code does not define the phrase "executory contract." The most frequently cited and most thorough discussion of executory contracts in bankruptcy is a two-part, 142-page article written prior to the enactment of the Bankruptcy Code by Professor Vern Countryman. Professor Countryman concludes that an executory contract for purposes of bankruptcy is one that is so far unperformed on both sides that the failure of either party to complete her performance would be a material breach excusing further performance from the other party.[6]

Most reported cases seem to follow the Countryman definition. There are, however, bankruptcy judges who have written opinions and

---

[6] Vern Countryman, *Executory Contracts In Bankruptcy*, 57 MINN.L.REV. 439 (1973); 58 MINN.L.REV. 479 (1974).

law professors who have written articles calling for a different definition of "executory contract." If your bankruptcy teacher is one of these judges or professors, then you need to read their opinions or articles.

CHAPTER XIII

DISCHARGE

Most debtors who file voluntary bankruptcy petitions expect that the bankruptcy case will wipe out all of their debts. These expectations are not always realized. Bankruptcy *discharges certain* debtors from *certain* debts.

As the italicized words in the last sentence suggest, there are three major discharge questions:

(1) Which debtors receive a discharge?

(2) Which debts are discharged?

(3) What is the effect of a discharge?

The answers to these three questions depend in substantial part on whether the bankruptcy case is a Chapter 7 case or a Chapter 11 case or a Chapter 13 case.

A. WHICH DEBTORS RECEIVE A DISCHARGE?

Not all people who file for bankruptcy receive a discharge.

1. CHAPTER 7

In counseling a beleaguered debtor about Chapter 7, it is very important to ascertain their eligibility for discharge—to determine whether any of the grounds for withholding discharge can be established by the bankruptcy trustee or a creditor. If after the debtor files for Chapter 7 relief the Chapter 7 trustee or a creditor can establish a ground for withholding discharge, the debtor loses two ways. The debtor will leave the bankruptcy case owing the same debts that they owed at the time of the filing of the bankruptcy case less any distribution that creditors received from the trustee. without (1) their section 541 property and (2) the amounts the debtor paid for filing fee and their attorney.

a. Substantive Grounds for Withholding a Chapter 7 Discharge

The grounds for withholding a discharge, i.e., objections to discharge, are set out in section 727(a). These grounds are exclusive. Unless the bankruptcy trustee or a creditor is able to establish one of these section 727(a) objections, the debtor in a Chapter 7 case will receive a bankruptcy discharge.

Only an individual is eligible to receive a discharge in a case under Chapter 7 of the Bankruptcy Code.[1] Section 727(a)(1) denies a discharge to corporations partnerships, and limited liability companies that are debtors in Chapter 7 cases.

Section 727(a)(1) is intended to prevent "trafficking in corporate shells and partnerships." Generally, the owners of a bankrupt corporation do not need a bankruptcy discharge. Since the corporation is a separate legal entity, its owners are

---

1 A corporation may receive a discharge under Chapter 11, section 1141(d).

protected from personal liability for the corporation's debts.

The next six grounds, section 727(a)(2) through (a)(7), for withholding discharge have as their foundation some form of bad act or lack of cooperation by the individual debtor either before or after the bankruptcy petition.

Certain fraudulent transfers can be the basis for an objection to discharge. Section 727(a)(2) denies a discharge to a debtor who transfers property "with an intent to hinder, delay or defraud" within the twelve months immediately preceding the filing of the bankruptcy petition or after the filing of the bankruptcy petition.

An objection to discharge may be based on the unjustified failure to keep or preserve financial records, section 727(a)(3). A section 727(a)(3) objection raises the following issues of fact: (1) Has the debtor failed to keep financial records? (2) Is such failure "justified under all of the circumstances of the case"? and (3) Is it still possible to ascertain the debtor's financial condition and business transactions? The standards applied in resolving these fact questions will reflect the nature of the debtor's business and his assets and liabilities.

Section 727(a)(4) lists four acts which tend to deprive the bankruptcy trustee of property of the estate or of information necessary to discover or collect property of the estate:

(1) Making a false oath or account in connection with the bankruptcy case;

(2) Presenting or using a false claim against the estate;

(3) Receiving or giving consideration for action or inaction in the bankruptcy case; or

(4) Withholding books and records from the bankruptcy trustee.

Proof that the debtor "knowingly and fraudulently" committed one of these acts will bar discharge.[2]

The fifth ground for denial of discharge is the failure to explain "satisfactorily" any loss or deficiency of assets, section 727(a)(5). Section 727(a)(5) focuses on the truth of the debtor's explanation, not on the wisdom of their expenditures.

Under section 727(a)(6), a debtor may be denied discharge if the debtor refuses to testify after having been granted immunity or after improperly invoking the constitutional privilege against self-incrimination.

The seventh ground for withholding discharge is the debtor's commission of any act specified in section 727(a)(2)–(6) no more than a year before the filing of the bankruptcy petition in connection with another bankruptcy case concerning an "insider," section

---

[2] Proof that the debtor "knowingly and fraudulently" committed one of these acts will also subject the debtor to criminal sanctions: a fine of not more than $5,000 and/or imprisonment for not more than five years, 18 USC § 152. The standard of proof under 18 USC is beyond a reasonable doubt; section 727(a)(4) merely requires a preponderance of the evidence. Accordingly, section 727(a)(4) focuses on commission of the act, not conviction for the crime.

727(a)(7). The term "insider" is defined in section 101(28). An individual's relatives, partners, partnership and corporation all come within the definition.

Section 727(a)(8) and section 727(a)(9) limit the frequency of Chapter 7 discharge relief. If a debtor has received a discharge in a Chapter 7 or Chapter 11 case in the past eight years, she will be denied discharge, section 727(a)(8). If a debtor has received a discharge in a Chapter 13 case within the past six years they will be denied a discharge unless (a) payments under the plan totaled at least 100% of the allowed unsecured claims, or (b) payments under the plan totaled at least 70% of the allowed unsecured claims *and* the plan was proposed in good faith *and* was the debtor's "best effort," section 727(a)(9).

The eight-year/six-year time period tests are measured from filing date to filing date. So, if *D* obtains a discharge on April 5, 2015, in a Chapter 7 case filed on January 15, 2015, section 728(a)(8) would not bar *D*'s bankruptcy discharge in a bankruptcy case filed in March of 2023.

Now that you understand what section 727(a)(8) and (9) do, be sure you understand what these provisions do not do. Section 727(a)(8) and section 727(a)(9) only limit the availability of a discharge in a Chapter 7 case. They do not affect the debtor's right to file a voluntary petition or creditors' right to file involuntary petitions under Chapter 7 or any other chapter. And, they do not affect the availability of a Chapter 13 discharge or a Chapter 11 debtor who "engages in business after consummation of the plan."[3]

Section 727(a)(10) recognizes certain waivers of discharge. A debtor's waiver will bar discharge only if it is:

(1) in writing; and

(2) executed after the filing of the bankruptcy petition, after the order for relief; and

(3) approved by the court.

Section 727(a)(11) denies a discharge for failure to complete an approved "instructional course concerning personal financial management." Section 727(a)(12) delays a discharge if there is a proceeding pending against the debtor and there is reasonable cause to believe that the debtor may be found guilty of a felony or liable for a debt arising from (I) violation of securities law, (II) RICO civil penalty, or (III) personal injury or death caused by the debtor's criminal act, intentional tort or willful or reckless misconduct.

b. Procedure for Objecting to a Chapter 7 Discharge

The Chapter 7 trustee, the United States trustee or a creditor may raise a section 727 objection to discharge, section 727(c)(1). Objections to discharge are initiated by complaints, filed with the bankruptcy court.

---

3 Section 1141(d)(3)(B).

Rule 4004 sets the time for filing complaints objecting to discharge. Any such complaint must be filed within 60 days of the first date set for the meeting of creditors. The court may "for cause" extend the time for filing a complaint objecting to discharge on motion of a party in interest. Such a motion, however, must be filed within the 60-day period.

If any creditor files an objection to discharge, the bankruptcy court tries the issue of the debtor's right to a discharge. Such a trial is an "adversary proceeding" governed by Part VII of the Bankruptcy Rules, Rule 4004(d). If no objection to discharge is filed, and the debtor has not waived his right to a discharge, has not failed to attend the meeting of creditors, and has paid the filing fees, the court shall grant the discharge, section 727(a), Rule 4004(c).

After the court has determined whether to grant a discharge, the court must hold a hearing and the debtor must appear in person, section 524(d). The hearing must be held within 30 days of the order granting or denying a discharge Rule 4008. At the hearing, the court informs the debtor that a discharge has been granted, or why a discharge has not been granted.

2. CHAPTER 11 CASES: BUSINESS ENTITY DEBTORS[4]

In Chapter 11 cases in which the debtor is a corporation, partnership or some other business entity, the confirmation of the plan operates as a discharge, section 1141(d). The following hypothetical points out the practical significance of this rule: *D* Corp. owes *X* $100,000. *D* Corp.'s Chapter 11 plan proposes to pay *X* $70,000 over three years. On confirmation, *D*'s only obligation to *X* is to pay it $70,000 over three years as provided in the plan. The remainder of the debt has been discharged.

The grounds for denying a discharge in a Chapter 11 case are different from the grounds for denying a discharge in a Chapter 7 case. A Chapter 11 debtor will be denied a discharge only if *all* of the following requirements are satisfied:

(1) The plan provides for liquidation of all or substantially all of the property of the estate; AND

(2) The debtor does not engage in business after consummation of the plan; AND

(3) The debtor would be denied a discharge if the case were in Chapter 7, section 1141(d)(3).

The following hypotheticals illustrate the application of section 1141(d)(3).

---

[4] There are some different rules for Subchapter V cases which are explained in Chapter XVI.

(1) *D* Corp. files a Chapter 11 petition. Its Chapter 11 plan provides for the sale of all of its assets, distribution of the proceeds from the sale to creditors, and termination of business operations. *D* Corp. would not receive a discharge.

(2) *D* Inc.'s Chapter 11 plan provides for the sale of six stores and continued operations of five stores. If its plan is confirmed, *D* Inc. will receive a discharge.

(3) *D*, an individual who owns and operates several small businesses as sole proprietorships, files a Chapter 11 petition. *D*'s Chapter 11 plan provides for the continued operation of these businesses. *D* had received a discharge in a Chapter 7 case commenced five years ago. Because of their "bankruptcy history," if *D* had filed for Chapter 7 relief instead of Chapter 11 *D* would have been denied a Chapter 7 discharge under section 727(a)(9). Because of section 1141(d)(3), *D* will not receive a discharge if its Chapter 11 plan is confirmed.

3. CHAPTER 13

In Chapter 13 cases, unlike Chapter 11 cases, the confirmation of the plan does not effect a discharge. In Chapter 13, the question of whether a debtor will receive a discharge cannot be resolved until the debtor either completes their payments under the plan or completes their efforts to make payments under the plan, section 1328.

Section 1328(a) provides for the discharge of a debtor who has completed all of the payments required by his Chapter 13 plan and all postpetition domestic support obligations. Note the word "shall" in section 1328(a).

Also note section 1328(b)'s use of the word "may." Section 1328(b) gives the court discretion to grant a "hardship discharge" to a debtor who has failed to make all of the payments required by their plan. Section 1328(b) lists three factors that the court should consider in exercising this discretion:

(1) holders of unsecured claims have already received at least as much as they would have received in a Chapter 7 case;

(2) debtor could not "justly be held accountable" for their inability to complete plan payments; and

(3) plan modification is not practicable.

While section 727 is not expressly applicable to Chapter 13 cases, there are three Chapter 13 discharge requirements that are similar to section 727 Chapter 7 discharge requirements.

First, in 13 cases, as in 7 cases, a debtor may be denied a discharge because of her bankruptcy history. Section 1328(f) denies a discharge because of what happened during (1) a Chapter 13 case in the 2 years prior to the filing or (2) another Chapter 7 or 11 case in the 4-year period prior to the filing.[5]

Second, section 1328(g), like 727(a)(11), denies a discharge for failure to complete an approved "instructional course concerning personal financial management.

Third, section 1328(h), like section 727(a)(12), delays a discharge if there is a proceeding pending against the debtor and there is reasonable cause to believe that the debtor may be found guilty of a felony or liable for a debt arising from (I) violation of securities law, (II) RICO civil penalty or (III) personal injury or death caused by the debtor's criminal act, intentional tort or willful or reckless misconduct.

4. CHAPTER 11 CASES: INDIVIDUAL DEBTORS

The discharge requirements for an individual debtor in Chapter 11 are very similar to the Chapter 13 discharge requirements. Section 1141(d)(5)(A) generally postpones discharge for individual debtors until completion of the plan. Section 1141(d)(5)(A) is thus much more similar to section 1328(a) than it is to section 1141(d)(1).

---

[5] It is not clear from the language in section 1328(f) whether what happened during that time period has to be merely the granting of a discharge in a prior case during that period or both the filing of the prior case and the granting of discharge in that case during that period.

And, just as in a Chapter 13 case, the court has discretion to grant a discharge to an individual 11 debtor even though they have not completed their plan payments. Compare section 1141(d)(5)(B) with section 1328(b).

5. CHAPTER 11 CASES: SUBCHAPTER 5

Since 2020, individuals and business entities that come within section 1182's definition of debtor can elect to proceed to under Subchapter V. In such Subchapter V cases, the confirmation of a "consensual plan" results in a discharge—even if the debtor is an individual.

Almost all confirmed Subchapter V plans are "consensual plans." Subchapter V "consensual plans" and Subchapter V more generally are discussed in Chapter XVI infra.

B. WHICH OBLIGATIONS ARE AFFECTED BY A BANKRUPTCY DISCHARGE?

Even when the debtor receives a discharge, they are not necessarily freed from all of their payment obligations. Certain payment obligations are not affected by a discharge. In determining whether a discharge affects an obligation, it is necessary to consider the following three questions:

(1) Is the obligation a "debt" as that term is defined in section 101?

Sections 727(b), 1141(d), and 1328 discharge the debtor from "debts." Remember that section 101 defines "debt" in terms of a "claim" and that section

101's definition of "claim" is very broad. Virtually all of a debtor's obligations will come within the term "debt."

(2) If so, when did the obligation become a debt?

Subject to limited exceptions, a Chapter 7 discharge reaches only "debts that arose before the date of the order for relief," section 727(b). A Chapter 11 discharge covers debts that "arose before the date of such confirmation," section 1141(d)(1)(A). A Chapter 13 discharge reaches debts "provided for by the plan," section 1328(a), (c). This includes prepetition debts and postpetition debts that come under section 1305.

(3) Is section 523 applicable?

Section 523 excepts certain debts from the operation of a discharge. Section 523 applies in all Chapter 7 cases, in all Chapter 11 cases involving individual debtors (including Subchapter V cases involving individual debtors), and in Chapter 13 cases in which the debtor receives a section 1328(b) "hardship discharge," section 727(b), 1141(d)(2), and 1328(c).

The next several pages cover section 523 and point out the extent to which Chapters 7, 11, and 13 differ with respect to debts affected by a discharge.

1. CHAPTER 7

In a Chapter 7 case, a discharge relieves a debtor from personal liability for debts that are both

(1) incurred prior to the time of the order for relief; and

(2) not within one of the exceptions to discharge set out in section 523.

It is very important to understand the difference between section 727(a) objections to discharge and section 523(a) exceptions to discharge. If an objection to discharge has been established, all creditors may attempt to collect the unpaid balance of their claims from the debtor. If a creditor establishes an exception to discharge, only that creditor may attempt to collect the unpaid portion of its claim from the debtor; all other prepetition claims remain discharged.

In other words, proof of an objection to discharge benefits all creditors while proof of an exception to discharge benefits only the creditor that establishes the exception.

Section 523(a) sets out nineteen exceptions to discharge. Some exceptions are based on the nature of the debt. Other exceptions are based on the conduct of the debtor in connection with the debt.

Bankruptcy affords very little relief to the delinquent taxpayer. Most taxes are not discharged in bankruptcy. Section 523(a)(1) excepts from the bankruptcy discharge all income and excise taxes for the three tax years immediately preceding bankruptcy.[6] And, taxes more than three years old

---

[6] Taxes that are entitled to a priority are excepted from discharge, section 523(a)(1)(A). Section 507(a) provides a priority for taxes for "a taxable year ending on or before the date of the filing of the petition for which a return, if required, is last due,

are nondischargeable if (a) a return was not filed, or (b) a return was filed within two years of the filing of the bankruptcy petition, or (c) a "fraudulent return" was filed.

Section 523(a)(1) needs to be read together with section 523(a)(14). A debt incurred to pay state or local taxes that would have been nondischargeable is itself nondischargeable. If, for example, *D* uses their American Express card to pay such a state or local tax bill, that portion of *D*'s American Express bill would be excepted from discharge under section 523(a)(14).

Section 523(a)(2), dealing with fraudulently incurred obligations, is the most frequently invoked exception to discharge. Section 523(a)(2)(A) and section 523(a)(2)(B) describe two different fact patterns.

Section 523(a)(2)(B) deals specifically with the fact pattern that includes the debtor's providing the creditor with a written false financial statement. Section 523(a)(2)(A) applies if the creditor alleges "false pretenses, a false representation, or actual fraud, other than a statement respecting the debtor's or an insider's financial condition."[7]

---

including extensions, after three years before the date of the filing of the petition."

[7] A close comparison of the language of section 523(a)(2)(A) with that of section 523(a)(2)(B) raises the question of whether a debtor's *oral* false representations about their financial condition falls between the two provisions.

It is easier to understand section 523(a)(2) by starting with section 523(a)(2)(B). A creditor faces difficult problems of proof under section 523(a)(2)(B). A creditor seeking an exception to discharge based on the debtor's providing false or incomplete financial information must establish:

(1) a materially false written statement respecting the financial condition of the debtor or an "insider";

(2) its reasonable reliance on the statement; and

(3) the debtor's intent to deceive.

Merely establishing the falsity of a written statement involving the debtor's financial condition will not suffice. The creditor will also have to establish its reliance, the reasonableness of the reliance, and, most difficult of all, the debtor's intent to deceive.

A close comparison of the language of section 523(a)(2)(B) with the language of section 523(a)(2)(A) raises the more important question of whether the reasonable reliance and intent to deceive requirements that are expressed in section 523(a)(2)(B) should be implied under section 523(a)(2)(A). Courts, including the Supreme Court in Field v. Mans, 516 U.S. 59 (1995), have held that section 523(a)(2)(A) does require proof of both the debtor's intent to deceive and the creditor's reasonable reliance.

Section 523(a)(2)(A) needs to be read together not only with section 523(a)(2)(B) but also together with section 523(a)(2)(C) which deals with luxury goods and services and cash advances. More specifically, consumer debts incurred for luxury goods and services owed to a single creditor in excess of $675[8] incurred within 90 days of the bankruptcy filing are "presumed nondischargeable." Similarly, obligations to pay cash advances of $950[9] obtained within 70 days of the bankruptcy filing are "presumed to be nondischargeable."

Note section 523(a)(2)(C)'s use of the phrase "presumed to be nondischargeable." How can this presumption be rebutted? Section 523(a)(2)(C) begins with the phrase "for purposes of subparagraph (A) of this subsection." Section 523(a)(2)(A) deals with false representations. When a person buys something on credit, he impliedly represents (1) an ability to pay and (2) an intent to repay. Section 523(a)(2)(C) seems to presume that with respect to the described luxury purchases and cash advances the debtor lacks that ability and/or intent. Accordingly, it would seem that the debtor can avoid section 523(a)(2)(C)'s exception from discharge by showing that he had both the ability and the intent to repay at the time of the transaction.

It is necessary to read section 523(a)(2) together with section 523(c) and section 523(d). Under section 523(c), discussed below, an exception to discharge based on section 523(a)(2) must be timely asserted during the bankruptcy case and adjudicated by the

---

[8] This amount is inflation indexed pursuant to section 104.

[9] Id.

bankruptcy judge. See Bankruptcy Rule 4007. Under section 523(d), a creditor who unsuccessfully asserts a section 523(a)(2) exception to the discharge of a consumer debt may be required to pay the debtor's costs including an attorney's fee. Section 523(d)'s test is whether the creditor was "not substantially justified." Even if the position of the creditor was "not substantially justified," it can avoid section 523(d) liability if "special circumstances would make the award unjust."

Unscheduled debts are excepted from discharge by section 523(a)(3). A creditor needs to know that its debtor is involved in a bankruptcy case. Only a creditor that timely files a proof of claim shares in the distribution of the "property of the estate."

How does a creditor learn that its debtor is in bankruptcy? Section 521 requires the debtor to file a schedule of liabilities, and the bankruptcy court sends a notice to each creditor on the list. A creditor whose debt was not scheduled will not receive any notice; a creditor that does not receive the notice will not file a proof of claim unless it knows of the bankruptcy case; a creditor that does not file a proof of claim will not be paid from the property of the estate. Accordingly, section 523(a)(3) excepts from discharge a debt not timely scheduled unless the creditor had notice or actual knowledge of the bankruptcy case.

Section 523(a)(4) excepts from bankruptcy discharge liabilities from "fraud or defalcation while acting in a fiduciary capacity." Proof of "fraud or defalcation" is not enough to establish the exception;

section 523(a)(4) requires proof that it occurred while the debtor was a fiduciary. Section 523(a)(4) also makes nondischargeable all embezzlement and larceny liabilities, whether the debtor is a fiduciary or not.

Section 523(a)(5) makes "domestic support obligations" dischargeable. Section 523(a)(5) needs to be read together with section 101 that defines domestic support obligations and section 523(a)(15) which excepts nonsupport obligations owed to a spouse, former spouse or child as a result of divorce or separation.

[It can be important to understand the differences between what comes within the section 523(a)(5) exception and what comes within the section 523(a)(15) exception. Section 523(a)(5)-type obligations but not section 523(a)(15)-type obligations are afforded a first priority under section 507. Similarly, sections 362(b)(2) and 522(f)(1) and section 547(c)(7) apply only to section 523(a)(5) obligations.]

Section 523(a)(6) excepts from the operation of the bankruptcy discharge any debt arising from the debtor's "willful and malicious" injury of person or property. There had been considerable confusion as to the meaning of the limiting phrase "willful and malicious."

In Kawaauhau v. Geiger, 523 U.S. 57 (1998), the Supreme Court limited that confusion; it held that a malpractice claim based on a doctor's choice of a less than optimal course of treatment in order to keep costs down was *not* excepted from discharge under section 523(a)(6). The Court reasoned that "willful" modifies "injury" so that section 523(a)(6) requires proof of the debtor's intent to injure, not just proof that the debtor did an act intentionally which caused injury. Now there is confusion over how to pronounce and spell "Kawaauhau."

Section 523(a)(6) needs to be read together with section 523(a)(9) and section 523(c). Personal injury and wrongful death claims based on a debtor's drunk driving are the subject of a separate exception from discharge, section 523(a)(9), which does not require proof of willfulness or maliciousness. Under section 523(c), discussed below, an exception to discharge based on section 523(a)(6), but not an exception to discharge based on section 523(a)(9), must be timely asserted during the bankruptcy case and adjudicated by the bankruptcy judge. See Bankruptcy Rule 4007.

And, section 523(a)(7) needs to be read together with section 726(a)(4). Under section 523(a)(7), fines, penalties, or forfeitures that the debtor owes to a governmental entity are nondischargeable unless the debt is compensation for an actual pecuniary loss or a tax penalty on a dischargeable tax, section 523(a)(7). Claims for fines, penalties and forfeitures have a very low priority in bankruptcy, section 726(a)(4).

Section 523(a)(8) excepts from discharge student loans and other obligations to repay "educational benefits." unless the debtor is able to show "undue hardship." In determining whether there is "undue hardship," most courts apply the *Brunner*[10] test which requires the debtor to show (i) inability to maintain a minimal standard of living at their current income level and (ii) likelihood that this will persist and (iii) good faith efforts to repay. And, in applying the *Brunner* test, most courts conclude no "undue hardship."

Exceptions to discharge based on section 523(a)(10)–(13) and (16)–(19) rarely arise in a bankruptcy case and never arise in a bankruptcy class.

2. CHAPTER 11

In two significant respects, the answer to the question which debts are affected by a discharge is different in Chapter 11 than in Chapter 7.

First, recall that generally a Chapter 7 discharge is limited to debts that arose before the date of the order for relief, section 727(b). A Chapter 11 discharge reaches debts that arose before the date of confirmation of the plan.

Second, every Chapter 7 discharge is subject to the exceptions to discharge of section 523. In Chapter 11, section 523 only applies if the debtor is an individual, section 1141(d)(2). Section 523 does not apply if the Chapter 11 debtor is a corporation or a partnership or a limited liability company.

---

[10] Brunner v. N.Y. State Higher Educ. Servs. Corp. 831 F.2d 395 (2d Cir. 1987).

3. CHAPTER 13

In Chapter 13 cases, the answer to the question which debts are covered by the discharge depends on the nature of the Chapter 13 discharge. Recall that section 1328(a) governs the discharge of the Chapter 13 debtor who has made all plan payments, and section 1328(b) permits a hardship discharge even though the debtor was not able to complete plan payments.

A section 1328(b) discharge is less comprehensive than a section 1328(a) discharge. If a debtor receives a discharge under section 1328(b), all of the exceptions to discharge in section 523 apply, section 1328(c). A section 1328(b) discharge then is no more comprehensive than a section 727 discharge.

A section 1328(a) discharge is more comprehensive than a section 1328(b) discharge. Some debts that would be excepted from discharge in a Chapter 7 case are still dischargeable under section 1328(a):

(1) section 523(a)(6) debts for willful and malicious injury to ***property***;[11]

(2) section 523(a)(14) debts incurred to pay nondischargeable tax obligations; and

(3) section 523(a)(15) divorce or separation property settlement obligations.

---

[11] Compare the language of 523(a)(6): "willful AND malicious . . . to another entity or the property of another entity" with the language of section 1328(a)(5) "willful OR malicious . . . that caused personal injury."

4. PROCEDURE FOR ASSERTING AN EXCEPTION TO DISCHARGE

Most exceptions to discharge can be asserted after the bankruptcy case is over, in litigation in courts other than the bankruptcy court. Only exceptions to discharge based on section 523(a)(2), (4) or (6) must be asserted during the bankruptcy case in the bankruptcy court. If and only if the creditor's exception to discharge is based on one of these three statutory exceptions, the creditor must timely file a motion in the bankruptcy court. When a creditor is relying on any other part of section 523(a), there is no requirement that the exception to discharge be asserted in the bankruptcy court during the bankruptcy case.

If no dischargeability complaint is filed with the bankruptcy court, the dischargeability issue may arise in connection with the creditor's collection efforts in a nonbankruptcy forum. For example, *D* owes *C* $1,000. *D* files a bankruptcy petition. *D* fails to list their debt to *C* on their schedule of liabilities. *D* receives a bankruptcy discharge. Six months later, *C* sues *D* in state court for the $1,000. If *D* asserts their bankruptcy discharge as a defense, *C* can counter by asserting a section 523(a)(3) exception to discharge.

C. EFFECT OF A DISCHARGE

1. WHAT A DISCHARGE DOES

A discharge protects the debtor from any further personal liability on discharged debts. Section 524(a) provides that a discharge voids a judgment on discharged debts and enjoins any legal "action" to collect such a debt from the debtor or property of the debtor. A discharge also bars extrajudicial collection "acts" such as dunning letters or telephone calls to collect discharged debts.

2. WHAT A DISCHARGE DOES *NOT* DO

A discharge does not cancel or extinguish debts. It only protects the debtors from further personal liability on the debt.

a. No Protection of Co-Debtors

Section 524(e) limits the protection of the discharge to the debtor. A bankruptcy discharge does not automatically affect the liability of other parties such as co-debtors or guarantors. For example, the discharge of an insured tortfeasor does not affect the liability of the insurance company.

b. No Effect on Liens

A bankruptcy discharge has no effect on a lien. Remember, a discharge only eliminates a creditor's right to collect a debt from the debtor personally. A discharge does not eliminate the debt; a discharge does not eliminate liens securing payment of the debt.

To illustrate, *D* owes *C* $20,000. The debt is secured in part by *D*'s car which is worth $16,000. D files for relief under Chapter 7. The trustee abandons the car to the debtor under section 554. *D* receives a discharge. The discharge does not extinguish *C*'s security interest. If *D* is in default, *C* can repossess the car. The discharge does, however, wipe out *C*'s rights against *D* personally. If *C* repossesses and resells the car, *C* cannot obtain a deficiency judgment against *D*.

3. REAFFIRMATION

Law students and lawyers need to be able to answer three questions about reaffirmation agreements: (1) what is a reaffirmation agreement, (2) why would a debtor enter into a reaffirmation agreement and (3) what are the bankruptcy law issues related to reaffirmation agreements?

First, a reaffirmation agreement is an agreement. It can't be done by the debtor alone; it can't be done by a creditor alone. It requires the assent of both the debtor and the creditor.

More specifically, a reaffirmation agreement is an agreement between a debtor and one of their creditors that the debtor will pay a debt they incurred before their bankruptcy filing that, but for the reaffirmation agreement, would have been dischargeable in the bankruptcy case. A reaffirmation agreement is legally enforceable even though there is no bargained-for exchange, i.e., no consideration.

Why would a debtor make such an agreement? The most common reason for a debtor's reaffirming a debt is to keep encumbered property. Assume, for example, that *D* owes GMAC $20,000 on their car loan at the time of their bankruptcy filing. *D*'s bankruptcy discharge will affect GMAC's contract rights against *D*—will eliminate GMAC's ability to collect the $16,000 from *D* personally. The bankruptcy discharge will not, however, affect GMAC's property interest in the car—will not eliminate GMAC's ability to foreclose on its lien and take the car. Accordingly, *D* might enter into a reaffirmation agreement with GMAC to keep their car.

A second common reason for reaffirmation is to protect co-debtors. What if *M*, *D*'s momma, *guaranteed* the car note? Neither the automatic stay in *D*'s Chapter 7 bankruptcy case nor any discharge that *D* might receive protects *M*. Accordingly, *D* might enter into a reaffirmation agreement with GMAC to keep GMAC from taking action against *M*.

Yet another common reason for reaffirmance is concern about dischargeability litigation. If, for example, *D* submitted a false financial statement to GMAC to get the car loan, *D* might enter into a reaffirmation agreement with GMAC to keep GMAC from filing a complaint under section 523(a)(2).

And, debtors might reaffirm a debt to preserve a relationship with that creditor. At the time of his bankruptcy filing, *D* owed D's proctologist *P* $1000. If *D* needs to be examined by *P* again, *D* might decide to reaffirm that debt.

Most of the bankruptcy law issues relating to reaffirmation relate to concern that a creditor might pressure a debtor into reaffirming its debt. Can a creditor ever contact a debtor about reaffirming its debt without violating section 362(a)(6)? Isn't that contact "an act to collect a claim"?

Section 362(b) does not expressly except reaffirmation efforts from the operation of the automatic stay. Yet, as the Sixth Circuit noted in its decision in In re Duke (1996): "The option of reaffirming would be empty if creditors were forbidden to engage in any communication whatsoever with debtors who have prepetition obligations." Case law has in essence created something of an exception to the automatic stay for some reaffirmation initiatives.

While the Bankruptcy Code has no provision as to what actions a creditor can take to obtain a reaffirmation agreement, section 524 has detailed provisions regarding the reaffirmation agreement.

Section 524(c) and (d) limit the enforceability of reaffirmation agreements by

(1) requiring that the agreement be executed before the discharge is granted, section 524(c)(1);

(2) giving the debtor a right to rescind, section 524(c)(4);

(3) requiring that, before any reaffirmation is signed, the creditor provided the debtor with disclosures detailed in section 524(k);

(4) requiring the agreement be filed with the court, section 524(c)(3);

(5) requiring a hearing if the debtor is an individual and not represented by an attorney in the reaffirmation negotiations, section 524(d), section 524(c)(6);

(6) requiring the attorney who represented the debtor in the reaffirmation to certify inter alia that the debtor was fully informed and that either the agreement does not impose an undue hardship or the debtor has the ability to make the reaffirmation payments, section 524(k)(5).

4. PROTECTION FROM DISCRIMINATORY TREATMENT

Section 525 is entitled "Protection From Discriminatory Treatment." The title promises more than the section actually provides.

The Boy Scouts could refuse to let someone serve as a scoutmaster because they filed for bankruptcy, More importantly[12], a store could refuse to extend credit or a bank could refuse to make a loan because of a person's bankruptcy history.

Notice that two of the three lettered subsections, 525(a) and 525(c), only apply to "governmental units." And, notice that two of the three subsections, 525(a) and 525(b), require proof that the adverse

12 Unless you were an Eagle Scout and have spent every summer since you completed the 8th grade at Philmont Scout Ranch.

action occurred "solely" because of the bankruptcy history.

More specifically, subject to very limited exceptions, a governmental unit may not deny a debtor a license or a franchise or otherwise discriminate against a debtor "*solely because*" the debtor (i) filed for bankruptcy, (ii) was insolvent prior to and/or during bankruptcy or (iii) refuses to pay debts *discharged* by his, her or its bankruptcy, section 525(a).

Similarly, a private employer cannot fire an employee or "discriminate with respect to employment" "*solely because*" (i) the employee filed for bankruptcy, (ii) was insolvent prior to or during the bankruptcy or (iii) refuses to pay debts *discharged* by his or her bankruptcy, section 525(b).

Section 525(c) prohibits a government unit operating a student loan program and any private lender making loans guaranteed under a student loan program from denying a loan because a person (i) filed for bankruptcy, (ii) was insolvent prior to or during the bankruptcy or (iii) refuses to pay debts discharged by his or her bankruptcy.[13]

---

[13] Section 525(c), unlike section 525(a) and (b) has a "because" and not a "solely because" standard.

CHAPTER XIV

CHAPTER 13

A. COMMENCEMENT OF THE CASE

Chapter 13 of the Bankruptcy Code replaced Chapter XIII of the Bankruptcy Act of 1898. Chapter XIII was limited to a "wage earner," i.e., "an individual whose principal income is derived from wages, salary, or commissions."

Chapter 13 is open to more debtors. Subject to limited exceptions,[1] the source of income is not an eligibility test. A debtor may file for Chapter 13 relief if the debtor

(1) *is an individual, and*

[Chapter 13 is not available to corporations or other business entities.]

(2) has a "regular income," and

[The phrase "individual with a regular income" is statutorily defined in section 101(30) as "an individual whose income is sufficiently stable and regular to enable such individual to make payments under a plan under Chapter 13 of this title."]

---

1 Neither a stockbroker nor a commodity broker may file a petition under Chapter 13, section 109(e).

(3) has noncontingent, liquidated unsecured debts of less than $419,725 and noncontingent, liquidated secured debts of less than $1,257, 850, section 109(e)[2].

[Note that the debt limitation only includes "fixed" debts. For example, Jimmy McGill is sued for $25,000,000 for malpractice on April 4. He could still file a Chapter 13 petition on April 5 The $25,000,000 unsecured claim is unliquidated and so does not affect Chapter 13 eligibility.]

While the means testing requirements of section 707 can and will prevent some individuals from filing for Chapter 7 relief, there is nothing in section 707 or section 109 or anywhere else in the Code that expressly requires anyone to file a Chapter 13 petition. Failing the means test simply means that an individual cannot use Chapter 7; it does not mean that they must use Chapter 13.

Obviously, failing the section 707 means test will mean that some debtors will file for Chapter 13 relief because they feel that they have no meaningful alternative: no protection from creditors under state law, no possibility of filing for Chapter 7 protection.

B. CO-DEBTOR STAY

An advantage of Chapter 13 over Chapter 7 is the co-debtor stay which is available only in Chapter 13 cases. Section 1301 restrains a creditor from attempting to collect a debt from the co-debtor of a Chapter 13 debtor.

---

2 The amounts are inflation indexed under section 104.

The following hypothetical illustrates the application of section 1301's co-debtor stay: *D* borrows money from *C* to buy a pair of contact lenses. *D*'s mother, *M*, signs the note as a co-maker. *D* later incurs financial problems and files a Chapter 13 petition. Section 362 stays *C* from attempting to collect from *D*; section 1301 stays *C* from attempting to collect from *M*.

Section 1301's stay of collection activities directed at co-debtors is applicable only if

(1) the debt is a consumer debt; and

(2) the co-debtor is not in the credit business.

This co-debtor stay automatically terminates when the case is closed, dismissed, or converted to Chapter 7 or 11.

Section 1301(c) sets out three grounds for relief from the co-debtor stay. Section 1301(c) requires notice and hearing and requires the court to grant relief if any of the three grounds are established.

First, the stay on collection from the co-debtor will be lifted if the co-debtor, not the Chapter 13 debtor, received the consideration for the claim, section 1301(c)(1). For example, if in the above hypothetical, *M*, not *D*, filed for Chapter 13 relief, *C* could petition for relief under section 1301(c)(1) so that it could attempt to collect from *D*. Section 1301(c)(1) also covers the situation in which the Chapter 13 debtor is merely an accommodation endorser.

Second, when the Chapter 13 plan has been filed, a creditor may obtain relief from the co-debtor stay to the extent that "the plan filed by the debtor proposes not to pay such claim," section 1301(c)(2). Assume, for example, that *D* still owes *C* $200. *D*'s Chapter 13 plan proposes to pay each holder of an unsecured claim 70¢ on the dollar. *C* will thus be paid $140 under the plan. As soon as such a plan is filed, *C* can obtain relief from the stay so that it can obtain $60 from *M*, the other 30¢ on the dollar. A motion to lift the stay under section 1301(c)(2) is deemed granted unless the debtor or co-debtor files a written objection within 20 days, section 1301(d).

Third, section 1301(c)(3) requires the court to grant relief from the co-debtor stay to the extent that "such creditor's interest would be irreparably harmed by continuation of such stay." The running of a state statute of limitations is not a basis for relief under section 1301(c)(3). Section 108(c) guarantees the creditor at least 30 days after the termination of the stay to file a state collection action against the co-debtor.

C. TRUSTEES

There will be a trustee appointed in every Chapter 13 case, section 1302(a). In almost all districts, the United States trustee appoint a standing trustee who serves as trustee in every Chapter 13 case, section 1302(d).

Being a Chapter 13 standing trustee is a full-time job, but it is not a government job. The Chapter 13 trustee is not a government employee. Rather, the Chapter 13 trustee operates a private business. The Chapter 13 trustee does not receive a salary from the government. Rather, they receives a percentage of the funds disbursed to creditors under the Chapter 13 plans in their district.

The trustee in a Chapter 13 case is an active trustee. Section 1302 imposes a number of duties on a trustee in a Chapter 13 case.

Section 1302 does not clearly indicate whether a Chapter 13 trustee can assert the avoidance provisions. The statutory arguments for a Chapter 13 trustee being able to avoid preferences and other prebankruptcy transfers are

(1) section 103 which indicates that provisions in chapter 5 such as section 547 are applicable in Chapters 7, 11, and 13;

(2) use of the word "trustee" in section 547 and the other avoidance provisions.

The statutory argument for a Chapter 13 trustee *not* being able to avoid preferences and other prebankruptcy transfers focuses on section 1302(b)'s exclusion of section 704(1). If a Chapter 13 trustee is not empowered to "collect the property of the estate," she should not be able to avoid prebankruptcy transfers.

Operation of the debtor's business is *not* one of the duties there enumerated. If a debtor engaged in business files a Chapter 13 petition, section 1304(b) contemplates that the business will be operated by the debtor, not by the trustee, "unless the court orders otherwise."

While a Chapter 13 trustee's duties are listed in section 1302, the exact role of a Chapter 13 trustee varies from district to district. And, while a Chapter 13 trustee does not collect property of the estate or bring avoidance actions or operate businesses, most Chapter 13 trustees play the leading role in most Chapter 13 cases.

Think about Chapter 13 in terms of amounts. First, the dollar amount of most claims. The amount owed by most Chapter 13 debtors to most of their creditors is too low for creditors to hire attorneys to represent them in the Chapter 13 case. Second, the amount of cases. The amount of cases handled by the typical bankruptcy judge is too high for the judge to be able to spend significant time on Chapter 13 cases.

Accordingly, creditors and the bankruptcy judges generally rely on the Chapter 13 trustee to (i) review the debtor's Chapter 13 plan, (ii) raise plan issues, if any, with the debtor's attorney and (iii) resolve those plan issues with the debtor's attorney. Most Chapter 13 plans are presented to the judge without any objection. And, to the extent that there is a plan confirmation objection, the objection is generally raised by the Chapter 13 trustee. After the plan is confirmed by the court, it is the Chapter 13 trustee's office that distributes the plan payments.

D. PREPARATION OF THE CHAPTER 13 PLAN

Only a debtor may file a Chapter 13 plan, section 1321. The court may dismiss a Chapter 13 case or convert it to Chapter 7 for "failure to file a plan *timely* under section 1321 of this title," section 1307(c)(3).

The Code leaves the question of the meaning of "timely"—how many days the debtor has to file such a plan—to the Rules. It's within 15 days after filing the petition, Bankruptcy Rule 3015.

The two most important plan preparation questions are (1) how much does the debtor have to pay under the plan and (2) how much do the various creditors get paid under the plan? To answer these questions, look primarily to sections 1322 and 1325.

Section 1322 governs the contents of a Chapter 13 plan. Section 1325 sets out the requirements for confirmation (court approval) of a plan. Since confirmation is a Chapter 13 debtor's objective, the debtor's attorney will want to look to both section 1322 and section 1325 in formulating the plan.

In looking at section 1325(b)(1)(B), you will see that the amount of a debtor's monthly plan payments depends on their "disposable income." In looking at section 1325(b)(2), section 1325(b)(4) and section 1322(d), you will see that the number of a debtor's monthly payments depends upon a debtor's "current monthly income" and "median family income." Generally, a debtor whose "current monthly income" multiplied by 12 is less than the "median family income" for the state for a family of the same size will make plan payments for three years, and a debtor whose "current monthly income" multiplied by 12 is more than the "median family income" for the state for a family of the same size will make plan payments for five years.

Looking more closely first at section 1322, notice that subsection (a) of section 1322 specifies what the plan must provide; subsection (b) specifies what the plan may provide. Generally, a Chapter 13 plan must provide for the full payment in cash of all claims entitled to priority under section 507 unless the holder of the claim otherwise agrees, section 1322(a)(2). There is a limited exception for assigned domestic support obligations, section 1322(a)(4).

A Chapter 13 plan may provide for less than full payment to other unsecured claims. It may not, however, arbitrarily pay some holders of unsecured claims less than others. Rather, the plan must either treat all unsecured claims the same or classify claims and provide for the same treatment of each unsecured claim within a particular class, sections 1322(a)(3), 1322(b)(4).

Section 1322(b)(2) indicates that a Chapter 13 plan can also modify the rights of most holders of secured claims.[3] The plan may modify the rights of creditor *A* who has a security interest on the Chapter 13 debtor's consumer goods, equipment, and inventory. The plan may modify the rights of Creditor *B* who has a mortgage on the Chapter 13 debtor's store.

[3] Section 1322(a)(2) needs to be read together with the 2005 amendments to section 1325(a)(5) which in essence modify or limit the extent to which a Chapter 13 plan can modify the rights of holders of most automobile secured claims. We will read about section 1325(a)(5) elimination of most Chapter 13 "strip downs" of car loans.

A Chapter 13 plan may not, however, modify the rights of Creditor *C* who has a mortgage *only*[4] on the Chapter 13 debtor's principal residence, section 1322(b)(2). If, for example, before bankruptcy, *D*'s home mortgage provided for a principal balance of $100,000, interest at 10% and monthly payments of $625, the debtor has exactly the same home mortgage obligation in Chapter 13. No plan modification of mortgages on the debtor's principal residence.

While a Chapter 13 plan cannot modify a claim secured only by the debtor's principal residence, it can cure defaults with respect to such a claim, section 1322(a)(3), (5). If, for example, *D* missed four home mortgage payments of $625 each before filing for Chapter 13 relief, *D*'s Chapter 13 plan can provide for periodic payments over the duration of the plan to "cure" that $2,500 default. We will do more examples of curing defaults on secured claims and do examples of modifying secured claims when we do more with confirmation of Chapter 13 plan provisions relating to claims secured by houses and other secured claims later in this chapter.

In the typical Chapter 13 case, the source of the payments proposed by the plan will be the debtor's wages. This is not, however, a statutory requirement. Payments under the plan may also be funded by other income such as social security benefits or even the sale of property of the estate, section 1322(b)(8). Section 1322(a)(1) only requires that the plan provide

---

4 Note the word "only" in section 1322(b)(2). If *C* loaned *D* $100,000 and obtained a mortgage on both *D*'s residence and *D*'s store, the plan could modify *D*'s rights.

for submission of "such portion of future earnings . . . of the debtor to the supervision and control of the trustee as is necessary for the execution of the plan." Section 1322(a)(1) needs to be read together with section 1325(b) which makes the commitment of disposable income necessary for the confirmation of the plan.

Again, in formulating a Chapter 13 plan or dealing with a law school exam question on a Chapter 13 plan, look not only at section 1322 which deals with the contents of the plan but also at section 1325 which covers confirmation of a plan. Section 1325 is covered below.

E. CONFIRMATION OF THE CHAPTER 13 PLAN

In Chapter 13, creditors do not vote on the plan. Chapter 13 requires only court approval. The standards for judicial confirmation of a Chapter 13 plan are set out in section 1325.

Section 1325(a)(1) requires that the plan satisfy the provisions of Chapter 13 and other applicable bankruptcy law requirements. Section 1325(a)(2) conditions confirmation on payment of the filing fee. Section 1325(a)(3) sets out a "good faith" standard.

Dicta in appellate court cases on section 1325(a)(3) (good faith) tend to list numerous factors. Holdings in bankruptcy court cases on section 1325(a)(3) tend to focus on the debtor's financial condition and the amount of payments proposed by the plan. Section

1325(a)(4) and section 1325(b) more directly address the adequacy of the plan payments.

Section 1325(a)(4) protects the holders of unsecured claims by imposing a "best interests of creditors" test: the present value of the proposed payments to a holder of an unsecured claim must be at least equal to the amount that the creditor would have received in a Chapter 7 liquidation. The following hypothetical illustrates the practical significance of the "present value" language in section 1325(a)(4). Assume the following four facts:

(1) *D* owes *C* $1,000;

(2) *D* files a Chapter 13 petition;

(3) If *D* had filed a Chapter 7 petition, the sale of the property of the estate would have yielded a sufficient sum to pay all priority creditors in full and pay unsecured creditors like *C* 36¢ on the dollar so that *C* will receive $360 in cash at the close of the Chapter 7 case;

(4) *D*'s Chapter 13 petition proposes to pay *C* $10 a month for 36 months.

This plan does not satisfy the requirement of section 1325(a)(4). Payment of $360 over a 36-month period does not have a "present value" of $360.

This hypothetical is probably somewhat unrealistic. In the typical Chapter 7 case, an unsecured creditor would receive little if anything. Accordingly, in the typical Chapter 13 case, section 1325(a)(4) will be easily satisfied.

Section 1325(a)(3) and (4) needs to be read together with section 1325(b). Section 1325(b) imposes a "best efforts" kind of requirement. More specifically, section 1325(b) requires either that the plan pay unsecured claims in full with interest or commit all of the debtor's "disposable income" to such payments for the "applicable commitment period" as defined in section 1325(b)(4).

Section 1325(b)(2) also defines "disposable income" as "current monthly income," other than child support income, that is not necessary to provide support for the debtor or the debtor's dependents. If (and only if) the Chapter 13 debtor's income is greater than the applicable "median family income," then it is necessary to read section 1325(b)(2) together with section 1325(b)(3) and necessary to limit the debtor's support needs by the Internal Revenue Service expense standards referenced in section 707(b)(2)(A)(ii)(I).

Section 1325(a)(5) protects the holders of secured claims "provided for by the plan" by requiring one of the following:

(1) Acceptance of the plan by such a creditor; or

(2) Continuation of the lien and proposed payments to such a creditor of a present value that at least equals the value of the collateral; [this "cram down" provision will be considered in Part F of this chapter]

(3) Surrender of the collateral to the creditor.

Section 1325(a)(6) requires a determination of ability to perform; it requires that the debtor "will be able to make all payments under the plan and to comply with the plan."

A confirmed Chapter 13 plan is binding on the debtor and all of his creditors, section 1327(a). Unless the plan or the order confirming the plan otherwise provides, confirmation of a plan vests all of the "property of the estate" in the debtor free and clear of "any claim or interest of any creditor provided for by the plan," section 1327(c).

After confirmation, the plan is put into effect with the debtor generally making the payments provided in the plan to a Chapter 13 trustee who acts as a disbursing agent.

A Chapter 13 plan can be modified after confirmation. Section 1329 expressly provides for post-confirmation modification on request of the debtor, the trustee, or the holder of an unsecured claim.

F. CRAMDOWN (OR CRAM DOWN) OF SECURED CLAIMS IN CHAPTER 13

A Chapter 13 plan can propose modifications of a secured claim to which the holder of the claim consents. For example, the creditor might agree to wait longer for payment if the payment is increased. If the modification is acceptable to the holder of the secured claim, it will be acceptable to the court, section 1325(a)(5)(A). No secured claim plan confirmation issue.

Alternatively, a Chapter 13 plan can propose to surrender the encumbered property to the holder of a secured claim. Assume, for example, that *D* owes *S* $200,000, secured by a first mortgage on Redacre. If *D*'s Chapter 13 plan surrenders Redacre to *S*, then *S* no longer has a secured claim. If Redacre's value is less than $200,000, then after S obtains Redacre. *S* might still have a claim. Just not a secured claim. Accordingly, a plan that "surrenders the property securing such claim" will be acceptable to the court, section 1325(a)(5)(C). Again, no secured claim plan confirmation issue.

Secured claim plan confirmation issues arise only if the plan proposes that (i) the debtor retain the encumbered property and (ii) the secured claim be modified and (iii) the holder of the secured claim does not agree. These issues are called cram down issues (or cramdown issues).

It's not the Bankruptcy Code that uses the phrase "cram down." Neither "cram down" (nor "cramdown") appears anywhere in the Bankruptcy Code. Rather it is the bankruptcy lawyers, judges and law professors who have come to use the term cram down to describe court approval of a plan provision that effects changes in the payment of a claim without claim holder approval.

In order to cram down a Chapter 13 modification of a secured claim, the bankruptcy court must apply section 1325(a)(5)(B). And, in order to apply section 1325(a)(5)(B), it is necessary to determine the nature of the proposed modification.

One form of cram down is a "strip down," i.e., reducing the amount that was to be paid to the holder of the secured debt to the value of its collateral. In applying section 1325(a)(5)(B) to a "strip down," the bankruptcy court makes the following two determinations:

(1) What is the value of the collateral?[5]

(2) Is the present value of the plan payments at least equal to the value of the collateral?[6]

To illustrate, *D*, an independent trucker, owes *S* $60,000. *S* has a security interest in *D*'s tractor and trailer rig. *D* files a Chapter 13 plan that proposes to pay *S* $1,000 a month for 36 months. *S* does not consent.

In applying section 1325(a)(5)(B) to this proposed strip down, the court would first have to determine the value of the collateral, i.e., the value of the tractor and trailer rig. Looking to *Associates Commercial Corp. v. Rash*, discussed in Chapter X, the court would look to the replacement value of the tractor and trailer rig.

If the replacement value of the tractor and trailer rig was $36,000, then the proposed plan payments must have a present value of $36,000. Obviously, a

---

5 The relevant language in section 1325(a)(5) is "allowed amount of SUCH CLAIM." The antecedent of "such claim" is "secured claim." Section 506 ties the amount of the secured claim to the value of the collateral.

6 The relevant language in section 1325(a)(5) is "value, as of the effective date of the plan, of property to be distributed under the plan . . . ."

Chapter 13 debtor's promise to pay $1,000 a month for 36 months has a present value significantly less than $36,000. The debtor would also have to pay cram down interest as measured by the "formula approach" of *Till v. SCS Credit Corp.*, discussed in Chapter X.

No strip down is allowed on a purchase money loan incurred within 910 days before the bankruptcy filing if it is secured by a motor vehicle acquired by the debtor for her personal use. Thus, a D, Chapter 13 debtor who owes $33,000 on a recently purchased personal car that *D* wants to keep will now have to make payments with a present value of $33,000.

While *D* cannot cram down a change in the principal to be paid, *D* can, consistent with *Till*, cram down a change in the interest rate, and *D* can, consistent with the requirements of section 1325(a)(5)(B)(iii)[7] change the number of payments and the amount of each payment.

Remember that strip down is simply one form of cram down. A cram down is any change in the payment obligation approved by the court over the creditor's objection. The change can be changes in the interest rate, changes in the number of payments, changes in the amount of payments, etc. Or the change can be a change in the amount to be paid, i.e., a strip down.

And, remember a strip down is still possible in a case with the same facts as *Rash*. A strip down of a

---

[7] Section 1325(a)(5)(B)(iii) requires that the payments be monthly and be adequate to provide "adequate protection."

motor vehicle loan is still possible so long as the collateral is not a personal use automobile.

G. TREATMENT OF HOME MORTGAGES IN CHAPTER 13 PLANS

Most home mortgages are protected from strip down or any other form of cram down. Section 1322(b) excepts from cramdown claims "secured only by a security interest in real property that is the debtor's principal residence" from plan modification.[8]

So, if *D* owes $100,000 on their home mortgage to *M* at the time that *D* files for Chapter 13 and her payments are $625 a month and the mortgage interest rate is 10%, *D* cannot use section 1322(b) to change the mortgage payment schedule or interest rate. Nor can *D* use section 1322 to reduce the amount of that secured claim, regardless of the value of the home. If, for example, the value of the home is only $70,000, *D* cannot use a Chapter 13 plan to "strip down" *M*'s secured claim to $70,000. Nobleman v. American Savings Bank, 508 U.S. 324 (1993).

---

[8] Reread the quoted language and identify the three "litigable" (i.e., "law school test-able") issues. First, is the residence the only security for the loan, or did the creditor take a lien on some other collateral such as the debtor? What if the home loan is secured not only by a mortgage on the home but also a lien on the debtor's bank account? By a credit life insurance policy? By fixtures or furniture? Second, is the double-wide mobile home that the debtor lives in "real property"? Third, is a mixed use property such as a combination home/business office protected?

In practice, a judge expects a lawyer to know how they have ruled on each of these questions. In law school, a law professor expects a student to "spot" and raise each of these questions.

Courts have distinguished between a "strip down" and a "strip off." Assume again that *M* has a $100,000 first mortgage on *D*'s $70,000 home. Now also assume that *S* has a $25,000 second mortgage. As noted above, *D* cannot use section 1322(b)(2) to strip down *M*'s secured claim to $70,000. How is *S*'s claim different from *M*'s? Under section 506, the amount of *S*'s secured claim is zero—the value of SUCH creditor's interest (i.e., the second mortgage interest) in the house. If *S* has a "zero" secured claim in *D*'s principal residence, courts reason that *S* gets "zero" protection from strip off from section 1322(b)(2).

In sum, no "strip down," i.e., no reduction of a first or second mortgage where that mortgage has some value but possibly a "strip off," an elimination of a second or third mortgage where the house has a value less than the amount of the mortgage(s) with priority, has no value.

Section 1322(b)(2) general prohibition against Chapter 13 plans making nonconsensual changes to mortgages on the debtor's principal residence is subject to an important statutory exception.

Section 1322(b)(5) permits a Chapter 13 plan to cure defaults on all home mortgages. Assume for example that *D* missed three home mortgage payments of $700 a month before *D* filed a Chapter 13 bankruptcy petition and under the terms of the mortgage D's default in making these three payments triggered an acceleration which made the entire loan balance immediately due. *D* can use their Chapter 13 plan to cure these defaults "within a reasonable time" and maintain the mortgage by continuing to make the usual monthly payments, section 1322(b)(5).

H. CLASSIFICATION OF UNSECURED CLAIMS

A Chapter 13 debtor often wants to make certain that some creditors are paid in full by their Chapter 13 plan. Especially debts guaranteed by a family member or friends and debts excepted from the Chapter 13 discharge.

To get credit, the debtor may have had to get someone more creditworthy—a relative or close friend[9]—to guarantee payment of the obligation. To the extent that the Chapter 13 plan does not pay that obligation, the creditor can and will collect from the co-debtor. Cf. section 1301(c)(2).

And, some debts such as student loans are not covered by a Chapter 13 discharge. The debtor will, of course, want to pay all such nondischargeable debts in full in her Chapter 13 plan; otherwise the debtor will have to pay the balance after completing the Chapter 13 plan payments.

A Chapter 13 debtor can use claim classification to pay one or more of their creditors in full even though they does not have sufficient disposable income to pay all of their creditors in full.[10] Under section

---

[9] There is no requirement that the guarantor be a relative or friend but. . . . How many of your loans have been guaranteed by strangers? How many loans have you guaranteed for strangers?

[10] A Chapter 13 debtor can also use section 1322(b)(5) to make preferential plan payments on long-term debts. Section 1322(b)(5) only applies if the last payment on the debt is due after

1322(b)(1), a Chapter 13 plan can divide unsecured claims into more than one class and treat the various classes differently.

The primary limitation on this discrimination in the plan treatment of unsecured claims is that the classification may not "discriminate unfairly." The key word is, of course, "unfairly": any classification discriminates—what is required is that the discrimination not be unfair.

Most reported opinions under section 1322(b)(1) set out some sort of multi-factor test. The factor that seems most important is the difference in the amount of payment to the various classes. Obviously, it will be easier to get court approval of a plan that pays Class 2 100% and all other classes 90% than a plan that pays Class 2 100% and all other classes 10%.

Put Chapter 13 plan classification in context. All Chapter 13 plans must meet the "best interests" test of section 1325(a)(4) with respect to all classes of unsecured claims. In other words, even the creditors in the class receiving least favorable Chapter 13 plan treatment are still receiving at least as much as they would have received if the debtor had filed for Chapter 7 relief instead of Chapter 13.

---

the last plan payment. With respect to such debts, a Chapter 13 debtor can simply make payments according to the contractual terms. The advantage to this approach is that more of the debt can be paid during the Chapter 13 case. The disadvantage to this approach is that, even if the debt was otherwise dischargeable, the debtor will have to complete the payments under the contract notwithstanding any Chapter 13 discharge. Cf. section 1328(a).

I. DISCHARGE

A Chapter 13 debtor will be denied a discharge because of their bankruptcy history. More specifically, a Chapter 13 debtor will be denied a discharge if they received a discharge in another Chapter 13 case in the two-year period preceding the filing of this Chapter 13 case, section 1328(f)(2). Similarly, a Chapter 13 debtor will be denied a discharge if they received a discharge in a Chapter 7, 11 or 12 case in the four years preceding the filing of this Chapter 13 case, section 1328(f)(1). And, any Chapter 13 discharge will be delayed until the debtor completes an "instructional course concerning personal financial management," sections 111, 1328(g).

Section 1328 contemplates that a Chapter 13 debtor will complete all plan payment obligations and certify that he has paid all postpetition domestic support obligations and then receive a discharge, section 1328(a). A section 1328(a) discharge is subject to most but not all of the exceptions to discharge in section 523. For example, a section 1328(a) discharge, unlike a discharge in a Chapter 7 case, will cover debts for willful and malicious injury to property and debts for divorce or separation property settlements. Cf. section 1328(a)(2), (4).

The bankruptcy court may grant a discharge in a Chapter 13 case even though the debtor has not completed payments called for by the plan. Section 1328(b) empowers the bankruptcy court to grant a "hardship" discharge if:

(1) the debtor's failure to complete the plan was due to circumstances for which she "should not justly be held accountable;" and

(2) the value of the payments made under the plan to each creditor at least equals what that creditor would have received under Chapter 7; and

(3) modification of the plan is not "practicable."

A section 1328(b) "hardship" discharge is not as comprehensive as a section 1328(a) discharge. A "hardship" discharge is limited by all of the section 523(a) exceptions to discharge, section 1328(c)(2).

J. DISMISSAL AND CONVERSION

Most Chapter 13 cases do *not* end in a discharge. Most bankruptcy cases filed as Chapter 13 cases are either dismissed or converted to Chapter 7 cases. A debtor who files a Chapter 13 petition may at any time request the bankruptcy court to dismiss the case or convert it to a case under Chapter 7, section 1307(a), (b).

The bankruptcy court may also dismiss a Chapter 13 case or convert it to a case under Chapter 7 on request of a creditor. The statutory standard for such creditor-requested conversion or dismissal is "for cause." Section 1307(c) sets out eight examples of "cause."

Section 1307(d) gives a bankruptcy court the power to convert from Chapter 13 to Chapter 11 before confirmation of the plan on request of a party in interest and after notice and hearing. There is no statutory standard to guide the court in deciding whether to convert from 13 to 11.

K. COMPARISON OF CHAPTERS 7 AND 13

Remember that in a Chapter 7 case, a debtor's unencumbered nonexempt property as of the time of the bankruptcy petition is sold by the Chapter 7 trustee and the proceeds are distributed to the holders of unsecured claims, What unencumbered nonexempt property do you have? Most individuals do not have much if any unencumbered nonexempt property. For most individuals, the only real costs of Chapter 7 bankruptcy are (i) the filing fee and (ii) their attorney's fee. And most Chapter 7 debtors receive a discharge within a few months of filing for bankruptcy.

Chapter 13 on the other hand puts the debtor on a strict budget and takes their "disposable income" for as long as five years. And, most Chapter 13 debtors do not receive a discharge until they complete their plan payments,

Accordingly, real lawyers will rarely be asked by clients to compare Chapters 7 and 13. For most individuals who pass the means test, Chapter 7 provides more immediate relief at a much lower cost than Chapter 13.

Nonetheless, law students will continue to be asked by law professors to compare Chapters 7 and 13 and so you might want to review the following chart:

		Chapter 7	Chapter 13
1.	**Automatic Stay**	Automatic stay of section 362 protects the debtor from creditors' collection efforts	Automatic stay of section 362 protects the debtor from creditors' collection efforts. Automatic stay of section 1301 protects certain co-debtors
2.	**Loss of Property**	"Property of the estate" as described in section 541 is distributed to creditors	Except as provided in the plan or in the order of confirmation, debtor keeps "property of the estate"
3.	**Availability of Discharge**	Section 727(a) lists grounds for objection to discharge	Section 727 is inapplicable. Discharge depends on completing payments required by the plan, section 1328(a). A "hardship" discharge to a debtor who makes some but not all payments required by the plan, section 1328(b).

		Chapter 7	Chapter 13
4.	**Debts Excepted from Discharge**	Section 523(a) excepts 19 classes of claims from operation of the discharge	A section 1328(a) discharge is subject to most of the important section 523(a) discharge exceptions. A section 1328(b) discharge is subject to all of section 523(a)'s exceptions to discharge
5.	**Effect on Future Chapter 7 Relief**	A debtor who receives a discharge in a Chapter 7 case may not obtain a discharge in another Chapter 7 case for eight years	A Chapter 13 discharge does not affect the availability of discharge in a future Chapter 7 case if the Chapter 13 plan was the debtor's "best effort" and paid 70% of all general claims, section 727(a)(9)
6.	**Whether Debtor's Postpetition Earnings are Property of the Estate**	No, section 541(a)(6) ("earnings from services performed by an individual")	Yes, section 1306

		Chapter 7	Chapter 13
7.	**Debtor's Ability to Terminate the Case**	"Only for cause," section 707	"On request of the debtor at any time," section 1307(b)
8.	**Amount Required to be Distributed to Holders of Claims**	Focus on property of the estate, section 541	Plan controls, confirmation requires that holders of claims receive at least as much as they would in Chapter 7 and that plan commits all focus on disposable income, section 1325(a)(4); 1325(b)

L. COMPARISON OF CHAPTERS 11 AND 13

Any debtor who files a Chapter 13 petition could instead have filed a Chapter 11 petition. We will learn about Chapter 11 and Chapter 11's special provisions for individual debtors in the next chapter.[11] Even if you read this next chapter casually and not carefully, you should see that a debtor who has a choice between Chapters 11 and 13 will almost always choose Chapter 13.[12]

---

[11] And Chapter XVI of this book will explain the special provisions for individual debtors who choose Subchapter V.

[12] Remember that Chapter 13 is not available to all debtors. Corporations and partnerships are not eligible for Chapter 13, and individuals have to meet the debt limits of section 109(e).

CHAPTER XV

CHAPTER 11

Any person can file a Chapter 11 petition, even individuals who do not own a business.

While the use of Chapter 11 is not restricted to business debtors, the typical Chapter 11 case involves a business debtor that is attempting to continue its business operations by restructuring its financial obligations. And, the typical business Chapter 11 case involves disputes among creditors as to the order and the amount of payment and disputes between creditors generally and the stockholders or other owners of the debtor as to how much if anything the owners can retain.

We know that in a Chapter 7 case, property of the estate is sold by the trustees and the net proceeds of the sale are distributed to creditors. In essence, in Chapter 7 cases, creditors' recovery is measured by the liquidation value.

And, we know from the overview in Chapter VI, supra, that Chapter 11 contemplates that a debtor keep its assets, continue its business and pay creditors from future business operations. The premise of Chapter 11 is that the going concern value of a business is greater than its liquidation value. The question in Chapter 11 is, how much of the difference between liquidation value and going concern value goes to creditors.

This question is answered by the debtor's Chapter 11 plan. To get to the answer, we need to learn about the stages of a Chapter 11 case:

A. Commencement of the Case

B. Operation of the Business

C. Preparation of the Plan

D. Creditor Acceptance of the Plan

E. Confirmation of the Plan

Subchapter V of Chapter 11 which became effective in 2020, makes significant changes to most of these stages. Subchapter V will be considered separately in the next chapter of the book.

A. COMMENCEMENT OF THE CASE

1. FILING THE PETITION

A case under Chapter 11 is commenced by the filing of a petition. The petition may be filed by either the debtor or creditors.

Insolvency is not a condition precedent to a voluntary Chapter 11 petition. With two minor exceptions[1], any "person" that is eligible to file a voluntary bankruptcy petition under Chapter 7 is also eligible to file a petition under Chapter 11.

---

[1] The first exception is stockbrokers and commodity brokers: they are eligible for Chapter 7, but not Chapter 11. The second exception is railroads: railroads are eligible for Chapter 11, but not Chapter 7.

If the Chapter 11 petition has been filed by an eligible debtor, no formal adjudication is necessary. The filing of the petition operates as an "order for relief," section 301.

The requirements for an involuntary, i.e., creditor-initiated, Chapter 11 case are the same as the requirements for an involuntary Chapter 7 case, section 303. These requirements are discussed supra in Chapter IV.

2. CONSEQUENCES OF COMMENCING A CHAPTER 11 CASE

As we have already seen, the filing of a Chapter 11 petition, like the filing of a Chapter 7 petition or a Chapter 13 petition, (i) triggers the section 362 automatic stay and section 541 property of the estate and (ii) is the "date of cleavage" for purposes of the avoiding powers and the treatment of claims.

As we will now see, the effects of filing of a Chapter 11 petition are unlike the effects of filing of a Chapter 7 petition or a Chapter 13 petition in that (i) the filing triggers business and legal issues that need to be resolved immediately and (ii) creditors have a statutory role in the resolution of those issues.

3. NOTIFYING AND ORGANIZING THE CREDITORS

How will creditors learn of a Chapter 11 filing? Sections 521 and 342 provide a partial answer.

Section 521 obligates the debtor to file a list of creditors. Section 342 requires appropriate notice of the order for relief. Rule 2002 governs the content of and time for the notice.

Generally, a creditor whose claim is included on a Chapter 11 debtor's list of creditors is not required to file a proof of claim, unless the claim is scheduled as disputed, contingent or unliquidated, a proof of claim is "deemed" filed by section 1111(a).

Nonetheless, holders of unsecured claims often file proofs of claim in Chapter 11 cases. Reasons for filing a proof of claim include (1) disagreement with the amount of the claim shown on the debtor's schedule and (2) concern that the Chapter 11 case will be converted to Chapter 7.

In some Chapter 11 cases, the debtor has hundreds, if not thousands, of creditors. It would not be practical for the Chapter 11 debtor to attempt to negotiate with each creditor individually.

Accordingly, section 1102 directs the United States trustee to appoint a committee of unsecured creditors as soon as practicable after the order for relief. Note that it is the United States trustee and not the bankruptcy court who appoints committee members. And, note that section 1102 suggests, but does not require, that the committee have seven members, and that the seven have the largest claims.

Section 1102(b)(1) does require that the committee members be "representative of the different kinds of claims." If, for example, *D* owed significant amounts to lenders, vendors and tort claimants, the creditors' committee should have representatives from each "kind" of claim.

A creditors' committee performs a number of functions. It may:

(1) consult with the trustee or debtor in possession concerning the administration of the case;

(2) investigate the debtor's acts and financial condition;

(3) participate in the formulation of the plan;

(4) request the appointment of a trustee;

(5) "perform such other services as are in the interest of those represented," section 1103(c).

The creditors' committee may also appear at various hearings as a party in interest, section 1109(b). And, the committee may file a plan in those situations where the debtor ceases to have the exclusive right to do so, section 1121.

To state the obvious, a creditors' committee acts on behalf of all the unsecured creditors. Case law has consistently held that members of a committee have a fiduciary duty to other holders of unsecured claims.

The Bankruptcy Code contemplates that there will be an active creditors' committee in all Chapter 11 cases. There is a difference between what Congress contemplated in 1978 and what actually happens more than 40 years later. Most Chapter 11 cases do not have an active creditors' committee.

4. FIRST DAY ORDERS

In some Chapter 11 cases, there are problems that need to be resolved immediately—on the first day of the case. The phrase "First Day Orders" does not appear in either the Bankruptcy Code or the Bankruptcy Rules. Nonetheless, "First Day Orders" appear in Chapter 11 cases.

"First Day Orders" are orders which the Chapter 11 debtor seeks to have entered by the bankruptcy court immediately, on the same day as the filing of the petition or soon thereafter. Many First Day Orders deal with administrative matters such as notices, bank accounts, employment of attorneys and other professionals and are usually noncontroversial.

More problematic are First Day Orders dealing with business emergencies such as obtaining financing and making payments to employees for work they have done prepetition and other essential prepetition creditors for goods or services they provided prepetition. In dealing with these business emergencies in the first day of the case, bankruptcy courts have to balance the argument by the debtor that immediate action is required or the business will close against the argument by creditors that they have the right to be heard and need more time and the argument by the U.S. Trustee that this early payment of some prepetition claims is inconsistent with the provisions and policies of the Bankruptcy Code.

B. OPERATION OF THE BUSINESS

Successful rehabilitation of a business under Chapter 11 generally requires the continued operation of the business. No court order is necessary in order to operate the debtor's business after the filing of a Chapter 11 petition. Section 1108 provides: "Unless the court . . . orders otherwise, the trustee may operate the debtor's business."

1. DEBTOR IN POSSESSION

Notwithstanding section 1108's use of the word "trustee," the debtor will remain in control of the business in most Chapter 11 cases. Prebankruptcy management will continue to operate the business as a "debtor in possession" unless a request is made for the appointment of a trustee and the court, after notice and a hearing, grants the request, section 1104. In Chapter 11 cases, the debtor in possession has "all of the rights and powers. and shall perform all of the functions and duties" of the trustee, section 1107.

2. TRUSTEE

a. Statutory Grounds for Appointment

Section 1104 sets out the grounds for the appointment of a trustee. A trustee is to be appointed if there is cause (fraud, dishonesty, mismanagement, or incompetence) or if the appointment of a trustee is "in the interest of creditors, any equity security holders, and other interests of the estate." Section 1104 specifically instructs the court to disregard the number of shareholders or the amount of assets and liabilities of the debtor in deciding whether to appoint a trustee.

b. Statutory Procedures for Appointment of Trustee

Under section 1104 the court decides whether to appoint a trustee in a Chapter 11 case. The United States trustee then decides which person to appoint, subject to the court's approval, unless the creditors act to select the trustee themselves.

c. Statutory Duties of a Chapter 11 Trustee

The duties of a trustee are enumerated in section 1106. Essentially, the trustee has responsibility for the operation of the business and formulation of the Chapter 11 plan.

Again, in most Chapter 11 cases there is a debtor in possession instead of a trustee, and the debtor in possession has the statutory duties of a trustee, section 1107.

d. Business Considerations

Who serves as trustee in Chapter 11 cases? Remember, the trustee has responsibility for operating the business. Are lawyers prepared to run a troubled business? What about appointing an outstanding, experienced business person as Chapter 11 trustee?

Even an outstanding, experienced business person is going to need time to familiarize herself with this particular business. And, if they are such an outstanding, experienced business person, why are they available to serve as trustee—why aren't they already running some other business?

These business considerations caused Congress to decide to keep the debtor in possession unless a party in interest establishes cause, section 1104. And, in almost all Chapter 11 cases, these business considerations cause the various parties in interest not to try to establish cause for the appointment of a Chapter 11 trustee.

3. EXAMINER

If a trustee is not appointed, the court can order the appointment of an "examiner." Again, the court decides whether to appoint and the United States trustee decides which person to appoint, with the court's approval.

Section 1104(c) sets out the requirements for the appointment of an examiner:

(1) a trustee was not appointed; *and*

(2) appointment of an examiner was requested by a party in interest; *and*

(3) the debtor's nontrade, nontax, unsecured debts exceed $5,000,000, *or* "such appointment is in the interests of creditors, any equity security holders, and other interests of the estate."

Read literally, section 1104(b)(2) compels the appointment of an examiner on request of a party in interest if the debtor has the requisite $5 million in debts. The cases, however, are divided.

In theory, the role of an examiner is different from that of a trustee. An examiner does not run the debtor's business or run the debtor's Chapter 11 case. An examiner merely examines: she investigates the competency and honesty of the debtor and files a report of the investigation, sections 1104(b), 1106(b). In practice, the bright lines between the roles of an examiner and the roles of a trustee are sometimes blurred.

And, in practice there is almost never an examiner in Chapter 11 cases. More important, in law school there is almost never an examiner in exam fact patterns.

4. CRITICAL VENDORS

a. Paying Critical Vendors for Prepetition Goods and Services

Most operating businesses have vendors who provide critical services and supplies. And most operating business that file a Chapter 11 petition are indebted to those critical vendors at the time they file the petition.

Recall that the section 362 automatic stay prevents any holder of a prepetition claim from taking any legal action or other acts to collect from the debtor. However, neither section 362 nor any other Bankruptcy Code provision compels vendors of services or supplies that are critical to the Chapter

11 debtor's business operations to continue to provide the critical services or supplies.

What if *C* supplies goods or services that are critical to Chapter 11 debtor *D* Furniture Store's business operations and *C* refuses to provide any further goods or services—even for payment in cash before delivery—until it is paid what it was owed at the time of *D* Furniture Store's Chapter 11?

Even though (i) the Bankruptcy Code contemplates that no creditor will be paid in a Chapter 11 case until a plan is confirmed (ii) most confirmed Chapter 11 plans provide for comparatively insignificant payments to holders of prepetition unsecured claims, Chapter 11 debtors request a First Day Order authorizing the immediate, full payment of the prepetition unsecured claims of their critical vendors. While reading the Code and reported cases gives the impression that bankruptcy judges cannot and do not authorize such payments, talking with lawyers gives a different impression.[2]

---

[2] The occasional reported opinion that authorizes immediate full payment of the unsecured claims of critical vendors references the "necessary and appropriate language" in section 105. And, there is dictum in a 2017 Supreme Court decision (which will probably be assigned) that can be read as supporting critical vendor payments. Czyzewski v. Jevic Holding Corp. 137 S.Ct. 973, 985 (2017) ("one can generally find significant Code-related objectives that the priority-violating distributions serve").

b. Obtaining Goods and Services Postpetition on Credit

Obtaining goods and services on credit is important for most businesses especially businesses that are Chapter 11 debtors.

Why would a vendor sell goods or services on credit to a business in bankruptcy? The MBA school short answer is to make money.

The law school exam answer begins with section 364(a) which empowers the debtor in possession to incur unsecured debt in the ordinary course of business" that will have an administrative expense priority and section 364(b) which provides that the bankruptcy court, may authorize the debtor in possession to incur non-ordinary unsecured debt that will have an administrative expense priority.

While we considered administrative expenses earlier, here are the four administrative expense priority concepts that you need to know:

(1) administrative expenses have priority over all unsecured claims other than "domestic support obligations" (and business entity debtors will not owe "domestic support obligations);

(2) section 1129(a)(9)(A) requires that a Chapter 11 plan provide for payment of all administrative expenses in full, in cash, at the time of confirmation of the plan (unless the holder of the administrative expense claim consents to different treatment);

(3) most Chapter 11 cases do not end in a confirmed Chapter 11 plan; many bankruptcy cases that are filed as Chapter 11 cases are converted to Chapter 7 cases;

(4) when a Chapter 11 case is converted to Chapter 7, section 726(b) requires that the administrative expenses incurred in the Chapter 7 part of the case be paid in full before the administrative expenses incurred in the Chapter 11 part of the case can be paid.

Nonetheless, an administrative expense priority is generally sufficient incentive for vendors to continue selling goods and services on credit to businesses that are Chapter 11 debtors

5. USE OF ENCUMBERED PROPERTY INCLUDING CASH COLLATERAL

a. In Bankruptcy Most Property Is Subject to Liens

In the typical Chapter 11 case, most of the property that the debtor owns at the time of the filing of the Chapter 11 petition is encumbered by liens.

The property that the debtor acquires after the filing of the Chapter 11 petition is generally protected from prepetition liens. Property acquired by the debtor after it files a Chapter 11 petition will not be "subject to any lien resulting from any security agreement entered into by the debtor before the commencement of the case," section 552(a). After-acquired property clauses are not recognized in cases under the Bankruptcy Code.

Assume, for example, that *D* Furniture Store files a Chapter 11 petition. If *S* contracted for a security interest in "all of *D* Furniture Store's inventory, now owned or hereafter acquired," section 552(a) will limit *S*'s lien to *D* Furniture Store's inventory as of the time before the Chapter 11 petition was filed.

S's lien will probably also reach the accounts receivable and other identifiable proceeds from the sale of such prepetition inventory. The Bankruptcy Code does recognize a secured creditor's right to "proceeds, product, offspring, rents, or profits" from the disposition of prepetition collateral, section 552(b). Under section 552(b), a prepetition security interest reaches proceeds acquired after the bankruptcy petition was filed "except to any extent that the court, after notice and a hearing and based on the equities of the case, orders otherwise."[3]

b. But 362 Stay Stops Creditor from Repossessing

Section 362(a) stays a creditor with a lien on the property of a Chapter 11 debtor from repossessing the encumbered property. Section 362(d) provides for

---

[3] The "equities of the case" exception covers situations in which postpetition labor or property of the estate is used in converting the collateral into proceeds. Assume, for example, that *S* has a security interest in the raw materials of Charlie Dunn, *D*, a boot maker. After filing for Chapter 11, *D* makes boots from the leather and sells the boots. A bankruptcy court could limit *S*'s security interest in the proceeds from the sale of the boots because of the postpetition labor.

relief from the stay in limited situations as discussed in Chapter V, supra.

c. And 363 Allows DIP to Use Collateral—with Conditions

Section 363 empowers the debtor in possession or trustee to continue using, selling, and leasing encumbered property. The interest of the lien creditor is safeguarded by section 363's requirement of "adequate protection," section 363(e).

Section 361 is entitled "adequate protection." Note that section 361 provides for "adequate protection" of "an interest of an entity in property," not adequate protection of an entity in having its debt repaid. Note further that section 361 does not define "adequate protection." Rather, it provides examples of "adequate protection."

And, examples are the easiest way to understand "adequate protection." Assume, for example, that *D* files for bankruptcy owing *S* $1 million secured by equipment, which is worth $800,000. *S* has an interest in property that is worth $800,000. The purpose of adequate protection is to assure that at the end of the bankruptcy case *S* has (i) collateral worth $800,000; or (ii) payments of $800,000 or (iii) a combination of collateral and payments that total $800,000.

In the equipment example, assume further that the court concludes that the value of the equipment is declining by $10,000 a month. Under sections 361 and 363, the bankruptcy court could require the debtor to make monthly payments to *S* of $10,000. If the bankruptcy lasts 14 months and the court was correct about the decline in the value of the equipment, then at the close of the bankruptcy case, *S* who had a lien on property worth $800,000 at the start of the bankruptcy case would have a lien on property worth $660,000 and $140,000 in adequate protection payments at the end of the bankruptcy case.

Consider a second example. *D* files for bankruptcy owing *M* $500,000 secured by a first mortgage on Greenacre which is worth $300,000. If the bankruptcy court concludes that the value of Greenacre will not decline during the course of the bankruptcy case, the bankruptcy court could conclude that Greenacre itself is adequate protection.

Adequate protection works so long as the bankruptcy judge correctly foresees the future of the encumbered property. What if the value of the creditor's interest in property drops more significantly than the bankruptcy judge anticipated?

Under section 507(b), a creditor may seek an administrative expense claim for the amount by which the adequate protection ordered proves to be inadequate. Section 507(b) should always be read together with section 726(b). If the debtor's Chapter 11 efforts are not successful and the case is converted from Chapter 11 to Chapter 7, the administrative expenses from the 11 are not paid until the administrative expenses from the 7 are paid in full.

While a Chapter 11 debtor's use or sale of encumbered property is always subject to "adequate protection" for creditors with liens on the property, the rules as to who has the burden of raising the adequate protection issue depend on the nature of the encumbered property and the nature of the debtor's use.

i. Encumbered Property That Is NOT "Cash Collateral"

Encumbered property that is not "cash collateral" as defined in section 363(a) may be used, sold, or leased in the ordinary course of business without a prior judicial determination of "adequate protection," section 363(c)(1).[4] On "request" of the lien creditor, the court shall condition the use, sale, or lease of encumbered property so as to provide "adequate protection," section 363(e).

To illustrate, if *D* Furniture Store, Inc. files a Chapter 11 petition and *C* Bank, *C*, has a perfected security interest in *D* Furniture Store's inventory, *D* Furniture Store may continue to sell inventory in the ordinary course of business. *D* Furniture Store will not have to obtain court permission in order to make such sales; rather, *C* will have the burden of requesting the court to prohibit or condition such sales so as to provide "adequate protection" of *C*'s security interest.

---

[4] Section 363(c)(1) is applicable only if "the business of the debtor is authorized to be operated." In a Chapter 11 case, the trustee or debtor in possession is authorized to operate the business "unless the court orders otherwise," section 1108.

Notice and a hearing[5] on the issue of "adequate protection" is required before a Chapter 11 debtor uses, sells, or leases encumbered property in a manner that is *not* in the ordinary course of business, section 363(b). If for example, *D* Furniture Store, after filing its Chapter 11 petition, decides to discontinue its oriental rug department and wants to make a bulk sale of its oriental rug inventory, *C* must be first given notice and the opportunity for a hearing on the issue of "*adequate protection.*"

ii. "Cash Collateral" Is Different

A debtor's use of cash collateral is treated different from the debtor's use of other collateral. Accordingly, it is necessary to understand (i) which collateral is "cash collateral" and (ii) when a debtor can use cash collateral.

(1) What Is It?

"Cash collateral" is defined in section 363(a). There are three components to the definition. First, cash collateral must be collateral, i.e., property that a creditor has an interest in because its lien extends to the property. Second, cash collateral must be cash or cash equivalent. Third, cash collateral can be derived from other collateral, e.g., cash received from the buyers of *D* Furniture Store's inventory that is collateral for *C*.

---

5 Remember that "notice and hearing" means "such notice as is appropriate in the particular circumstances, and such *opportunity* for a hearing as is appropriate in the particular circumstances," section 102(1)(A).

In the above hypothetical of *D* Furniture Store, cash received by *D* Furniture Store from the postpetition sale of prepetition encumbered inventory would be *C*'s cash collateral. Cash received from the sale of *D* Furniture Store's parking lot or other property not subject to *C*'s lien would not be cash collateral. And, accounts receivable generated by the postpetition sale of prepetition inventory would be *C*'s cash collateral only when collected.

(2) Use of Cash Collateral Only upon Consent or Adequate Protection

Cash collateral may be used only if the lienholder *C* consents, or if the court, after notice and hearing, finds that *C*'s collateral position is adequately protected and authorizes such use under section 363(c)(2). Until the use of cash collateral is authorized under section 363(c)(2), the debtor in possession must segregate and account for all cash collateral, section 363(c)(4).

To understand how section 363(c) typically works, it is necessary to understand (i) how the Uniform Commercial Code works, (ii) how the Bankruptcy Code works and (iii) how the real world works.

First, how the Uniform Commercial Code works. Under Article 9 of the UCC, a creditor who extends credit secured by inventory or accounts receivable can (and usually does) obtain a security interest in not only the accounts and inventory a debtor has at the time it extends credit but also the accounts and inventory that the debtor later acquires. Thus, in the

D Furniture Store example, *C*'s collateral could be all of *D* Furniture Store's inventory, whenever acquired.

Now, how the Bankruptcy Code works. If *D* Furniture Store files for Chapter 11, section 552(a) limits the extent to which *C*'s lien can "float" to after-acquired property. More specifically, under section 552(a), *C*'s prepetition security interest does not cover inventory that *D* Furniture Store acquires after the date of the Chapter 11 filing.

Accordingly, a Chapter 11 debtor such as *D* Furniture Store can offer its prepetition secured creditors a replacement lien in postpetition inventory as "adequate protection" for *D* Furniture Store's use of cash collateral. In essence a debtor in possession such as *D* Store simply offers to give back what section 552(a) took away as the necessary "adequate protection."

And, if you understand how the "real world" works you will understand that such an offer is generally the proverbial "offer he cannot refuse."

Recall that a Chapter 11 debtor cannot use cash collateral unless the creditor with a lien on the cash collateral consents or the court approves the use, section 363(c). *D* Furniture Store is like most Chapter 11 debtors in that most of the cash it generates from business operations is cash collateral. Unless the business can use the cash collateral, the business will close.

Understandably, bankruptcy judges are sympathetic to the debtor's argument that unless it is permitted to use cash collateral, it will close and all of its employees will lose their jobs, their health insurance, their retirement benefits, etc. Understanding this, creditors generally agree to the debtor's use of cash collateral in exchange for some sort of replacement lien on postpetition inventory and receivables and some sort of administrative expense priority. Most court orders approving the use of cash collateral are consent orders.

While use of cash collateral is typically the debtor's initial source of credit, cash collateral alone is often not a sufficient source of credit. Accordingly, one of the first problems confronting a business contemplating a Chapter 11 reorganization is financing the operation of the business pending the formulation and approval of a plan of rehabilitation.

6. DEBTOR-IN-POSSESSION FINANCING (A/K/A DIP FINANCING)[6]

a. Possible Sources of DIP Financing

Section 365(c)(2) prevents the Chapter 11 debtor from making use of prebankruptcy lines of credit. Accordingly, a Chapter 11 debtor in possession needs to persuade creditors to make new loans.

---

[6] If you are going to work in this area, the terms "DIP," "DIP financing" and "DIP loan" need to be a part of your working vocabulary. And, if you want to be paid for your work, the term "Carve out" needs to be a part of your working vocabulary. "Carve out" describes a provision in a Chapter 11 financing agreement or order that sets aside a portion of the funding or a portion of the debtor's postpetition assets to pay the attorneys and other professionals working on the case for the debtor and the creditors' committee.

While an administrative priority is sufficient incentive for vendors to continue selling goods on credit. an administrative expense priority is generally not sufficient incentive for lenders to make new loans. Debtors in possession need to be able to offer lenders more than an administrative expense priority.

Under section 364(c), a debtor in possession needing additional financing can offer a DIP lender (1) priority over any or all other administrative expenses, (2) a lien on property that is "not otherwise subject to a lien" and/or (3) a junior lien on property already subject to a lien

Think about the section 364(c)(2) phrase "property of the estate not otherwise subject to a lien." Remember that (i) most financially troubled businesses grant liens on all of their assets, including all of the assets that they acquire in the future to borrow as much as they can, (ii) section 552(a) of the Bankruptcy Code extinguishes prepetition liens on property acquired by the debtor in possession postpetition and (iii) under section 541(a)(7) property that the debtor in possession acquires postpetition is "property of the estate."

Accordingly, to induce a lender to make a DIP loan, *D* Furniture Store can offer a first lien on the inventory that it acquired postpetition.

Or can it?

A few pages ago, *D* Furniture Store offered a lien on that same postpetition inventory as "adequate protection" so that it could use cash collateral. If *D*

Furniture Store offers creditor *C* a lien on its postpetition inventory so that *D* Furniture Store can use *C*'s "cash collateral" and then *D* Furniture offers creditor *Y* a lien on that same postpetition inventory so that it can obtain a DIP loan from *Y*, what are the relative rights of *C* and *Y*?

In most Chapter 11 cases, that question does not arise because in most cases, it is the prepetition creditor that a has a security interest in the cash collateral that makes the DIP loan.

b. Roll-Up

A prepetition creditor that makes the DIP loan often tries to improve its prepetition loan by conditioning its DIP loan on a "roll-up."

The term "roll-up" does not appear in the Bankruptcy Code. I can most easily explain roll-up with an example.

Assume that *D* Furniture Store, a debtor in possession, needs an additional $2M to continue operating its business until a plan is confirmed and so needs a $2M DIP loan. *C*, who is owed $5M on its prepetition loan to *D* Furniture Store is willing to provide DIP financing if the amount of DIP loan is $7M and $5M of the $7M is used to pay off *C*'s $5M prepetition loan

You need to understand why *C* wants this roll-up and why the Bankruptcy Judge should not approve the roll-up.

If *C* makes a $2M DIP Loan and (i) *D* Furniture Store is unable to reorganize and (ii) *C*'s collateral is worth less than $7M, then *C*'s claim for the deficiency is a prepetition unsecured claim. But, if *C* makes a $7M DIP loan with $5M of the $7M being used to pay off *C*'s prepetition loan, then if *D* Furniture Store is unable to reorganize and *C*'s collateral is worth less than $7M, then *C*'s claim for the deficiency is a postpetition administrative expense claim.

Like First Day Orders authorizing payment of prepetition claims of critical vendors, roll-ups are inconsistent with the bankruptcy policy that creditors cannot improve their legal rights during the bankruptcy case. And, like with First Day Orders authorizing payment of prepetition claims of critical vendors, reading the Code and reported cases gives the impression that bankruptcy judges cannot and do not authorize roll-ups, but talking with lawyers gives a different impression.[7]

c. Obtaining Priming Lien

What can induce a new creditor to make a loan to a Chapter 11 debtor in possession who, like most Chapter 11 debtors in possession has no unencumbered property?

Under section 364(d), a DIP lender can obtain a "priming lien", i.e., a first lien on property of the

---

[7] And like First Day Orders, there is dictum in a 2017 Supreme Court decision (which will probably be assigned) that can be read as supporting roll-ups. Czyzewski v. Jevic Holding Corp. 137 S.Ct. 973, 985 (2017) ("one can generally find significant Code-related objectives that the priority-violating distributions serve").

Chapter 11 debtor in possession that is already encumbered by a prepetition lien. Section 364(d) was discussed in Chapter X.

Recall that section 364(d) has two requirements: (1) the debtor in possession is unable to obtain such credit otherwise and (2) the interests of prepetition lienholders on the property whose liens are subordinated to the DIP loan are adequately protected.

A new creditor seeking a section 364(d) priming lien typically argues that the existing lien holder is adequately protected because either (i) there is an equity cushion (i.e. value of collateral exceeds the amount of the prepetition secured debts) or (ii) its new loan will create more value than the amount of the loan. The existing lender's obvious response is that if a second lien is adequately protected why does the new lender insist on its lien being the first lien.

Most DIP lenders do not even try for a section 364(d) priming lien.

d. DIP Lender "Control" of Chapter 11 Cases

Often businesses negotiate for a DIP loan before filing a Chapter 11 petition. Regardless of when the DIP loan was negotiated, the lender generally has all of the leverage in the negotiations. DIP loan agreements commonly include terms such as

- financial covenants which if violated give the DIP lender the right to terminate the financing;

- waiver of the Debtor's right later to seek a section 364(d) priming lien;
- deadlines for the Debtor's filing a plan and obtaining creditor acceptance of the plan;
- termination of the financing if the Debtor fails to sell all of its assets under section 363 by a specified date. (Section 363 sales of all of the assets of a business are explained in Chapter XVII, infra).

Regardless of when the DIP loan was negotiated, the terms of the DIP loan agreement must be approved by the Bankruptcy Judge after notice and hearing, section 364(c). And, in the hearing, the lender generally has the leverage. At the "urging" of the lender, the debtor will ask the judge to approve the DIP loan agreement because (i) no one else is willing to make it a DIP loan (or no one else is willing to make a DIP loan on better terms), (ii) this lender is only willing to make the DIP loan on these terms, and (iii) the debtor cannot continue business operations without the DIP loan.

Some judges will approve a DIP loan agreement notwithstanding these terms that give the DIP lender effective control of the Chapter 11 case because they are concerned that if they don't the DIP loan will not be made, the Chapter 11 will fail and people will lose their jobs. And, some judges will approve such a DIP loan agreement because they are concerned that if they don't the DIP loan will not be made, the Chapter 11 will fail, and this will be the last big Chapter 11 case ever filed in their court. [As you will learn in Chapter XVIII of this book, the bankruptcy venue rules gives businesses considerable discretion as to where to file.]

C. PREPARATION OF THE CHAPTER 11 PLAN

1. EXCLUSIVITY

A Chapter 11 plan may be filed at the same time as the petition or any time thereafter. Section 1121 answers the question who can file a Chapter 11 plan.

Section 1121 gives a Chapter 11 debtor a period of exclusivity in which only it can file a plan. Being the only party able to file a plan can be a very significant advantage to a debtor. So long as the debtor has exclusivity, creditors have the limited options of (i) accepting what the debtor proposes or (ii) moving to convert the case to Chapter 7 and liquidating all of the assets or (iii) moving to end the debtor's exclusivity.

Section 1121(b) grants the debtor exclusivity for the first 120 days of the case. If the debtor files its plan within that 120-day period, no other plan may be filed during the first 180 days of the case while the debtor tries to obtain creditor acceptance of its plan, section 1121(c)(3). Section 1121(d) empowers the bankruptcy court to extend or reduce the 120-day and 180-day periods.[8]

---

[8] Note the relationship between the 120-day and the 180-day periods. Both begin running at the same time—the date of the order for relief. If, for example, the debtor files a plan 30 days after

The 120-day period to file a plan and disclosure statement may not be extended beyond 18 months, and the 180-day period to obtain acceptances may not be extended beyond 20 months, section 1122(d)(2).

Section 1121's provisions on exclusivity are of limited practical significance. Remember that in larger cases, the debtor in possession financing agreement often dictates a shorter deadline for the debtor's filing a plan. In smaller case, the debtor's limited financial resources often dictates a shorter deadline.

If a trustee is appointed, the trustee, the debtor, a creditor, the creditors' committee, and any other party in interest may file a plan, section 1121(c). More than one plan may be filed. Similarly, if the debtor fails to file a plan and obtain creditor acceptances within the specified exclusivity time periods, the debtor and any other "party in interest' may file a plan and more than one plan may be filed.

Regardless of who files the plan, the Bankruptcy Code contemplates that the creditors' committee will play a role in formulating the plan, cf. section 1103(c)(3). Again remember that most Chapter 11 cases do not have a creditors' committee.

2. CONTENTS OF THE PLAN

A lawyer's questions about the contents of a plan are typically (i) what is my client getting under the plan and (ii) what are others getting under the plan.

---

the order for relief, the debtor will have 150 more days of exclusivity to obtain creditor acceptance.

A law professor's question about the contents of a plan is typically does the plan comply with section 1123.

Section 1123 is entitled "Contents of Plan." Paragraph (a) sets out the mandatory provisions of a Chapter 11 plan ("shall"); paragraph (b) of section 1123 indicates the permissive provisions of a Chapter 11 plan ("may").

3. FUNDING FOR THE PLAN

Compliance with the requirements of section 1123 is not the difficult part of preparing a plan for the rehabilitation of a business under Chapter 11. Rather, the hard question is usually how will the debtor fund the payments? Possible sources of such funding include

(1) new borrowing from creditors;

(2) new equity capital from investors;

(3) sales of assets.[9]

[While assets may be sold as a part of the Chapter 11 plan process, Chapter 11 asset sales more commonly occur earlier in the case, pursuant to section 363. As noted earlier, section 363 sales of businesses are explained in Chapter XVII infra.

Debtors prefer to use Chapter 11 and section 363 sales instead of Chapter 7 trustee liquidation sales

---

9 While Chapter 11 is generally thought of as a reorganization rather than liquidation, a Chapter 11 plan may provide for the sale of all of the debtor's assets, section 1123(b)(4).

because the debtor in possession (i.e., existing management) can continue to operate the business until its sale and can negotiate the terms of the sale. Both debtors and buyers prefer to use section 363 instead of sales pursuant to a Chapter 11 plan because section 363 sale procedures are more time efficient and more cost efficient than Chapter 11 plan procedures.]

A Chapter 11 plan does not always provide for cash payments to creditors. A plan can offer creditors new debt in different amount with different terms or equity securities[10] instead of cash.

4. CLASSIFICATION OF CLAIMS

Classification of claims is important. It can affect not only who gets what under the plan but also whether there is a plan.

Look at section 1123(a) and section 1122. Section 1123(a)(1) requires that the claims be classified, and section 1123(a)(4) requires the "same treatment" for

---

[10] Generally, the issuance of a security requires expensive and time consuming federal and state registration. Section 1145(a)(1) exempts the issuance of the debtor's securities under a Chapter 11 plan from federal and state registration requirements. A creditor's resale of a security received under a Chapter 11 is also exempted from federal and state registration requirements, section 1145(b). Section 4(1) of the Securities Act of 1933 states in essence that transactions by any person who is not an "issuer, underwriter, or dealer" need not be registered. Section 1145(b)(2) provides an exemption to creditors who resell securities obtained under a Chapter 11 plan by indicating that such creditors are not "underwriters."

all claims within a class. Section 1122 governs classification of claims in Chapter 11 plans.

Section 1122(b) is easy to apply so let's start with that. Section 1122(b) says that the plan can segregate all small claims into a single class if "reasonable and necessary for administrative convenience." A plan proponent may use such an "administrative convenience class" to pay small claims in cash at the time of confirmation, instead of incurring the cost and inconvenience of processing and mailing monthly checks for dollars or even pennies over the course of the Chapter 11 plan.

Section 1122(a) is hard to apply because of what it does not say. While section 1122(a) says that the test for whether claims can be included in the same class is "substantially similar," it does not define "substantially similar."

In determining whether claims are "substantially similar" for purposes of section 1122(a), courts look primarily at legal rights. A claim with a section 507 priority has different legal rights from an unsecured claim and so priority claims and unsecured claims cannot be placed in the same class. Similarly, a secured claim has different legal rights than an unsecured claim or a priority claim and so secured claims cannot be placed in the same class with priority claims or unsecured claims. And, *B*'s first mortgage on Blueacre has different legal rights from *W*'s first mortgage on Whiteacre or *S*'s second mortgage on both Blueacre and Whiteacre.

Accordingly, each secured claim is placed in a separate class in most[11] Chapter 11 plans.

And, section 1122(a) is hard to apply because it does not say anything about whether claims must be included in the same class. Section 1122(a) states that all claims in a class must be "substantially similar"; it does not state whether all claims that are "substantially similar" must be in the same class.

To illustrate, assume that *X, Y* and *Z* are unsecured creditors of Chapter 11 debtor, *D*. If *D*'s plan places all three creditors' claims in the same class, section 1122(a) controls. It is clear from section 1122(a) that *D* cannot place the claims of *X, Y* and *Z* in a single class unless all three claims are "substantially similar." The limits on *D*'s discretion in placing claims in a separate class are not clear from the Bankruptcy Code. Can *D* place *X* in a class different from *Y* and *Z* even though their claims are substantially similar?

There are both business reasons and a legal reason that a debtor might want to divide its unsecured debts into various classes.

First, a possible business reason. Some creditors such as long-term lenders or large vendors that are continuing to sell to the debtor might be willing to take long-term notes or even stock while other creditors such as short-term lenders or discontinued

---

[11] If a debtor has issued public debt secured by its assets, the claims of the various debenture holders are "substantially similar" and can be placed in a single class.

vendors might insist on short-term notes or even cash.

Second, a possible legal reason for classification of claims. A plan proponent will sometimes place claims that will vote for the plan in a separate class so that at least one class of claims accepts the plan. As discussed below, the Chapter 11 plan approval process requires that (i) creditors vote on Chapter 11 plans, (ii) the creditor vote be tabulated by classes and by number of claims and amount of claims in that class, and (iii) at least one class of claims vote for the plan by the requisite majorities in number and amount.

This legal reason for classification and legal battles over classification often arise in cases in which the debtor's principal significant asset is a building. Assume, for example, that *D* is a limited partnership that owns an apartment complex valued at $12.2 million. *M* has a mortgage on the apartment complex to secure its $15 million claim. *M* thus has both a $12.2 million secured claim and a $2.8 million unsecured claim. *M* is not only *D*'s only secured creditor; it is also *D*'s largest unsecured creditor. *M*'s $2.8 million unsecured, deficiency claim is larger than all other unsecured debts combined. Unless *D* can classify *M*'s unsecured deficiency claim different from the claims of its other unsecured creditors, *M* can effectively veto any Chapter 11 plan.

The cases are divided on whether the deficiency claim of a single asset real estate debtor's secured creditor can be classified separately from other unsecured claims. Some of the cases approving such classification rely on *M*'s section 1111(b) rights as making *M* different from other holders of unsecured claims, Section 1111(b) is considered later in this Chapter.

D. ACCEPTANCE OF THE PLAN

Chapter 11 contemplates a restructuring of the debtor's financial obligations with the creditors' consent. Creditors vote on the Chapter 11 plan before the plan is approved by the bankruptcy judge. The term "acceptance" is used to describe the creditors' voting process.

1. DISCLOSURE

Section 1125 requires full disclosure before postpetition solicitation of acceptances of a Chapter 11 plan. Creditors and shareholders must be provided:

(1) a copy of the plan or a summary of the plan; and

(2) "a written disclosure statement approved, after notice and a hearing, by the court as containing adequate information," section 1125(b).

"Adequate information" is defined in section 1125(a) as information which it is "reasonably practicable" for this debtor to provide to enable a "hypothetical reasonable investor" who is typical of the holders of the claims or interests to make an informed judgment on the plan. What constitutes "adequate information" thus depends on the circumstances of each case—on factors such as (1) the condition of the debtor's books or records, (2) the sophistication of the creditors and stockholders, and (3) the nature of the plan.

2. WHO VOTES?

Both creditors and shareholders vote on Chapter 11 plans. According to section 1126(a), creditors with claims "allowed under section 502" and shareholders with interests "allowed under section 502" vote on Chapter 11 plans. The statutory requirement of "allowed under section 502" is generally satisfied by the Bankruptcy Code's "double-deeming."

In a Chapter 11 case, section 1111(a) deems filed a claim or interest that is scheduled and is not shown as disputed, contingent, or unliquidated. And, section 502 deems allowed any claim or interest that is filed and not objected to by a party in interest.

Statutory "deeming" also eliminates voting by two classes of claims or interests. First, if a class is to receive nothing under the plan, it is deemed to have rejected the plan, and its vote need not be solicited, section 1126(g). Second, if a class is not "impaired" under the plan, the class is deemed to have accepted the plan and again its vote need not be solicited, section 1126(f).

a. Impairment of Claims

The concept of "impairment" is unique to Chapter 11. Section 1124 is entitled "Impairment of Claims or

Interests." Under section 1124 a class of claims or interests is impaired unless

(1) the legal, equitable, and contractual rights of the holder are left "unaltered"; [If the plan in any way changes the rights of the holder, it alters and thus impairs the holder. It is not necessary to determine whether the change adversely affects the holder.] *or*

(2) the only alteration of legal, equitable, or contractual rights is reversal of an acceleration on default by curing the default and reinstating the debt.

b. Section 1111(b) Elections

Section 1111(b), like section 1124, deals with a concept that is unique to Chapter 11. Generally, a creditor whose debt is only partially secured has two claims—a secured claim measured by the value of its collateral and an unsecured claim for the remainder, section 506(a).

Assume, for example, that *C*'s $100,000 claim against *D* is secured by Blueacre, real property owned by *D*, that is valued at $70,000. Under section 506(a), *C* has a $70,000 secured claim and a $30,000 unsecured claim. Under section 1111(b), *C* can elect to have a $100,000 secured claim and no unsecured claim.[12]

---

[12] Note that section 1111(b) provides for election by classes of secured claims, not by individual holders of secured claims. Generally, each holder of a secured claim will be in a separate

Let's use the hypothetical in the previous paragraph to consider some of the advantages and the disadvantages of a section 1111(b) election:

If C makes the section 1111(b) election,

(1) C will not be able to vote its $30,000 unsecured claim and will not receive the plan distribution that it would otherwise receive for its unsecured claim; and

(2) the only plan distribution to C will probably be a long-term note for $100,000 at below-market interest. Section 1129(b) requires that the payments to C under the plan total $100,000,[13] and that the payments have a present value of $70,000[14]. This can be done by giving the creditor that makes a section 1111(b) election a long-term note that bears a below market interest rate.

Generally a section 1111(b) election benefits a secured creditor such as *C* only if Blueacre later increases in value and there is default or a sale of Blueacre that accelerates the $100,000 obligation.

3. NEEDED MAJORITIES

A class of claims has accepted a plan when more than one half in number and at least two thirds in

---

class. Note also that some classes of secured claims are not eligible to make a section 1111(b) election.

[13] "Allowed amount of such claim" after an 1111(b) election is $100,000.

[14] Value of such holder's interest in the estate's interest in such property" remains $700,000, even after an 1111(b) election.

amount of the allowed claims actually voting on the plan approve the plan, section 1126(c). The following hypotheticals illustrates the application of section 1126(c):

D files a Chapter 11 petition. *D*'s schedule of creditors shows 222 different creditors and $1 million of debt. *D*'s Chapter 11 plan divides creditors into four classes. Class 3 consists of 55 creditors, with claims totaling $650,000. Only 29 of the creditors in Class 3 vote on the plan. Their claims total $450,000. If at least 15 Class 3 creditors (more than 1/2 of 29) with claims totaling at least $300,000 (2/3 of $450,000) vote for *D*'s plan, the plan has been accepted by Class 3.

What if *D* plan's Class 4 consists of 7 creditors with claims totaling $210,000 and 6 of the Class 4 creditors vote for the plan but the other creditor with claim of $71,000 votes against the plan? Class 4 did not accept the plan.

A class of interests has accepted a plan when at least two thirds in amount of the allowed interests actually voting on the plan approve the plan, section 1126(d).

E. CONFIRMATION OF THE PLAN

Approval of a Chapter 11 plan involves not only creditor acceptance but also court confirmation. A bankruptcy judge has the power to confirm a Chapter 11 plan that has not received the needed majorities; a bankruptcy judge has the power not to confirm a

Chapter 11 plan that has been accepted by all holders of claims and interests.

Section 1128 requires that the bankruptcy court hold a hearing on confirmation and give parties in interest notice of the hearing so that they might raise objections to confirmation.

While it is possible for more than one plan to be filed and accepted, only one plan may be confirmed. If more than one plan meets the confirmation standards of section 1129, the court "shall consider the preferences of creditors and equity security holders in determining which plan to confirm," section 1129(c).

Subparagraphs (a), (b), and (d) of section 1129 contain the confirmation standards. Section 1129(d) prohibits confirmation of a plan whose "principal purpose" is the avoidance of taxes or the avoidance of registration of securities. Subparagraph (a) and (b) are discussed below.

1. STANDARDS FOR CONFIRMATION

a. Plans Accepted by Every Class

Section 1129(a) sets out 16 confirmation requirements for plans accepted by every class. Subject to the limited exception of sections 1129(c) and 1129(d), a plan that has been accepted by every class of claims and every class of interests must be confirmed by the bankruptcy court if the 16 enumerated requirements of section 1129(a) are satisfied. Section 1129(b) does not apply to plans that have been accepted by every class of claims and every class of interests.

Most of the requirements of section 1129(a) are easy to understand, easy to apply. Law school bankruptcy courses tend to cover only four of the requirements.

First, section 1129(a)(7) creates a "best interests of creditors" test.[15] It requires that each dissenting member of a class—even dissenting members of classes that approve the plan—receive at least as much under the plan as it would have received in a Chapter 7 liquidation.[16]

Second, section 1129(a)(9) provides special treatment for priority claims. A holder of an administrative expense claim or a claim for certain postpetition expenses in an involuntary case must be paid in cash on the effective date of the plan unless the *claim holder* otherwise agrees, section 1129(a)(9)(A). Wage claims, claims for fringe benefits, and certain claims of consumer creditors must be paid in cash on the effective date of the plan unless the *class* agrees to accept deferred cash payments that have a present value equal to the amount of the claims, section 1129(a)(9)(B). Each

---

[15] Section 1129(a)(7) does not use the term "best interest." Courts and commentators use the term "best interests" in applying section 1129(a)(7).

[16] Section 1129(a)(7) looks to the value of the distribution under the plan as of the effective date of the plan. If for example the plan calls for payment to Creditor *X* of $100 a month for 20 months, the value of the payment to *X* "as of the effective date of the plan" is clearly less than $2,000.

priority tax claim must receive deferred cash payments that have a present value equal to the amount of the claim, section 1129(a)(9)(C).

Third, section 1129(a)(11) imposes a feasibility requirement.[17] It requires that the court determine that the debtor can meet its plan commitments—that confirmation is not likely to be followed by liquidation or the need for further financial reorganization. Obviously, the court's determination of whether a plan is feasible will necessarily depend on the facts of the case.

Fourth, section 1129(a)(10) requires that there be at least one consenting impaired class. Section 1129(a)(10) is confusing when read together with section 1129(a)(8) which requires the consent of all impaired classes. Section 1129(a)(10) is less confusing when read together with section 1129(b).

A plan can be confirmed if all of the requirements of section 1129(a) are satisfied including the section 1129(a)(8) requirement of consent of all impaired classes. Alternatively, a plan can be confirmed if all of the requirements of section 1129(a) other than section 1129(a)(8) are satisfied and the requirements of section 1129(b) are also satisfied. In other words, if section 1129(a)(10)'s requirement of one consenting impaired class is satisfied, then satisfaction of the cram down requirements of section 1129(b) can

---

[17] Like the "best interests" test of section 1129(a)(7) which does not use the term "best interests," section 1129(a)(11) does not use the word "feasibility."

override section 1129(a)(8)'s requirement of consent of all impaired classes.

b. Plans Accepted by Less than Every Class

Plans accepted by less than every class can be confirmed only if the additional requirements of section 1129(b) are satisfied. This is commonly called a cram down.[18]

Section 1129(b) does not use the term "cram down." Section 1129(b) does use two terms that you need to understand: (1) "not discriminate unfairly" and (2) "fair and equitable."

There are three things that you need to know about "not discriminate unfairly:"

(1) it only applies if section 1129(b) applies (If all impaired class have accepted the plan, the 1129(b) does not apply and "not discriminate unfairly" does not apply.)

(2) it only applies to the nonassenting class (If classes 4, 5, and 6 assent but class 7 does not, "not discriminate unfairly" only applies to class 7.)

(3) it is not enough that the plan discriminates against class 7 that discrimination must be so harsh as to be "unfairly."

Whether discrimination is unfair is a fact question and so not likely to be a law school exam question.

---

[18] Or "cramdown" or "cram-down." Neither "cram down" nor "cram-down" nor "cramdown" appears in the Bankruptcy Code.

The other section 1129(b) term, "Fair and equitable", is more likely to be on your exam.

Section 1129(b)(2) sets out three different tests for determining whether a plan is "fair and equitable" depending on whether the dissenting class is a (A) secured claim class, or (B) a class of unsecured claims, or (C) ownership interests.

First, cram down of secured claims and section 1129(b)(2)(A). We need distinguish between a Chapter 11 plan that provides that the secured creditor will retain its lien from a Chapter 11 plan that provides the debtor will sell the encumbered property free and clear of liens. The former triggers section 1129(b)(2)(A)(i); the latter triggers section 1129(b)(2)(A)(ii).

First, section 1129(b)(2)(A)(i).

We have already learned about cram down of secured claims in Chapter 13 cases. Compare the language of section 1325(a)(5)(B) with the language of section 1129(b)(2)(A)(i). Basically the same. The law governing cram down of a secured claim under an 11 plan that provides for the creditor retaining its lien works basically the same as the law governing cram down in a Chapter 13 case.

First, it is necessary to determine the amount of the secured claim. Under section 506, that is keyed to the value of the collateral. Second, it is necessary to determine a cram down interest rate—to determine how much more than just the replacement value the debtor must pay over the life of the plan so that the proposed plan payments have a discounted present value equal to the value of the collateral.

If, for example, Chapter 11 debtor *D* owes *S* $100,000 and that debt is secured by Redacre which is valued at $70,000,a cram down of *S*'s secured claim would require plan payments that have a discounted present value of $70,000, with S retaining its mortgage on Redacre.

So far, Chapter 11 cram down of secured claims is identical to Chapter 13 cram down of secured claims. Now compare sections 1325(a)(5)(B) and section 1129(b)(2)(A)(i)(II)) more closely. Note that section 1129(a)(2)(A)(i)(II) has an additional requirement that the amount of the plan payments must be at least equal to the amount of the secured claim.

In most Chapter 11 cases, this additional requirement is meaningless. Generally, a stream of payments that have a discounted present value equal to the value of the collateral will exceed the amount of the secured claim.

This additional Chapter 11 cram down requirement will only matter if the Chapter 11 debtor has made a section 1111(b) election. Recall that under section 1111(b), a creditor with a lien can elect to have its entire claim treated as secured, regardless of the value of its collateral. If, for example, *D* owes *S* $100,000 and the debt is secured by Redacre with a value of $70,000, then under section 506, *S* has a $70,000 secured claim. But by making a section 1111(b) election, *S* can have a $100,000 secured claim. If *S* so elects, then a cram down of *S*'s secured claim would require both that the stream of payments under the plan have a discounted present value of $70,000—"the value of such holder's interest in the estate's interest in such property"—and that the face amount of the plan payments total at least $100,000.

Now, let's consider section 1129(b)(2)(A)(ii) and the cram down of the holder of a secured claim under a plan that provides for the sale of that creditor's collateral free and clear of liens. What if the plan provides for the sale of Redacre to *T*, free and clear of *S*'s lien? What does section 1129(b)(2)(A)(ii) require be distributed to *S*?

The requirements for amount and present value of the plan distribution are exactly the same as section 1129(b)(2)(A)(i) except that the plan distributions are secured by a lien on the proceeds from the sale of Redacre to *T* instead of on Redacre.

The more significant difference between cram down of a plan providing that *D* retains Redacre and a plan providing that *D* sells Redacre free and clear of liens is that if *S* believes the sales price is too low, then *S* can bid in all or some of its claim and end up owning Redacre. This "credit bidding "will be more fully explained in Chapter XVII.

Again, section 1129(b)(2)(A) only applies if there is a nonassenting class of secured claims. If the nonassenting class is unsecured claims, then section 1129(b)(2)(B) sets out the requirements for "fair and equitable." So let's consider section 1129(b)(2)(B) and cram down of unsecured claims.

Bankruptcy law professors, lawyers and judges (but not the Bankruptcy Code) use the phrase "absolute priority" to describe the standard for "fair and equitable" treatment of unsecured claims.

Section 1129(b)'s "fair and equitable" standard is satisfied with respect to a dissenting class of unsecured claims if "the holder of any claim or interest that is junior to the claims of such class will not receive or retain under the plan on account of such junior claim or interest any property." What does the quoted language mean? Who is "junior" to an unsecured creditor?

Under the Bankruptcy Code, as under corporate codes, stockholders are "junior" to unsecured creditors. Accordingly, the "absolute priority" rule of section 1129(b)(2)(B) requires payment in full[19] to all holders of unsecured claims before distributions to shareholders. Accordingly, a Chapter 11 plan cannot be crammed down on unsecured creditors unless stockholders get nothing. lose all of their interests in the debtor.

Consider the following illustration of section 1129(b)(2)(B): *D* Corp. files for Chapter 11 relief. Its Chapter 11 plan provides for 70 cents on the dollar to a class of holders of unsecured claims and also provides for its shareholders to retain their *D* Corp. stock. Can the plan be confirmed? Yes, if accepted by the requisite majorities of all classes of claims. If *D*

[19] By "payment in full," I mean (or, more importantly, section 1129(b)(2)(B) requires) that the plan distributions to the dissenting class have a present value that at least equals the face amount of the claim.

Corp.'s plan is accepted by all classes, then section 1129(b) does not apply. If, however, *D* Corp.'s plan is not accepted by all classes, section 1129(b) will apply and will preclude confirmation. This plan is not "fair and equitable" under section 1129(b)(2)(B): stockholders are junior to the dissenting class and are retaining property under the plan.

Reconsider the language of section 1129(b)(2)(B) set out above, particularly the phrase "on account of such junior claim or interest." Can shareholders retain their stock notwithstanding nonassenting classes and section 1129(b)(2)(B) by making a new capital contribution to the corporation? In Case v. Los Angeles Lumber Products Co., 308 U.S. 106 (1939), the Supreme Court, in dicta, recognized a "new value" exception to the absolute priority rule: shareholders of an insolvent debtor could retain an interest in a reorganized entity if their "participation [is] based on a contribution in money or money's worth, reasonably equivalent in view of all of the circumstances to the participation of the shareholder."

Case is a case under the Bankruptcy Act of 1898. There has not been a Supreme Court decision on whether "new value" exception to the absolute priority rule was eliminated by the 1978 Bankruptcy Code. . .

In Bank of America v. 203 North LaSalle Street Partnership, 526 U.S. 434 (1999), the Supreme Court again declined to rule whether the Bankruptcy Code eliminated the "new value" exception to the "absolute priority" rule. Instead, the Court limited its overruling of the Seventh Circuit's use of the new value exception to the specific facts of the case. More specifically, to the fact in the case that the debtor still enjoyed section 1121 exclusivity. The Supreme Court held that a debtor could not simultaneously retain the exclusive right to file a plan and then propose in its plan that its owners (and only its owners) could contribute new capital to obtain the ownership of the reorganized debtor. The Court reasoned that the exclusive opportunity to buy the ownership must be considered property received "on account of" old equity interests in the entity and so prohibited by 1129(a)(2)(B).

In sum, it is still not clear whether the Bankruptcy Code precludes use of a new value exception. All that is now clear is that the Supreme Court precludes use of both exclusivity and a new value exception.

Finally, cram down of equity under section 1129(b)(2)(C). Cram down of equity will not be covered in this basic student text because this (1) rarely arises in bankruptcy cases, and (2) even more rarely is covered in basic bankruptcy courses and (3) can be[20] really hard stuff.

---

[20] In its basic form, section 1129(b)(2)(C) is a form of absolute priority rule: While dissenting classes of claims must be paid in full before classes of equity interests receive anything, equity must receive what is left after dissenting classes of claims are paid in full. For example, D Corp owes creditors $2M. D Corp's plan provides that all equity is to be transferred to D Corp's creditors. Shareholders object to confirmation, contending that the value of D Corp is more than $2M. If the court concludes that D Corp is worth more than $2M, then the plan cannot be confirmed: the plan

2. EFFECT OF CONFIRMATION

After confirmation of a Chapter 11 plan, the debtor's performance obligations are governed by the terms of the plan. The provisions of a confirmed Chapter 11 plan bind not only the debtor but also the debtor's creditors and shareholders "whether or not such creditor, equity security holder, or general partner has accepted the plan," section 1141(a). Subject to limitations noted below, confirmation of a Chapter 11 plan operates as a discharge, section 1141(d). The following hypothetical illustrates the possible application of section 1141(a) and section 1141(d).

D's confirmed Chapter 11 plan provides for monthly payments to creditors. Each creditor in Class 2 is to receive 5% of its claim each month for 15 months. After making two payments under the plan, *D* defaults. At the time of the filing of the petition *D* owed *C* $10,000. *C* has received $1,000 under the plan. *C*'s claim against *D* is now limited to $6,500. (75% × $10,000 – 1,000).

Chapter 11 withholds discharge from some debtors and some debts. The plan may limit discharge, section 1141(d)(1). The order of confirmation may limit discharge, section 1141(d)(1). The exceptions to discharge in section 523 are applicable to individual debtors, section 1141(d)(2). The objections to discharge in section 727 are applicable only if (1) the plan provides for the sale of all or substantially all of

---

is not "fair and equitable" because creditors are receiving more than what they are owed at the expense of equity.

the debtor's property, *and* (2) the debtor does not engage in business after the consummation of the plan, section 1141(d)(3).

To illustrate, *D* Corp. owns and operates both motels and movie theaters. *D* Corp. files for Chapter 11. Its reorganization plan provides sale of the motels and continued ownership and operation of its movie theaters. On confirmation of the plan, *D* Corp. would receive a discharge. While section 727(a)(1) denies a corporation a discharge in Chapter 7 cases, that provision does not apply here because *D* Corp. will engage in business after consummation of its plan, section 1141(d)(3). And, since *D* Corp. is a corporate debtor and not an individual debtor, the section 523 exceptions do not apply to it, section 1141(d)(2).

The following chart compares Chapter 11 discharge rules with those of Chapter 7.

	Chapter 7	Chapter 11
Corporations, partnerships	Not eligible for discharge	Eligible for discharge unless plan is a liquidating plan and the debtor terminates business
Section 523	Applicable to individuals	Applicable to individuals
Grounds for withholding discharge	Section 727	1. provision in plan 2. provision in confirmation order 3. Section 727 if a. liquidating plan, and b. termination of business operation

F. SPECIAL FORMS OF CHAPTER 11 CASES

1. PREPACKAGED

A prepackaged plan is a bankruptcy plan of reorganization which has been negotiated and accepted by the requisite number of creditors prior to the commencement of the bankruptcy case. A prepackaged Chapter 11 involves the same legal requirements as any other Chapter 11 case; a prepackaged differs only in the sequence in which the requirements are satisfied.

The prepackaged process contemplates that debtor-creditor negotiations, disclosure statement preparation, and creditor acceptance all occur before a bankruptcy petition is filed. The statutory bases for a prepackaged plan include (i) section 1102 which recognizes prepetition creditors' committees, (ii) section 1121 which permits a debtor to file a plan of reorganization together with its petition, and (iii) section 1126(b) which provides for solicitation of acceptances prior to bankruptcy.

The benefits of a prepackaged Chapter 11 are obvious. Prepackaged plans minimize the amount of time that the debtor operates in bankruptcy because the time-consuming negotiations occur prior to any bankruptcy filing. Less disruption to the debtor's business. Moreover, a debtor has more control over the process. A plan is finalized before the debtor submits to the bankruptcy court's jurisdiction.

The disadvantages of a prepackaged Chapter 11 should be equally obvious. The debtor does not have any of the protections of Chapter 11 during the negotiations. No automatic stay, no ability to reject unfavorable contracts, no moratorium on the accrual of interest on unsecured debts, no ability to obtain needed funding by using the super-priority provision until the bankruptcy petition is filed. In general, prepackaged bankruptcy is better suited for a debtor looking for help with its highly leveraged capital structure rather than a debtor looking for help with its trade debt, a debtor with financial problems rather than operational problems.

2. SINGLE ASSET REAL ESTATE CASES

The phrase "single asset real estate" is a part of the language of section 101 and of section 362 and part of the language of bankruptcy judges and lawyers. The phrase "single asset real estate" is not, however, a phrase that actually appears in Chapter 11.

The definition in section 101(51B) is straightforward:

(1) single property or project;

(2) real property;

(3) no substantial business other than the business of operating the real property.

Note the third requirement. A hotel or a nursing home cannot be a single asset real estate case. Taking care of the guests or residents is not "business of operating the real property."

The stay provision for single asset real estate cases in section 362(d) needs to be read together with section 1121. Even though section 1121 provides for an initial 120-day exclusivity period, in a single asset real estate Chapter 11, the deadline is sometimes 90, not 120. In a single asset real estate case, lenders secured by the real property are entitled to stay relief 90 days after the bankruptcy filing unless the debtor has filed a plan and that plan has a reasonable possibility of being confirmed within a reasonable time or the debtor is making monthly payments to those lenders.

Even though there is no statutory basis for otherwise treating Chapter 11 cases involving a "single asset real estate" different from other Chapter 11 cases, single asset real estate case law has developed. Facts common to these cases include

(1) debtor's only asset is a piece of real estate, i.e., a shopping center, office building, apartment complex, raw land;

(2) debtor's only secured creditor and only significant creditor is the lender that holds the mortgage on the real estate;

(3) that lender is seriously under-secured;

(4) the amount of the mortgage lender's unsecured claim is substantially larger than the claims of all other unsecured creditors combined.

In sum, the typical single asset real estate case is a dispute between a debtor and one creditor over one asset. For some law professors and judges, such single asset real estate cases raise a bankruptcy policy question: should bankruptcy be used to resolve a dispute between a debtor and only one of its creditors?

3. INDIVIDUAL CHAPTER 11 CASES

Generally Chapter 13 is more favorable to individual debtors than Chapter 11. or Chapter 13 cases are quicker and less expensive.

Remember creditors are more involved in Chapter 11 cases than in Chapter 13 cases and that takes time, including time spent and billed for by attorneys. For example, there is no creditor voting in Chapter 13, but a Chapter 11 plan proponent must solicit creditors for their votes after obtaining bankruptcy court approval of a disclosure statements.

Some individuals file for Chapter 11 because they are not eligible for Chapter 13. If an individual's debts exceed the dollar limits in section 109(e), they cannot file for Chapter 13. Chapter 11, however, has no debt limits.

A Chapter 11 case in which the debtor is an individual is like a Chapter 13 case in three major respects that are favorable to creditors:

(1) section 1123(a)(8) and 1129(a)(15), like section 1325(b), impose a "best efforts" kind of test, requiring commitment of "disposable income" to plan payments;

(2) section 1141(d)(5), like section 1328(a), defers discharge until completion of plan payments;

(3) section 1123(b), like section 1322(b), prevents cram down of debts, secured by the debtor's principal residence.

There are of course differences between Chapter 13 cases and individual Chapter 11 cases. other than Chapter 11's creditor acceptance process. Chapter 11, unlike Chapter 13, does not protect car loans from strip down.

Yet another possible difference between a Chapter 13 case and an individual Chapter 11 case is section 1129(b)'s "absolute priority rule. The absolute priority does not apply in Chapter 13 cases Courts are divided as to whether the absolute priority rule applies to individual Chapter 11 debtors.

More specifically the courts are divided over the meaning of the following language in section 1129(b)(2)(B)(ii): "except that the debtor may retain property included in the estate under section 1115." Does it mean that under the absolute priority rule an individual debtor in a Chapter 11 cases may keep only property that is not property of the estate under section 541, but is added to property of the estate by section 1115, namely, only "property of the kind specified in section 541 that the debtor acquires after the commencement of the case" (emphasis added) and "earnings from services performed by the debtor after the commencement of the case" (collectively, "section 1115 property"). Or, does the quoted language from section 1129(b)(2)(B)(ii) mean that an individual debtor may keep all property of the estate, thus effectively exempting individual Chapter 11 debtors from the absolute priority rule?

4. SMALL BUSINESS CASES

A small business Chapter 11 case is a Chapter 11 case involving a debtor who comes within the Bankruptcy Code's definition of "small business debtor."

That definition in section 101 focuses primarily on the amount of unsecured debt and not the size of the business operations. More specifically, in order to be a "small business debtor" the debtor must meet the two requirements in the definition.

(1) Debt not more than $2,726,625.[21] [This includes both secured and unsecured debt; it does not include contingent or unliquidated debt.]

(2) Person engaged in "commercial or business activities" other than simply "owning or operating real property."

Any debtor who meets these two requirements is also eligible to use Subchapter V which is explained in the next Chapter of this book, Subchapter V became effective in 2020 and since it became effective, debtors eligible for 'Subchapter V have chosen Subchapter V.

So, because of Subchapter V, the following comparison of small business cases and standard Chapter 11 cases is of limited value to practicing lawyers and law clerks and should be of no value to law students. But, as you undoubtedly have already discovered, some professors have no sense—or at least no sense of what you should be learning, And so I provide the following comparison.

A small business Chapter 11 case is different from other Chapter 11 cases in that

(1) United States Trustee has additional oversight duties, as described in section 1116 and 28 USC § 586; and

(2) a small business debtor has additional reporting requirements detailed in section

---

21 This amount is inflation-indexed under section 104 and so will change

308 and other duties set out in section 1116; and

(3) the plan process can be simpler because section 1125(f) permits courts to

- determine that a plan itself provides adequate information so that no disclosure statement is necessary;
- approve a standard form disclosure statement;
- combine approval of the disclosure statement with confirmation.

(4) time periods and deadlines are different

- 180 days of debtor exclusivity, section 1121(e);
- 300-day deadline for filing plan and disclosure statement, section 1121(e);
- 45 days after filing for confirmation of the plan, section 1129(e).

Failure to meet the deadlines is "cause" for a motion to dismiss by the United States Trustee or a creditor.

Again, debtors are choosing Subchapter V instead of the small business alternative.

CHAPTER XVI

SUBCHAPTER V

Subchapter V became effective in 2020. Subchapter V was added to make Chapter 11 "timely and cost-effective" for small businesses.

Subchapter V sounds a lot of like the small business debtor provisions in the last part of the prior Chapter of the book.

Subchapter V does not literally replace the small business debtor provisions. A debtor who comes within the section 101 definition of "small business debtor" can choose Subchapter V which will be explained in this Chapter of the book or can choose the small business case provisions explained at the end of the previous Chapter of this book. Thus *D*, a "person engaged in commercial or business activities" with debts of no more than $2,725,625, can be either a "small business debtor" or what this book will call a "Subchapter V debtor."

But if *D* is a "person engaged in commercial or business activities" with debts of more than $2,725,625 but less than $7,500,000 then *D* can be a "Subchapter V debtor" even though *D* is not eligible to be a "small business debtor." Subchapter V has a different debt limit.

This Chapter will explain how a Subchapter V Chapter 11 case is different from "standard Chapter 11 cases" (i.e., other Chapter 11 cases) in each of the five stages of a Chapter 11 case.

A. COMMENCEMENT OF THE CASE

As in every bankruptcy case, the filing of a bankruptcy petition commences the case. Subchapter V is different in that it applies only if (i) the debtor is eligible for Subchapter V and (ii) elects for Subchapter V to apply.

There will not be a creditors' committee in Subchapter V cases unless the court orders otherwise.

In Subchapter V cases, there will be a debtor in possession of the assets and control of the business but there will also be a trustee from a panel of Subchapter V trustees appointed by the United States Trustee. While the Subchapter V trustee will have monitoring and oversight duties, Subchapter V contemplates that the debtor will be the person that runs the business, and the debtor in possession will be the person who prepares and files the plan.

Under section 1185, the court "shall" remove the debtor in possession, if specified grounds exist.

B. OPERATING THE BUSINESS

Unless the court has removed the debtor in possession, in Subchapter V cases, it will be the debtor in possession that operates the business. if the court has removed the debtor in possession, the Subchapter V trustee has the duty to operate the business.

A Subchapter V debtor has the same section 308 periodic reporting requirements relating to cash receipts, cash disbursement, profitability as a small business debtor. And the Subchapter V debtor in possession operating the business has the same section 362 stay protection and the same sections 363, 364 and 365 options as a debtor in possession in a standard Chapter 11 case.

C. PREPARATION OF THE CHAPTER 11 PLAN

Preparation of a plan in a Subchapter V case is different from the preparation of a plan in a standard Chapter 11 case. There are both procedural differences and substantive differences.

1. PROCEDURAL DIFFERENCES IN THE PLAN PROCESS

The procedural differences are different time deadlines and different people participating.

The deadline for a Subchapter V debtor to file a plan is 90 days from the commencement of the case, although the court may extend the time. There are two other important deadlines.

The court must hold a status conference within 60 days of the petition "to further the expeditious and economical resolution" of the case. And, not later than 14 days before the status conference the Subchapter V debtor must report its efforts to achieve as "consensual plan" of reorganization." [As will be explained later in this Chapter, "consensual plan" is an important Subchapter V term.]

The Subchapter V trustee is also involved the plan process. The Subchapter V trustee has the duty "to facilitate the development of a consensual plan of reorganization," section 1183(b)(7). The Subchapter V trustee cannot file the plan, even if the court has removed the debtor in possession; only the debtor can file a plan, section 1189(a)

2. SUBSTANTIVE DIFFERENCES IN PLAN PROVISIONS

A Subchapter V plan may spread administrative expense priority payments over the life of the plan instead of paying all administrative expense priority claims in full in cash as of confirmation as is required in standard Chapter 11 plans.

And, a Subchapter V for an individual debtor may modify a claim secured by a mortgage only the debtor's principal residence if the mortgage proceeds were not used to acquire the real property but were used in connection with debtor's business.[1] Such modification is not permitted in standard individual Chapter 11 cases or in Chapter 13 cases.

Subchapter V eliminates the requirement of a disclosure statement and a disclosure statement hearing.[2] Instead, a Subchapter V plan must contain the information a disclosure statement usually contains including

- brief history of the business;

---

1 Section 1190(3).

2 Section 1181(b).

- a liquidation analysis;
- financial projections showing how proposed plan payments will be made.[3]

D. ACCEPTANCE OF THE CHAPTER 11 PLAN

As in standard Chapter 11 cases, in Subchapter V cases, creditors vote on the plan and the necessary majorities of more than ½ in number and at least 2/3 in amount are determined based on claims voted in each class.

E. CONFIRMATION OF THE PLAN

1. REQUIREMENTS FOR CONFIRMATION

As in standard Chapter 11 cases, in Subchapter V cases, there are confirmation requirements set out in section 1129(a) that must always be satisfied and additional requirements in section 1129(b) that must be satisfied only if one or more classes of impaired claims do not accept the plan.

Subchapter V provisions use the term "consensual plans." While that term is not defined, it seems clear that "consensual plans" are plans that all impaired classes have accepted.

a. Consensual Plans

The requirements for confirmation of a consensual plan in Subchapter V are essentially the same as the

---

[3] Section 1181(a)

requirements for confirmation of a standard Chapter 11 plan. All of the requirements of section 1129(a) must be satisfied except for section 1129(a)(15). Section 1129(a)(15) is of limited practical significance and no law school significance. It imposes a projected disposable income requirement on an individual debtor.

Almost all Subchapter V confirmed plans are consensual plans.

b. Nonconsensual Plans

Section 1129(b) applies if, and only if one or more impaired classes do not assent. The application of section 1129(b) In Subchapter V cases differs from in standard Chapter 11 cases in two important respects.

First, in Subchapter V cases, the bankruptcy court can confirm a plan under section 1129(b) even if no class of impaired claims has assented. In standard Chapter 11 cases, section 1129(b) requires at least one assenting impaired class.

Second, the requirements for cram down of a plan with one or more non-assenting classes of unsecured claims is different in standard Chapter 11 cases than in Subchapter V cases. Recall, that in standard Chapter 11 cases, section 1129(b)(2)(B) imposes an absolute priority rule, i.e., owners cannot retain their ownership interest such as stock if there is a non-assenting impaired class. In a Subchapter V case, the owners of a business can retain their ownership interest and cram down their plan notwithstanding a nonassenting class of unsecured claims if the plan provides for payments to the non-assenting unsecured class equal to three to five years of "disposable income."[4]

2. CONSEQUENCES OF CONFIRMATION

a. Consensual

The primary consequence of confirmation of a consensual Subchapter V plan is that the debtor receives a discharge, Even an individual debtor in a Subchapter V case receives a discharge on confirmation of a consensual plan, section 1183. In a standard Chapter 11 case, an individual debtor receives a discharge only after plan payments are completed.

Less important, the confirmation of a consensual plan ends the work of the Subchapter V trustee.

b. Nonconsensual

If the plan that is confirmed is nonconsensual, i.e., one more nonassenting classes of impaired claims, then confirmation does not result in a discharge in a Subchapter V case. There is no discharge until the last plan payment is made, section 1192. And, the

---

[4] If the debtor is a business entity such as a corporation or limited liability company, disposable income is the entity's income less "the payment of expenditures necessary for the continuation, preservation or operation of the debtor," section 1191(d)(2). If the debtor is an individual, disposable income is income less amounts "reasonably necessary . . . [for] maintenance and support." section 1191(c)(1).

Subchapter V trustee has the statutory duty to collect and distribute the plan payments.

CHAPTER XVII

SECTION 363 SALES OF ALL OF THE ASSETS

Recapitalization and debt restructuring by the existing owner under a creditor approved/court approved plan or the sale of the business to a new owner are two different ways that a Chapter 11 debtor can address its financial distress. And, there are two different ways that a Chapter 11 debtor can sell its assets to a new owner.

Section 1129(b)(8) provides for sale of a debtor's assets under a Chapter 11 plan, and section 363(b) provides for a sale of a debtor's assets "after a notice and hearing. Increasingly, Chapter 11 cases are primarily section 363(b) sales.

The Bankruptcy Code was not written with the idea that section 363(b) sales would be the alternative to the Chapter 11 plan process in many cases. Section 363(b), unlike the various Bankruptcy Code sections governing the Chapter 11 plan process, is incomplete.

Let's consider five section 363(b) questions that your client or prof might expect you to answer that are not FULLY answered by section 363(b).

1. What if a creditor or the United States trustee objects to the debtor's selling its assets under section 363 instead of using the Chapter 11 plan process?

At an earlier time, this question was regularly raised. Creditors and the United States trustee argued that permitting a Chapter 11 debtor to sell all of its assets in section 363 was unfair to creditors who had the power to vote on Chapter 11 plans and had the protection of section 1129(b)'s plan confirmation standards. Since the Second Circuit's decision in In re Lionel Corp., 722 F.2d 1063 (2d Cir. 1983), courts have approved preplan, section 363 sales of all of a Chapter 11 debtor's assets if the sale proponent provides a "good business reason" for the sale. And, there is always a "good business reason."

2. What if another buyer appears at the bankruptcy court's hearing on the section 363(b) sale?

Not only does section 363 say nothing about what standards a bankruptcy court should use to decide whether a section 363 sale of all of the debtor's assets should be conducted, it is also silent as to ow a section 363 sale should be conducted.

Typically, the debtor files a Sale Motion that includes (1) a proposed sale agreement and (2) sale procedures. For example, D, a Chapter 11 debtor, enters into agreement to sell all of its assets to P for $10M, subject to court approval. D then files the Sale Motion and the agreement with P, and the court holds a hearing. If T, a third party, comes to hearing and offers $20M cash for D's assets, then the bankruptcy court will order the sale of the assets to T, not P.

In negotiating with D to buy its assets in a section 363 sale, potential purchasers such as P are aware of the risk of a third party such as T's "piggybacking" on P's due diligence and valuation and making a higher offer at the hearing. No buyer wants to spend time and money valuing the debtor's assets and business and negotiating a purchase agreement only to have someone else make a higher bid at the hearing on the section 363 sale and walk away with the business, Accordingly, a Sale Motion often asks the court to enter an order authorizing compensation to the initial bidder if the section 363 hearing results in a sale to someone else.

In practice, the initial bidder is often times referred to as the "stalking horse"; the compensation is referred to as a "breakup fee"; and the argument for a breakup fee frequently includes the phrase "level playing field . . ." The Bankruptcy Code does not mention stalking horses, breakup fees or level playing fields.

There are numerous opinions by bankruptcy judges and state court judges that address breakup fees. The promise of a breakup fee can entice someone to make a firm bid that in turn generates other bids; on the other hand, the breakup fee can have a chilling effect, discouraging others from bidding. For example, D agrees to sell its assets to P under section 363 for $10M, subject to bankruptcy court approval. The agreement provides that if someone else buys the assets at the section 363 hearing then P receives a breakup fee of $500,000. As a result of this breakup fee agreement, some third party such as T will have to bid at least $10.5M+ to prevail.

3. What is credit bidding?

The Bankruptcy Code does not use the term "credit bidding." Bankruptcy lawyers and judges use the term "credit bidding" to describe the effect of the following language in section 363(k): "may offset such claim against the purchase price of such property."

Let me use an example to explain how and why credit bidding works: *D* owes *C* $3M, and *C* has a first lien on all of D's equipment and inventory. If *X* buys that equipment and inventory for $2M, *C* should ultimately get the $2M.

What if *C* believes that its collateral is worth $2.5M, not just $2M? Shouldn't *C* be able to buy the equipment and inventory for $2.5M? And, if *C* buys the equipment for $2.5M, shouldn't *C* ultimately get the $2.5M?

Does it make sense to require *C* to incur the costs of borrowing $2.5M to buy the equipment and inventory if that $2.M is ultimately going to *C*?

Section 363(k) answer to the question is to enable *C* to "offset such claim against the purchase price of such property," i.e. credit bidding.

Permitting *C* to credit bid up to $3M simply saves *C* the costs of obtaining a loan for $2.5, paying $2.5M at the section 363 sale and waiting for the $2.5to be distributed to it so it can repay the loan.

Note *C* can credit bid under section 363(k) only if it has a lien on the property being sold. A creditor with a lien on Redcare cannot credit bid on a section 363 sale of Blueacre.

4. Can the buyer at a section 363 sale acquire the debtor's assets free and clear of liens? Free and clear of successor liability claims?

Section 363(f) expressly provides an affirmative answer to the first question. If the section 363 sale satisfies any of the five requirements of section 363(f), the buyer takes the assets free and clear of liens.

Of these five requirements, section 363(f)(3) is invoked most often in law school and in practice. Section 363(f)(3) conditions a sale free and clear of liens on "the price is greater than . . . the value of all liens on such property."

The troublesome word in section 363(f)(3) is the word "value." What if the debt owed to the lien creditor is greater than the value of the collateral securing the debt?

For example, *D* owes *S* 100. *S*'s debt is secured by Redacre. The value of Redacre is 70. Can *D* sell the assets free and clear of *S*'s lien for 70? Courts are split as to whether 100, the face amount of the debt.is the "value" of *S*'s lien or 70, economic value of the lien, is the "value" of *S*'s lien as the word "value" in section 363(f)(3).

The answer to the question of whether a section 363 buyer can acquire assets free and clear of claims such as successor liability claims is even more problematic. The relevant statutory language is "free and clear of interests."

There are circuit court decisions which have interpreted that quoted language as including claims that might arise out of state successor liability law.

Such a result is easier to justify as a matter of policy than as a matter of statutory interpretation.

Policy arguments for a section 363 buyer's being able to acquire assets free and clear of claims can be based on (1) bankruptcy's providing a fresh start and (2) bankruptcy's being a collective proceeding resolving all liabilities.

Statutory interpretation problems with reading "free and clear of interests" as including claims are created by section 1141(c) which uses the phrase "free and clear of all claims and interests" and sections 1122, 1124 and others which use the phrase "claims or interests." If the word "interests" in Bankruptcy Code section 363(f) included "claims," then other provisions of the Bankruptcy Code would not use the phrase "claims and interests" or the phrase "claims or interests."

5. What happens after a section 363 sale?

If *P* buys all of the assets of *D*, a Chapter 11 debtor, through a section 363(b) sale, *D*'s bankruptcy case is not over. The sale proceeds have to be distributed, and, the section 363 sale agreement cannot provide who gets what.

In re Braniff Airways, Inc., 700 F.2d 935 (5th Cir. 1983), is often cited to support the proposition that a section 363 sale order cannot specify any particular distribution of the sale proceeds—cannot be a "sub rosa plan." A section 363 sale which specifies which of the sale proceeds is to be distributed to whom is in essence a Chapter 11 plan but is not subject to all of the protection of the plan confirmation process.

Generally, one of three things happens after a section 363 sale of all of the debtor's assets: (1) the debtor files a Chapter 11 plan distributing the sale proceeds that must be accepted by creditors and confirmed by the court or (2) the case is converted to Chapter 7 and the trustee distributes the sale proceeds as mandated by Chapter 7 priority rules or (3) the case is dismissed and the debtor and creditors later work out what happens to the sale proceeds.

If your professor covered Czyzewski v. Jevic Holding Corp. 137 S.Ct. 973 (2017), then you need to consider "structured dismissals"—a fourth possible section 363(b) end game. In a structured dismissal of a Chapter 11 case after a section 363(b), the dismissal includes payments of sale proceeds to some parties before the dismissal is effective.

In *Jevic*, the Court described the "basic question" that the Court was answering as "Can a bankruptcy court approve a structured dismissal that provides for distributions that do not follow ordinary priority rules without the affected creditors' consent?" The Court's answer to this question was simply "no."

Jevic involved dismissal and the distribution of the proceeds of the settlement of litigation over a leveraged buyout and not a section 363 sale and so Jevic leaves the following three questions unanswered

(1) Does *Jevic* apply to a structured settlement and distribution of the proceeds of a section 363 sale?

(2) Does *Jevic* affect a structured dismissal that follows ordinary priory rules?

(3) Is the approval of every affected creditor necessary for "affected creditors' consent"?

And, these questions are still unanswered. There are relatively few appellate court decisions reviewing section 363 sale orders. Section 363(m) limits appellate court jurisdiction of an unstayed sale order issued by a bankruptcy judge to the narrow question of whether the property was sold to a good faith purchaser.

CHAPTER XVIII

ALLOCATION OF JUDICIAL POWER OVER BANKRUPTCY MATTERS

In the main, the substantive law of bankruptcy is in title 11 of the United States Code. Questions of judicial power over bankruptcy-related matters are, in the main, answered in title 28 of the United States Code.

The question of which court has the power to adjudicate the litigation that arises in bankruptcy can be an important one. Many attorneys that represent parties with claims against a debtor in a bankruptcy case or parties against whom the debtor has claims prefer to litigate in some forum other than the bankruptcy court. Some believe that the bankruptcy judge has a pro-debtor bias; others are simply more comfortable or more familiar with state court procedures; others prefer state court for reasons of delay—a state court generally has a larger backlog of cases than a bankruptcy court so that filing in state court delays any litigation.

In considering the question of which court has the power to adjudicate the litigation that arises in bankruptcy, it is helpful to consider the kinds of matters that can arise in bankruptcy.

Some matters will involve only bankruptcy law. For example, *D* files a Chapter 7 petition. The Chapter 7 trustee alleges that *B*'s payment of $40,000 to *C* a month before bankruptcy is recoverable by the estate under section 550 as a section 547 voidable preference. *C* contends that the $40,000 payment is protected from avoidance as a section 547(c)(2) ordinary course of business payment.

Other matters will involve both bankruptcy law and nonbankruptcy law. For example, *D* files a Chapter 7 petition. *C* files a secured claim that describes its Article 9 security interest. The bankruptcy trustee takes the position that *C*'s security interest is invalid because it was not properly perfected. If this is litigated, it will probably involve both the Bankruptcy Code's invalidation provisions and the Uniform Commercial Code's perfection provisions.

And, still other matters will not involve substantive bankruptcy law. For example, *D*, Inc., a Chapter 11 debtor, files a breach of contract claim against *X*.

A. HISTORY

The allocation of judicial power over bankruptcy matters has been one of the most controversial bankruptcy issues. Historically, lawyers have believed that bankruptcy judges favor (1) the debtor over creditors and (2) lawyers who regularly appear before them over lawyers who do not generally appear before. Accordingly, cases as to what a bankruptcy judge can decide have been appealed all of the way up to the United States Supreme Court. A general familiarity with prior statutory schemes and prior legal and political controversies is helpful to understanding the present situation.

1. 1898 ACT

Under the Bankruptcy Act of 1898, bankruptcy courts had limited jurisdiction. This jurisdiction was commonly referred to as "summary jurisdiction." (The phrase "summary jurisdiction" is somewhat misleading. First, it incorrectly implies that under the Bankruptcy Act of 1898, bankruptcy courts had a second, nonsummary form of jurisdiction. Summary jurisdiction is the only form of jurisdiction that a bankruptcy judge possessed under the Bankruptcy Act of 1898. Bankruptcy courts had only summary jurisdiction; other courts had plenary jurisdiction. Second, it incorrectly implies that in resolving controversies the bankruptcy judge always conducted summary proceedings.)

Summary jurisdiction extended to (1) *all* matters concerned with the administration of the bankruptcy estate and (2) *some* disputes between the bankruptcy trustee and third parties involving rights to money and other property in which the bankrupt estate claimed an interest. The tests for which disputes with third parties were within the bankruptcy judge's summary jurisdiction turned on issues such as whether (1) the property in question was in the actual possession of the bankrupt at the time of the commencement of the case, (2) the property in question was in the constructive possession of the bankrupt at the time of the commencement of the case, and (3) the third party actually or impliedly consented to bankruptcy court jurisdiction.

There was considerable uncertainty over which disputes were within the summary jurisdiction of the bankruptcy court. This uncertainty gave rise to considerable litigation.

2. 1978 CODE

Apparently for the above reasons, Congress in 1978 decided to create a bankruptcy court with pervasive jurisdiction. Apparently for political reasons, Congress also decided that this bankruptcy court should *not* be an Article III court.

As you recall from your Constitutional Law course in law school or civics course in high school, Article III of the Constitution vests the judicial power of the United States in the United States Supreme Court and such inferior tribunals as Congress might create. To insure the independence of the judges appointed under Article III (the so-called constitutional courts), Article III provides them with certain protections. These include tenure for life, removal from office only by congressional impeachment, and assurance that their compensation will not be diminished.

The constitutional courts created under Article III include the United States Supreme Court, the United States Courts of Appeal, and the United States District Courts. The United States Customs Court (now the Court of International Trade) is also an Article III court; its judges may be, and often are, assigned to hear cases in the district courts and the courts of appeal.

Congress, in the exercise of its legislative powers enumerated in Article I of the Constitution, may create other inferior federal tribunals—the so-called legislative courts. Judges of these legislative courts need not be granted tenure for life. In addition, they can be removed by mechanisms other than congressional impeachment, and their salaries are subject to congressional reduction.

Historically, these Article I legislative courts and their judges have been granted jurisdiction over limited and narrowly defined subject matters, like the Tax Court. In other instances, jurisdiction has been limited to narrowly defined geographical territories, such as the territorial courts, the District of Columbia courts, etc.

In amending title 28 in 1978, Congress gave bankruptcy judges none of the protections found in Article III of the Constitution. Nevertheless, the 1978 amendments to title 28 gave bankruptcy judges much of the power and responsibilities of an Article III judge. Since bankruptcy debtors can be just about any kind of individual or business entity, this meant that litigation in the bankruptcy courts could deal with almost every facet of business and personal activity.

3. *MARATHON PIPE LINE* DECISION

The 1978 grant of pervasive jurisdiction to a non-Article III bankruptcy court was successfully challenged in the *Marathon* case.

Northern Pipeline, a Chapter 11 debtor, filed a breach of contract lawsuit against Marathon Pipe Line in bankruptcy court. There was no question as to whether the bankruptcy court had jurisdiction over this lawsuit under 28 USCA § 1471(c). Marathon Pipe Line did, however, question whether section 1471(c) conferred Article III judicial power on non-Article III courts in violation of the separation of powers doctrine and filed a motion to dismiss. A divided Supreme Court sustained Marathon's challenge in Northern Pipeline Constr. Co. v. Marathon Pipe Line Co., 458 U.S. 50 (1982).

The Court in *Marathon* was so divided that there was no majority opinion. Justice Brennan's opinion was joined by three other justices. Additionally, two justices concurred in the result. The holding of these six is perhaps best summarized in footnote 40 of Justice Brennan's plurality opinion which indicates that (1) the 1978 legislation does grant the bankruptcy court the power to hear Northern Pipeline's breach of contract claim, (2) the bankruptcy court, a non-Article III court, cannot constitutionally be vested with jurisdiction to decide such state law claims, and (3) this grant of authority to the bankruptcy court is not severable from the remaining grant of authority to the bankruptcy court.

After *Marathon*, Congress was urged to solve the constitutional dilemma by establishing bankruptcy courts as Article III courts. Congress rejected this solution. Instead, Congress in 1984[1] made the bankruptcy court a part of the federal district court, conferred jurisdiction in bankruptcy on the district

---

1 In the two-year gap between the 1982 *Marathon* decision and the 1984 legislation, the allocation of judicial power over bankruptcy was governed by an Emergency Rule adopted by all district courts.

court, and allocated judicial power in bankruptcy matters between the federal district judge and the bankruptcy judge.

It is easy for any lawyer or law student to criticize the provisions allocating judicial power over bankruptcy matters. It is more difficult (but probably more important) for a lawyer or law student to understand how these provisions operate.

B. OPERATION OF PRESENT LAW

In understanding the present law allocating judicial powers over bankruptcy matters, it is necessary to understand three separate sections in title 28: (1) 151, (2) 1334 and (3) 157. By understanding these three provisions you will understand that (1) bankruptcy courts are a part of the United States District Court but bankruptcy judges are different from district court judges, (2) bankruptcy cases are different from bankruptcy proceedings, (3) bankruptcy cases can be handled by either bankruptcy judges or federal district judges (depending on withdrawal of the reference), but not by state court judges and (4) bankruptcy proceedings can be tried by bankruptcy judges or federal district judges (depending on withdrawal of the reference) or even state court judges (depending on where the lawsuit was filed and removal and abstention). To understand even more, please read the following descriptions of the three key sections in title 28:

1. BANKRUPTCY COURT AS PART OF THE DISTRICT COURT, SECTION 151

Section 151 refers to a bankruptcy judge and a bankruptcy court as a "unit" of the district court. It is important to keep this reference in mind when reading other sections in title 28 dealing with the allocation of judicial power in bankruptcy matters. When the term "district court" appears in section 1334 or section 157, it could be referring to the United States district judge and/or the bankruptcy judge. After all, the bankruptcy judge is a part of the district court—a "unit" of the district court.

2. GRANTS OF JURISDICTION TO THE DISTRICT COURT, SECTION 1334(a) AND (b)[2]

Section 1334(a) vests original and exclusive jurisdiction in the district court over all cases arising under the Bankruptcy Code. "Case" is a term of art used in both the Bankruptcy Code and the Bankruptcy Rules. "Case" refers to the entire Chapter 7, 9, 11, 12 or 13—not just some controversy that arises in connection with it.

The term "case" is to be distinguished from the term "proceeding." A specific dispute that arises during the pendency of a case is referred to as a "proceeding." Section 1334(b) provides that the district courts have original but not exclusive jurisdiction over all civil proceedings, "arising under

[2] Section 1334(c) which deals with abstention will be separately considered later in this chapter.

title 11, or arising in or related to cases under title 11."

"Proceedings" include "contested matters" (motions brought in the main bankruptcy case) and "adversary proceedings" (lawsuits). Section 1334(b) grants the district court original but not exclusive jurisdiction over three types of "civil proceedings":

(1) "arising under" title 11

This involves adjudication of rights or obligations created by the Bankruptcy Code. For example, stay relief. Another example, objections to discharge.

(2) "arising in" a case under title 11

This covers matters peculiar to bankruptcy but based on rights or obligations created by the Bankruptcy Code. For example, allowance or disallowance of claims. Another example, assumption or rejection of executory contracts.

(3) "related to" a case under title 11

This covers matters that impact on the bankruptcy case.[3] While it is not a "catch-all," it certainly catches a lot. In Celotex Corp. v. Edwards, 514 U.S. 300 (1995), the Supreme Court held that entry of an injunction prohibiting a judgment creditor from

---

[3] Reported decisions on "related to" commonly quote from the Third Circuit's decision in Pacor, Inc. v. Higgins, 743 F.2d 984 (1984): "The test for determining whether a civil proceeding is related to bankruptcy is whether the outcome of the proceeding could conceivably have any effect on the estate being administered in bankruptcy."

executing on a supersedeas bond of a third party surety of the debtor was "related to."

3. ROLE OF THE BANKRUPTCY COURT, SECTION 157

Clearly, section 1334 confers jurisdiction over bankruptcy matters to the district court. It is equally clear that most federal district judges have neither the time nor the inclination to exercise this jurisdiction. Accordingly, section 157 empowers the district judge to refer bankruptcy matters to the bankruptcy judge.

Note the title of section 157, "Procedures." As this title suggests, section 157 is not a jurisdictional provision. It does not confer jurisdiction on the bankruptcy judge. Rather, it deals with procedure—the role that the bankruptcy judge, a unit of the district court under section 151, is to play in exercising the jurisdiction conferred by section 1334 on the district court.

Section 157 differentiates between "core" and "noncore" proceedings. A nonexclusive list of core proceedings is set out in section 157(b)(2). The bankruptcy court can enter a final judgment in core proceedings.

A nonexclusive list of core proceedings is set out in section 157(b)(2). The list includes "counterclaims by the estate against persons filing claims against the estate," section 157(b)(2)(C).

If a matter is not a core proceeding, it is a "noncore proceeding." "Noncore proceeding" is neither defined nor illustrated in the statute. In noncore proceedings, the bankruptcy judge still can hold the trial or hearing, but and submits, proposed findings of fact and law to the district court for review, section 157(c)(1). The bankruptcy judge can enter a final order or judgment in a noncore matter only if the parties consent, 28 section 157(c)(2).

The bankruptcy judge is empowered to determine whether a matter is a core proceeding or a noncore proceeding, section 157(b)(3). Remember that a determination that a proceeding is noncore does not mean that the matter is withdrawn from the bankruptcy judge. Remember that a bankruptcy judge can hear noncore proceedings and prepare findings of facts and law.

The statutory list of core proceedings includes "counterclaims by the estate against persons filing claims against the estate, section 157(b)(2). In Stern v. Marshall, 564 U.S. 462 (2011) a divided Supreme Court held that section 157(b)(2) was unconstitutional—at least as applied to a counterclaim based on state law. The decision is based on constitutional law, not bankruptcy law. Justice Roberts, writing for the majority, looks to the core constitutional law concept of separation of powers to conclude that a bankruptcy judge, who is an "Article 1 judge," can enter final judgment only on matters of "public right."

While the holding in *Stern* is limited, Justice Roberts broad reasoning has caused lower courts judges to question which other matters identified as "core proceedings" in section 157(b) are not "public right" matters and so vulnerable to a Stern challenge so that a bankruptcy judge cannot constitutionally enter a final order. Such matters are commonly referred to as "*Stern* claims."

The Supreme Court has not yet definitively answered the question of what are "*Stern* claims" i.e., what other matters statutorily classified as "core proceedings" are not "public right matters." There are, however, two later Supreme Court cases that limit the practical impact of *Stern*.

First, in Executive Benefits Ins. Agency v. Arkison, 573 U.S. 25 (2014), the Court held that Stern claims can be treated as non-core proceedings, meaning that the bankruptcy judge can hear such matters and submit findings of fact and conclusions of law that will be approved by the district judge. Second, in Wellness Int'l Network Ltd. v. Sharif, 575 U.S. 665 (2015), the Court held that a bankruptcy judge can enter a final order on a *Stern* claim with the knowing and voluntary consent of the parties and that consent can be inferred from conduct.

Remember that Congress conferred bankruptcy jurisdiction on the district court and the district judge retains ultimate control over the role of the bankruptcy judge. Section 157(d) authorizes the district judge to withdraw a case or proceeding from a bankruptcy judge. The first sentence of section 157(d) provides for permissive withdrawal "for cause shown." Under the second sentence of section 157(d), withdrawal of the reference is mandatory if "resolution of the proceeding requires consideration of both Title 11 and other laws of the United States regulating . . . interstate commerce."

In applying this provision, most courts disregard the "plain language" quoted above. The plain language of section 157(d) indicates that withdrawal of the reference is mandatory only if both the Bankruptcy Code and another federal statute must be construed to resolve the proceeding. Under the statute's "plain language," a district court would be required to withdraw the reference only in actions involving both bankruptcy and nonbankruptcy law—not in matters involving nonbankruptcy law alone. And, under the statute's plain language, the bankruptcy court would have to abstain on all matters that involve both bankruptcy law and a nonfederal statute regulating interstate commerce, regardless of how simple and straight forward the application of the other statute.

Because the "plain language" of section 157(d)'s second sentence plainly does not work, most courts have ignored the literal language of section 157(d) for mandatory withdrawal. Instead, these courts require that the reference be withdrawn if an action involves a "substantial and material" consideration of a nonbankruptcy federal statute regulating interstate commerce, regardless of whether the action also involves consideration of the Bankruptcy Code.

Withdrawal of the reference from the district court to the bankruptcy judge is also mandatory for (1) claims for wrongful death or other personal injuries, section 157(a)(3)(5), or (2) matters in which a party has a right to a jury trial unless the district court has authorized the bankruptcy judge to conduct the jury trial and the parties have consented, section 157(e).

Remember that withdrawal under section 157(d) merely moves a matter from the bankruptcy judge to the federal district judge. Withdrawal under section 157(d) does not move a matter to a state court. That requires abstention.

4. ABSTENTION UNDER SECTION 1334(c)

Abstention under section 1334(c) moves litigation from bankruptcy court to a state court. In considering and applying the abstention provisions of section 1334(c), it is important to recall the jurisdictional provisions of section 1334(b). As you learned from your readings in constitutional law and/or federal courts, a federal court with jurisdiction over a matter or controversy must exercise that jurisdiction except under unusual circumstances. And, as you learned from reading this book, Congress provided for broad, pervasive bankruptcy jurisdiction in section 1334(b) to eliminate the costly litigation over jurisdiction that occurred under the Bankruptcy Act of 1898. As a result, some of the matters covered by the jurisdictional grant in section 1334(b) are not really bankruptcy matters, are matters that would be better left to other courts. Section 1334(c) empowers the bankruptcy judge to leave such matters to other courts by abstaining.

Section 1334(c)(1) provides for permissive abstention. If the district court believes that abstention would be "in the interest of justice" or "in the interest of comity with State courts or respect for

State law," it has the option of abstaining. Section 1334(c)(2) provides for mandatory abstention; if the following six requirements of section 1334(c)(2) are satisfied, the district court must abstain:

1. A party to the proceeding must timely file a motion to abstain.

2. The proceeding is based on a state law claim or cause of action.

3. The matter is a "related to" proceeding, as contrasted with an "arising under" or "arising in" proceeding.

[Section 1334(b) uses all three of these phrases. Section 1334(c)(2) limits mandatory abstention to its certain "related to" proceedings. There is no statutory definition of "arising under," "arising in" or "related to."]

4. The action could not have been commenced in federal court in the absence of the jurisdiction conferred by section 1334. If there is any other basis for federal court jurisdiction, mandatory abstention is not available. This requirement means that mandatory abstention would not be available in the *Marathon* case because of the diversity of citizenship between the parties.

5. An action is commenced in state court. There is a question as to whether this means that the state court action must be

pending at the time of the bankruptcy filing.

6. The state court action can be timely adjudicated.

5. JURY TRIALS

There are two questions about jury trials in bankruptcy proceedings. First, when is there a right to a jury trial. Second, can the bankruptcy judge conduct the jury trial.

The Seventh Amendment to the Constitution governs the right to jury trials in federal courts—"suits at common law, where the value in controversy shall exceed twenty dollars." Note the phrase "at common law." The Seventh Amendment does not confer a right to jury trial to equitable actions or to those who seek equitable remedies. Which bankruptcy proceedings are "suits at common law"? When does a debtor or holder of a claim in a bankruptcy case seek an equitable remedy?

The Supreme Court addressed these questions (sort of) in Granfinanciera, S.A. v. Nordberg, 492 U.S. 33 (1989), which found a right to jury trial in fraudulent conveyance litigation where (1) the trustee is seeking a money judgment and (2) the transferee has not filed a proof of claim. In so ruling, the Court compared "the statutory action to 18th-century actions brought in the courts of England prior to the merger of the courts of law and equity" and concluded that "actions to recover preferential or fraudulent transfers were often brought at law in late 18th-century England."

Section 157(e) answers the second question of whether a bankruptcy judge can hold a jury trial. Actually, the federal district judge and the parties to the proceeding answer the question of who holds the jury trial. Under section 157(e), the bankruptcy judge can conduct the jury trial only if she has been "specially designated" by the district judge and "all of the parties" consent.

6. FOREIGN CASES

Chapter 15 establishes a set of protocols for bankruptcies that touch more than one country. A case under Chapter 15 is commenced by a "foreign representative" seeking "recognition" of a "foreign proceeding."

The quoted terms in the last sentence are defined in section 101. Applying these definitions, a person with a trustee-like status in a foreign insolvency case commenced in another jurisdiction has standing to file a Chapter 15 proceeding in the United States to protect assets in the United States for administration and distribution in that foreign insolvency case. If the United States bankruptcy court "recognizes" the foreign case under the requirements set out in Chapter 15, the automatic stay and certain other protections of the Bankruptcy Code will apply.

INDEX

References are to Pages